YOU ARE WHAT YOU SPEAK

YOU ARE
WHAT YOU
SPEAK

Grammar Grouches,
Language Laws, and the
Politics of Identity

Robert Lane Greene

DELACORTE PRESS ▬ NEW YORK

Published in the United States by Delacorte Press,
an imprint of The Random House Publishing Group,
a division of Random House, Inc., New York.

DELACORTE PRESS is a registered trademark of Random House, Inc.,
and the colophon is a trademark of Random House, Inc.

Portions of this book have appeared previously, in different form,
in *The Economist* and *Slate*.

LIBRARY OF CONGRESS CATALOGING-IN-PUBLICATION DATA
Greene, Robert Lane.
You are what you speak: grammar grouches, language laws,
and the politics of identity/Robert Lane Greene.
Delacorte Press: New York, 2010.
p. cm.
Includes index.
ISBN 978-0-553-80787-5
eBook ISBN 978-0-440-33976-2
1. Historical linguistics.   I. Title.
P140.G74 2010
417'.7—dc22   2010038891

Printed in the United States of America on acid-free paper

www.bantamdell.com

1 2 3 4 5 6 7 8 9

FIRST EDITION

Book design by Susan Turner

To my father, Wayne Greene

Foreword

by John McWhorter

When I was eight years old, my family, as most from Philadelphia will on occasion, took a day trip to New York City. We visited, as most families on such trips will at least once, the Empire State Building.

From that afternoon almost forty years ago, I retain only a vague recollection of what Connecticut looked like from the 101st-floor observatory (it was indeed the kind of clear day that allowed one that classic vista). To me, the highlight of the day, still sitting among assorted memorabilia in a box in my study closet, was the brochure for the tour. More specifically, the versions of the brochure in five languages other than English!

To me, the fact that there were ways of speaking other than English had been mesmerizing since I had first realized it a few years earlier. That sense of wonder never left me for some reason. That by my late twenties I was on a linguistics faculty and devoting a career to studying languages was not as much of a happenstance as it felt at the time.

Perhaps that sense of happenstance was due in part to the fact that being a linguist requires grappling ceaselessly with a dissonance between how you see language and how almost everyone around you does beyond the hallway where you work. You feel, in trying to discuss your career, vaguely unmoored, "different."

The astrophysicist understands the composition and movements of heavenly bodies with a degree of detail unattainable by most. However, all readily understand in a basic sense why those heavenly bodies would interest him, and quite a few even share the interest from a fellow-traveler planetarium-style perspective. The architect wants to create buildings; we know she does and understand why. The mechanic fixes our cars, and we're glad. There is no disjunction between the mechanic's sense of mission and our sense of it.

Things are different for the linguist. Linguists marvel at the basic fact that human speech is complex, in a fashion that combines the sprawling with the elegant. The linguist seeks to identify the system amid what seems to be chaos. The fundamental sentiment is one of wonder.

And of a global variety. The marvels are not only German and Russian, but the Hausa of Nigeria or the virtually unknown language of the Amazonian tribe. Seeing Myanmar cut off from outsiders indefinitely, we sometimes think of the fascinating linguistic richnesses that remain to be discovered there in some distant day.

Yet as time passes, the linguist finds that to most of the general public, language comes down less to wonder than to a rather censorious bifurcated sentiment—namely, that the vast majority of the world's humans either speak something primitive or speak something badly.

Few would put it that way, of course. Rather, it "falls out of," to put it in the terms of the scientist, their basic assumptions.

For example, the common idea is that a language is not "real" unless it is written. Language, under this view, is letters, not sounds. An unwritten language is "undeveloped," typically ranked as such even by its speakers.

However, given that there are about six thousand languages and only a few hundred at most are written in any serious way, the common consensus is that all but a few of the languages spoken by humans are larval. Primitive.

Primitive like, say, the tiny language of Papua, Berik, in which you have to pack onto a verb not only a person marker like English's *s* but another one specifying what time of day the action happened, whether it involved a small or big thing, *and* whether that thing wound up up high or down low.

Or primitive like the language of the Caucasus Mountains, Kabardian, where the whole sentence "He gave it to me" is one word, with each piece of meaning composed of one syllable or even sound, pronounced roughly "Kuh-s-a-y-uh-tuh-agh-s." Now, that's "primitive." And then, when you put them all together and say the word, it actually comes out as just "Kih-ZEE-tas"—even when you say it slowly! It all happens because of the same kinds of regular processes that make us say "leaves" instead of "leafs," all and many more of which you have to learn if you want to speak Kabardian.

Linguists have found, in fact, no "primitive" language. By and large, unwritten languages are likely to be more complicated than English. Writing is ultimately just scratches on paper, a useful but flawed approximation of the *sound* of language. And sound, after all, is what language was from the dawn of modern humanity 80,000 years ago or before until just 5,500 years ago, when writing first emerged.

We perhaps find it easy to understand the folly of equating writing with linguistic "reality" from the common Chinese perception that Mandarin, Cantonese, and other varieties are "dialects" of "the same language" because they are all written with the same Chinese characters. Clearly, we think, even if all of the Chineses use a character 我 for *I*, if Mandarin's rendition of the word is *wǒ*, Cantonese's is *ngóh*, Taiwanese's *góa*, Shanghainese's *ngú*, Hakka's *ngái*, and Gan's *ǎ*, these are no more dialects of one language than French, Spanish, and Italian are. The writing is something quite different from the languages.

Yet in the same way, the idea is equally contingent that even a single language "is" the way that it happens to be written and that a language unwritten is therefore less of a language than one that is. Berik has barely ever been written, yet it most certainly "is," with a complexity that, if anything, makes it appear in closer touch with "reality" than English. The sense of writing as what language really consists of is a modern twist of mind, like the sense that conventional travel occurs at the rate of at least sixty miles per hour.

Then there is the idea that as far as one's own "developed" language is concerned, you would never know it was developed from the way most people actually speak it. Linguists are familiar with the fact that after giving a presentation, they find that the audience's most urgent questions are about the fact that so many people speak incorrectly.

Lynne Truss's *Eats, Shoots & Leaves,* decrying the untutored usage of language, was a massive bestseller in mining this vein, to the dismay of Lane Greene in this book. Truss's publisher is also my own, and I highly suspect that they wish I would come up with a book that would stir up the same brand of indignation!

But I just can't, because the things that seemed like mistakes in earlier stages of English are precisely what are today considered proper grammar. One can only imagine how Old English speakers felt hearing people letting go of the language's Latin-style case endings. Certainly they felt as Cicero did hearing the same thing happening to Latin itself, as Lane also recounts. Yet what happened to Old English was that it became what I am writing in, and what happened to Latin was that it became the language of *The Divine Comedy.*

Yet the idea that the casual speech of most people is faulty dies so hard that I have seen immigrants to America accept that the argument is invalid about English but then insist that in their home countries the way people talk in this region or that one "really is terrible—they don't speak their own language." It would seem that especially once the frozen standards of writing are introduced, it is human to think of language as something uniquely susceptible to shirking and flouting, like posture, payment of taxes, and telling the truth.

Lane Greene's flinty, fact-packed funhouse of a book truly gets across the peculiarity of this way of thinking about language, why linguists do not share it, and what the advantages are of letting it go. Lane goes about the task in the only way that can really work—by romping through a wide variety of the world's languages and their histories. In the end we can see that the legions of people assessing whether languages' development is "good" or not have been but bystanders at a gorgeous parade whose magnificence has always been clear to anyone not trained to look past it. In that light, Lane's book will increase the ranks of the felicitously untrained.

We learn that language is interesting not only in the notoriously writerly regions of Europe, the Middle East, and perhaps China and Japan, with a nod to the Rig Veda, some "writing systems" used elsewhere in South Asia, and the hieroglyphics of ancient Egypt and the Mayans, but the world over. Lane shows us that the languages of the world are actually a smudge of dialects bleeding into and out of one another across the globe. The true stories of how French became French and Serbo-Croatian became (or didn't become) Serbo-Croatian show how standard languages are just dialects out of many that happened to be singled out as lingua francas amidst the coalescence of nation-states.

There are actually signs that America's sense of the wonder of language as a worldwide phenomenon is opening up. Students study Arabic, Chinese, Russian, and Japanese to an extent unthinkable when those Empire State Building brochures were printed. Of those four languages, for example, only Chinese got a brochure at the time. Also, the Immigration Act of

1965 was only eight years old. Since then, massive numbers of immigrants and their children have become a part of the American fabric. It is ever clearer, such as in urban school districts where children speak dozens of different languages at home, that "language" is more than the few behemoths that Berlitz published its classic hardback self-teachers for in the old days.

As it happens, Lane and I have of late shared in an experience that neatly encapsulates both the delightful difficulty of even lesser-known languages and the loose connection between writing and a language's essence. Both Lane and my sister happen to have married Danes. Both Lane and I have enjoyed grappling with a language where the word for "better" is spelled *bedre*, but is actually pronounced something like "bihl-thruh" and requires several dozen repetitions to even approximate closely enough for a Dane to sweetly pretend you're close. And that's just one word.

This language, spoken by fewer people than live in New York City, is murderously difficult to pronounce—and its spelling system seems designed for another language (and basically was). Lane has gotten further with it than I ever will, but for both of us it has been a lesson in what languages really are—even when spoken by few, and with its written form, like English's, more an irritation than a badge of maturity.

This book is a perfect introduction to seeing language plain. Ironically, this is so very much more gratifying—you'll see—than the conception of language as a grab bag of also-rans and bad habits.

JOHN MCWHORTER, a columnist for *The New Republic* and contributing editor of *City Journal*, earned his Ph.D. in linguistics from Stanford University in 1993. He currently teaches linguistics at Columbia University, specializing in language change and language contact. He is the author of the *New York Times* bestseller *Losing the Race: Self-Sabotage in Black America*.

PREFACE

My two language teachers taught me different things. My grandfather Robert Wilson Lane was a colonel in the army, a fact you never forgot. Years after he retired, he still answered his telephone with a stern "Colonel Lane." I worshiped him, having fingered his uniforms hanging in the hall closet, and considered a career in the military to make myself more like him. My mom and dad would stash my brother and me in San Antonio, where my grandparents had retired, for a few weeks every summer, and it was there that my first thoughts about language were formed.

Grandpa was endless entertainment. He knew French and German and delighted in trotting those languages out to no end but enjoyment. He taught me that *Hottentotenpotentatenmuttermörderattentatsverrater* meant, in German, "the betrayer of the murderer of the mother of the king of the Hottentots." I thought it pretty amazing that Germans had come up with such a word. (Never did it occur to me that they hadn't, and that this was a party trick of English-speakers charmed with the Germans' habit of concatenating words to make compounds.)

He also taught us hundred-dollar words as playthings: Why say "a little" when you could say "a paucity"? Why say "a lot" when "a plethora" was so much fun? One of our summer games involved him instructing me and my brother, Hank, to "mosey," "sidle," "amble," "strut," and "skulk" across the room—forcing us to put physical sensations to those words we'd only read. How did it actually feel to sidle? Do you do it sideways?

But Grandpa's real legacy with me was a strong dose of what I will call in this book "sticklerism." "Hank and me are going to the mall," I'd say, heading out. "*Who's* going to the mall?" would come the thundering reply. "Hank and *I* are going to the mall." Only then could we go.

So from my first days of thinking of it, I had internalized the stickler's code: big words are better than plain ones and grammatical mistakes are shoddy habits, like leaving the bathroom light on.

But I also grew up closer to a very different English. My father, Wayne Greene, grew up in Macon, Georgia. He dropped out of high school and ran with the wrong boys, and everyone knew that he would turn out no good. Surprising everyone, he would instead join the navy, learn a trade as an electrician, and go back to finish a GED and then college. He spent his career at General Electric as a successful salesman and was proud of bringing up his boys in a middle-class comfort he hadn't known.

But while you can take the boy out of the country, you can't take the country out of the boy. Dad was Macon, distilled. I never realized how southern his English was until I was far from home. At graduate school in Oxford, when a friend from New Zealand visited my place, I pressed "Play" on my answering machine, responding to a blinking light. To my surprise I heard "Boy, what the *hell* you doin'? This is your Dad, callin' to check up on you, but you probably out in one a' them bars . . ." I explained sheepishly to my friend that he didn't always talk that way. The next day, I called my mom. "Mom, has Dad's accent gotten a lot stronger?" I was sure it had, but she said calmly, "No, I don't think so."

Dad was, to put it mildly, no linguist. Besides his southern diction, unfamiliar words and names utterly flummoxed him, even if they were fairly straightforward. He couldn't pronounce the names of the players for the Atlanta sports teams we caught up on over the phone. Jon Koncak, the gangly center for the Hawks, became "Konchak" in his mouth, even though "Kon-cak" is hardly difficult to say. Once he talked up a middle-infield prospect the Braves were hopeful about: "Wilfredo Benitez." Only knowing the Braves' farm prospects did I guess that he meant our Dominican shortstop, Wilson Betemit.

Thousands of miles from Georgia, beginning that night in England, my dad became a foreign-language speaker to me—and I was utterly charmed by it. I had found the foreigner in myself; like so many Italian Americans, Irish Americans and so on, in my early adulthood I had uncovered an exotic background that I would cling to like a favorite shirt, one that everyone else thought was a bit silly or dingy. To me, my half-southernness all of a sudden meant the world. I probably started sounding a little bit more southern then, in Oxford of all places, trying on a heritage I had only just decided to love.

But he was proud that I had learned several languages in college. Introducing me to a German customer of his, he would say, "Now, y'all speak German," and the red-faced, fluently English-speaking customer and I would sheepishly talk in German while Dad looked on. By that point he had accepted that I wouldn't join the navy, and would find my way in civilian clothes instead. If I hadn't quite turned out like him, I had become something he could tell friends about, anyway.

Languages became something of a calling card of mine. Someone would say "Lane speaks like nine languages," and someone else would say, "Really, which ones?" I'd start to explain with the outward sheepishness and inner pride of the nerd.

I started with Spanish, in high school. Unlike for most kids at fourteen, it was a joy from the start, like cracking a code, English put through a funky processor. I went on to German in college and spent my junior year in Hamburg. Every other free elective I had in college I plowed into language classes, working up decent French and basic Russian. Later I began learning Arabic, shortly after September 11, 2001. It seemed like a good idea at the time. By then, I'd been hired as a Web editor at *The Economist*. Arabic, I hoped, might give me a jump ahead in foreign-affairs journalism. Over several years, I've learned to read a newspaper and to chat in colloquial spoken Arabic, but this, the hardest language I've studied, is a work in progress.

Finally, I met a six-foot blonde with a smile as wide as the sky at another linguistically significant Fourth of July, in 2005. My wife, Eva, is Danish, and I have spent the last few years working on that language while I also learn Arabic. Danish takes a backseat to the more professionally useful Semitic language, and my wife's English would be the envy of most Americans, so there's little incentive to learn it. Besides, Danish is a beast to pronounce. But when my wife leaves me alone in Copenhagen, I realize that I know more than I think and can get through half an hour of conversation without struggling too badly. It's not Kierkegaard, but it works.

What made me want to write this book, though, was not all the languages I know. It was all those I don't. My experiences trying to speak new languages and often failing made me realize what an amazing faculty the average human child has for learning language. (Nothing humbles you like an eight-year-old in another country treating you like an idiot for your broken language.) My son is nine at this writing, and his linguistic ability is through the roof—not just for a nine-year-old but compared to the many intelligent immigrant adults who struggle with English in America. Most people, especially the "sticklers" I poke gentle fun at in this book, see linguistic incompetence everywhere. I see what seems like a never-ending miracle.

Like most people, I was first educated to think that "real" language was a codified, formal thing that educated people got right and most people got wrong. But gradually, as I struggled with different languages, the English rules I had been taught started to seem a little arbitrary. That "Hank and me" that my grandfather taught me never to say? The French say *Henri et moi*, "Henry and me," never *Henri et je*. Sticklers say you can't end a sentence with a preposition, but Danes do. (*Hvad taler du om?*, or "What talk you about?") The English rules were taught to me as self-evident and logical, yet people broke them all the time speaking the "correct" version of their own languages. Were French and Danish illogical, or were the rules I had been taught in English based on something else besides logic?

Putting languages side by side made me start to see *language,* not languages. Listening to the languages of the world, not with an ear for mistakes but with a curiosity for the new, the world begins to be a much more interesting place. I hope readers of this book will discover the fascinating variety of language not as a problem but as a treasure.

What does this kind of thinking about language have to do with politics? Language is a powerful marker of our identity: our social group, our class, and our nation. Virtually since we have had written records, and no doubt before, language has distinguished Us from Them. But the connection between language and politics has become ever more explicit with the rise of modern nationalism. We will see that while sticklerism has been with us for a long time, it has been wedded to a particular kind of conservative nationalism in the modern era. Not all sticklers are political conservatives or nationalists. But the rigid thinking behind sticklerism—"you must speak and write this way, and *only* this way"—dovetails with a rigid thinking about group belonging.

Once people in the modern era started thinking of themselves as belonging to nations, they developed a bad habit of trying to chase out diversity, including linguistic diversity. At the more harmless end of things, this has meant nuisances like ineffective and even humorous attempts to reform language, prescribing this usage and proscribing that one. But things get more serious when modern nationalism has meant trying to destroy minority languages, expel speakers of neighboring languages from the country, or make life miserable for people who don't know the standard language. And at the extreme, modern nationalism has also been at the root of our most violent wars, especially in the twentieth century. We will see examples from dozens of countries on every continent. I hope this global approach will make the reader realize that concerns about language and languages are universal and old as the written record itself. But they have been sharpened in the modern age by the idea of nationalism.

Sticklers who will object to much in this book: I hear you. The standard languages that are the vehicles of great writing and formal speech are a valuable heritage that we must teach children, so that they gain access to their heritage and history and can distinguish themselves with their words. But as I hope to make clear here, standard languages are inventions, most of them confined to a recent period in human history. They are codes that give access not to clear thinking and basic decency but to the structured parts of our lives such as job interviews, political speeches, literary essays, novels, and the like. They signal education and learning, but they are not the same thing as education and learning.

This book will attempt to connect fretful thinking about language with modern identity politics, looking at some of the characteristics the two share. It will encourage a different way of thinking about language: not neat, clear-cut boxes ("This is English, this is not"; "This is quality language, this is not") but as overlapping and moving clouds ("This is how these people here speak, not unlike, but interestingly a bit distinct from, the people here next to them"). I think flexibility, humility, and multilingualism should take the place of sticklerism, arrogance, and nationalism when we think about language. I believe this is a more human way to think about our most human faculty, not to mention a source of much more sheer joy. Too many people are too angry about language too much of the time. That time that could be better spent listening, learning, and enjoying the vast variety of human language around them.

And so we return to the two men who taught me language and who represent the two poles of language in this book. I hope my grandfather, the proud colonel and stickler of sticklers, would have enjoyed it. I doubt I would have changed his mind completely, but I hope I would have made him think twice about where some of the rules he liked to enforce came from, and what was really worth fighting for: not compliance but communication, not rules, but rhetoric. His captivating speech came not from his grammar or vocabulary but from the joy he took in wielding them well.

And my father? A stickler could have found fault with much of what he said. His grammar was nonstandard, his pronunciation southern, his vocabulary earthy and frequently not the type you want your three-year-old learning. He was also the best talker I ever knew. Dad could tell the same joke again and again and make it funny every time. And the stories he told of growing up, getting in trouble, and fighting his way through life got more outlandish every time I heard them. Yet I couldn't wait to hear them again. He could spellbind any audience.

I learned what poor language use really looks like. Dad died of cancer, which traveled slowly to his brain until he made little sense. He would ask non-sequitur questions or worry about things that hadn't happened. Over time, it came so that words just poured out of him, the remnants of grammar still there for a while, then just words, then just sounds.

But that wasn't my father. My father was an absolute genius with language: funny, fiery, persuasive, enchanting, and most of all, charming. To anyone who would hear his southern English at its peak and say, "He can't speak properly," I'd say, "The hell he can't." And there's just enough southern in me to look for a fight over it. He didn't speak French or German, but he taught me that there's more than one way to put two words together. Language isn't just rules and words, but communication. And my father was a master talker. This book is for him.

CONTENTS

YOU ARE WHAT YOU SPEAK

Babel and the Damage Done

Language and Myth

The Gileadites captured the fords of the Jordan leading to Ephraim, and whenever a survivor of Ephraim said, "Let me cross over," the men of Gilead asked him, "Are you an Ephraimite?" If he replied, "No," they said, "All right, say 'Shibboleth.'" If he said, "Sibboleth," because he could not pronounce the word correctly, they seized him and killed him at the fords of the Jordan. Forty-two thousand Ephraimites were killed at that time.

—JUDGES 12

The power of language in the human imagination is illustrated by one of the best-known stories of Genesis. Men, in their arrogance, began to build a tower that would reach to Heaven, rivaling even the glory of God. God, who admits he is "a jealous God," is not amused and resolves to take action. But what does he do? Does he smite the tower builders, as he does a host of other unfortunates throughout the Old Testament? Does he send an unforgettable visible sign, like the writing on King Belshazzar's wall or the pillar of fire that led the Israelites through the desert?

These things, well in God's power, would have been more

direct ways of impeding the arrogant tower builders. But instead, God makes a decision that will have lasting consequences, deciding to "confound the language of all the earth." Before the birth of historical linguistics, the Babel story explained how the world came to speak a multitude of languages. Adam and Eve presumably spoke the same one. Genesis tells us how this happy state of affairs ended and we got Akkadian, Hittite, and Hebrew.

But the more interesting part of this story is what it shows about the power of language in the eyes of its authors. God worries that with one common language for humankind, "nothing will be restrained from them." This, remember, is *God:* he can flood the world, rain frogs on the Egyptians, turn rivers to blood, and raise the dead. Communication through language must be mighty indeed to worry the Supreme Being into doing something about it.

The epigraph beginning this chapter may be the first recorded, but certainly not the last, story of language differences getting violent. Militant Protestants and Catholics distinguished one another in Northern Ireland in part by the modern-day equivalent of "shibboleth": Protestants pronounce the eighth letter of the alphabet "aitch," while Catholics say "haitch." Minor differences in the Serb, Croat, and Bosniak pronunciations of the language once known as Serbo-Croat were played up by ethnic nationalists in the run-up to the wars in the former Yugoslavia. (The former Yugoslavs have abandoned "Serbo-Croat," now insisting they speak Serbian, Bosnian, and Croat.) And after a horrifying multiday spree of shootings and bombings in Mumbai in December 2008, Indian police insisted that Pakistanis were behind the massacres. Though the killers had attempted to appear Indian, Indian authorities noted spelling mistakes in their letter of demands. Pakistanis retorted that certain pronunciations— "zoror" versus "jurur"—marked the terrorists as Indians. The two nuclear-armed rival countries mobilized troops amid talk of war, as the shibboleth appeared again in its most life-or-death form.

If language is enough to get God himself involved and a terrifically powerful marker of who belongs to what tribe, we would expect humans to try to control it by raising one language above all others—and sometimes even restricting who can use it and when and how.

Hebrew died out as a standard language almost two thousand years ago. As Aramaic became more common in the ancient Middle East, Jews began using the holy language of the Torah mainly for religious purposes. Hebrew was effectively dead for those millennia, until Eliezer Ben Yehuda began the revival of it in Palestine. But the idea of using the holy tongue for scolding a child or ordering food offended the most Orthodox Jews, who resisted violently. It is those same ultrareligious types who don't even speak the name of their god. Modern scholars can only guess (from the Hebrew text, which omitted vowels) that the Jewish deity's name is "Yahweh." When reading the Torah aloud, religious Jews replace YHWH, the four letters of God's name, with *adonai,* "Lord." Elsewhere, they simply refer to him as *haShem:* the name. Jews are famous for revering their holy books; less famously but just as fervently, they revere the language itself, too. They once revered it so much that they resisted its revival: to see it spoken in the street would inevitably mean seeing it profaned.

Judaism's Abrahamic rival took the opposite path: not restricting the language of religion but flinging it far and wide. The archangel Gabriel's first word to the prophet Muhammad was *Iqra'!,* "Recite!" Muhammad took dictation of the Qur'an from Heaven in his native language, Arabic, then spoken only in the Arabian Peninsula. From there, he and his successors spread the new religion of Islam spectacularly in just a few centuries. And Arabic was the essential language of Islam. So important was the original language of the text that true Muslims had to read it only in Arabic. (The Qur'an itself states, in God's own words, "And if We had sent this as a Quran in a foreign language other than Arabic, they would have said: 'Why are not its Verses explained in detail in our language? What! A Book not in Arabic and the Messenger an Arab?' " [41:44])

The religious role of the language helped Arabize the lands from Morocco to Iraq. Pious Muslims the rest of the world over must know Arabic to read their holy book too. Any translation is by definition inauthentic—in 2009 an Afghan court upheld the twenty-year prison sentence of a man who had translated the Qur'an into the local dialect of Persian without the Arabic text alongside. This means that hundreds of millions of Muslims—a majority of the world's Muslims, in fact—can access their religion today only in a foreign language.

Different though the Jewish and Islamic approaches are, both faiths revere their sacred language. Being a true Jew means mastering the Hebrew language in order to interact with the texts and learning Aramaic to read Judaism's lengthy exegeses on the Bible. Meanwhile, Arabs so venerate the language of the Qur'an that one of the highest honorifics in Islam is *hafiz*: one who has memorized the entire book.

This is a book about language, not religion, so why all this talk about the sacred? The interplay between religion and language illustrates a core point: language is tightly bound with the things we hold dearest. It makes us human; if united through language, we can be as great as God. But language also defines us as religious tribes: we are those who read the holy texts in their original sacred languages, and you are not. Finally, religious-linguistic taboos reveal some of our magical thinking: using a word, the name of God, risks the sin of taking that holy name in vain. Jews avoid it entirely. Christians make sure that when they are angry they say "Jiminy cricket!" or "Jeez!" The fact that God made this one of only ten commandments tells us something.

The point is that even today, we both worship the power of language and approach it with a dose of fear. People believe that words matter intensely. They often think that the way they speak is inimitable and superior, and that their language is the clearest outward sign of who they are. These two beliefs taken together form a secular religion of language today—and make language an inviting target for mythmaking and manipulation. Often these myths come from those who care most about language, great writers and wordsmiths who should really know better.

For example, did you know that the Arabs have six thousand words for camels and camel equipment; that "muscatel" is an Italian word meaning "wine with flies in it"; and that the Maoris of New Zealand have thirty-five words for dung?

Actually, you couldn't know any of these things, because verbs such as "know" (and "learn" and "discover" and the like) require the following statements to be true. None of these statements is. And they all come from the same source: the entertaining and wide-ranging journalist Bill Bryson, in his book *The Mother Tongue*. This book, meant to be an entertaining but serious look at the English language, begins with an introduction so packed with manifest silliness that it makes for an excellent illustration of why smart people believe so many odd things about language.

The Mother Tongue first takes the reader on a magical mystery tour of foreign languages. Bryson says that "we tend to regard other people's languages as we regard their cultures—with ill-hidden disdain." Too true. Unfortunately, Bryson proves himself right with a series of stories that should have set off his own too-bizarre-to-be-true detector. "In Japanese, the word for foreigner means 'stinking of foreign hair'," he tells us. No. *Gaikokujin* means foreign-country-person. "To the Czechs, a Hungarian is 'a pimple.' " No, to the Czechs, a Hungarian is a *Mad'ar,* related to the Hungarians' name for themselves, Magyars. (A less-common variant, *uhersky,* looks a bit like *uher,* "pimple," but only coincidentally.)

Bryson goes on, "The French, for instance, cannot distinguish between house and home, between mind and brain, between man and gentleman." All three claims are wrong. "Mind" is *esprit*, brain is *cerveau*, and the French can certainly tell them apart. Man is *homme*, but the French have the (English-derived calque) *gentilhomme* for a well-bred man, as well as the word *monsieur* for situations such as "The gentleman would like a cup of coffee." *Maison* does mean both house and home, but that doesn't mean the French "cannot distinguish" them any more than it means that Americans "cannot distinguish" "house," a dwelling, from "house," a kind of electronic dance music.

The "X people have no word for" trope is a staple of curious but only half-informed language writing. It is based on the expectation that a foreign lexicon is mysteriously different if one word in that language equates to two or more of ours (*maison* for "house" and "home") or if we need two English words or more to translate a foreign one. Bryson says we have no word for the Danish *hygge*, then goes on to tell us exactly what it means: "instantly satisfying and cozy" (though he's confused parts of speech: *hygge* is a noun, and so it's "coziness"). Since we have no word for the French *sang-froid* or Spanish *macho*, Bryson says, "we must borrow the term or do without the sentiment." Really? Was there no way to think about cool under pressure or swaggering masculinity, before those words entered English? Bryson is indulging here in a pop form of the theory called "Whorfianism": the notion that without a word for something, you can't think about it.

What about thirty-five Maori words for "dung"? I don't know Maori, so I found a dictionary, which included three: *haumuti, hamuti,* and *tuutae.* "Piece of dung" also came in with *parakaeto* and *paratutae.* Perhaps in every dialect of every Maori, including slang words and euphemisms and animal-related terms, and throwing in adjectives and verbs related to it, you could, at a stretch, turn up thirty-five. But how easy would it be in English? Polite words would be *dung, fertilizer, manure, feces, stool, defecation*; euphemisms would include *poo, poop, doo-doo,* and *number two;* animal terms would include *cow patty, buffalo chip, rabbit pellet,* and *guano;* semi-taboo words would include *turd* and *crap;* silly words would encompass *malarkey* and *caca;* and let's not forget good old *shit.*

What of "muscatel" being Italian for "wine with flies in it"? Not remotely, though Bryson may have been misled by the fact that *mosca* means "fly" in Italian. If you want a fun fact for muscatel, here's one: the name comes from muscat, a type of grape. "Muscat" shares an etymology with "musk." And "musk"? It comes from Middle English *muske,* which comes from Middle French *musc,* which comes from Late Latin *muscus,* from Late Greek *moschos,* from Middle Persian *mušk-,* from Sanskrit *muska,* meaning—wait for it—"testicle." And *muska* comes from the diminuitive of *mūs,* meaning "mouse." So Sanskrit speakers many, many years ago euphemized "testicle" as "little mouse," and through many years of natural language change, the word "musk" evolved along one track and the words "muscat" and "muscatel" developed from another. This doesn't mean that "muscatel" means "testicle wine" or "wine with mice in it" or any such ridiculousness. It means that "muscatel" shares a distant past with Sanskrit words for "testicle" and "mouse"—a story just as interesting as Bryson's, with the virtue of being true.

I can't resist one last Bryson foreign-language story, perhaps the most preposterous of all: "In Cantonese, *hae* means 'yes.' But with a fractional change of pitch, it also describes the female pudenda. The resulting scope for confusion can safely be left to the imagination." This requires a tremendous imagination indeed. I have tried and totally failed to imagine a context in which both "yes" and "female pudenda" might both be appropriate responses to the same question and hilarity could ensue from the wrong understanding. In any case, the "fractional change of pitch" Bryson describes is one of the Chinese "tones," rising, falling, level, or dipping pitch. These tones make one Chinese word as different from another as "bit" and "beet" are in English, and the Chinese have no trouble distinguishing them.

Somewhere out there, a Chinese journalist-cum-humorist may be writing "In English one word means 'cotton or cotton-blend cloths used to cover a bed.' But with a fractional change in vowel quality, it means excrement. The resulting scope for confusion can safely be left to the imagination." Except how often do you really confuse "sheet" and "shit," even when, as many foreigners do, they are pronounced similarly?

Having exoticized—call it amiable bullsheet—every foreign language he has ever heard a tall tale about, Bryson moves on to English, the real subject of *The Mother Tongue*. Here the talented writer is on firmer ground, and by and large the book is an accurate and enjoyable popular history. But first he feels compelled to set up the unique story of English with a list of supposedly mind-bending quirks:

> English is full of booby traps for the unwary foreigner. . . .
> Imagine being a foreigner and having to learn that in English one tells *a* lie but *the* truth. . . . The complexities of the English language are such that even native speakers cannot always communicate effectively. . . . English also has a distinctive capacity to extract maximum work from a word by making it do double duty as both a noun and a verb . . . *drink, fight, fire, sleep, run.* . . .
> There is an occasional tendency in English, particularly in academic and political circles, to resort to waffle and jargon . . . one of the great curses of modern English.

Which of these things couldn't be said of French or German, or a vast number of other languages for that matter?

That is quite enough picking on Bill Bryson. He is, after all, more of a commentator and a humorist than a serious journalist. His writing is laugh-out-loud funny, he has remarkable powers of observation, and he is obviously a highly intelligent man. But being a humorist doesn't get him off the hook; he wrote not just *The Mother Tongue* but several other books trying to entertainingly teach people things they did not know about English. Humorist or not, Bryson really wants to share the things he "knows." The problem is, as the nineteenth-century American writer Josh Billings wrote (though it's often put into the mouth of Mark Twain), it's not the things people don't know; it's the things they know that ain't so.

It seems nobody knows more things that ain't so about language than journalists. No journalist would switch from writing about politics to a writing about physics without checking the facts carefully. But thoughtful and brainy writers think that because they know how to *use* language well, they can suspend their nonsense detector when they write *about* language. Legends get dredged from magazine articles and other secondary sources, themselves badly informed. For the writer passing them along, some stories are too good to check or even to think critically about for several seconds. All a writer needs, when writing about language, is the sense of being a good writer with a fine vocabulary and style. Forget research, dictionaries, etymologies, the insights of linguistics—just use your intuition to decide what to believe or, when in doubt, just wing it. Journalists writing about language without getting the facts, just because they themselves are adept at using language, are like top athletes who think they are physiologists. I, of course, am a journalist too. But I've learned (not least by making my own mistakes) that language really deserves proper study in its own right, not just the odd dashed-off column on a linguistic topic between other endeavors.

If you want entertaining language punditry without too much worry about the facts, I prefer punditry that knows it's fake. Take Dave Barry's "Ask Mr. Language Person," an advice column:

Q: I am a speechwriter for a leading presidential candidate, and I need to know which is correct: "integrity OUT the wazoo," or "integrity UP the wazoo."

A: We checked with both the Oxford English Dictionary and the Rev. Billy Graham, and they agree that the correct word is "wazooty."

But those interested in language don't need to choose between dry academia, too-good-to-check "facts," and satire. There are many fascinating real-world facts about language, including those still being discovered about language's origins, its possibilities, and its global varieties. No enemy of fun facts, I absolutely glory in them. But fun facts are fun only when they're true.

Language myths serve to define "us" and distance "them." Many myths are about one's native tongue. People around the world often describe their own language or dialect as the clearest, most beautiful, most logical, and most expressive. You will also commonly hear speakers of a language you don't know tell you, "Oh, this word is very special in our language. It cannot be translated." Almost immediately, though, they will tell you what the word means, proving themselves wrong. Virtually anything can be translated—"X cannot be translated" usually means nothing more exciting than "We have a word, X, that you need three or four words for in your language." But it is thinking like this, for example, that makes Arab Muslims think the Qur'an cannot be translated. Of course it can.

Other "no-word-for" and "can't-be-translated" myths include the stories that the Irish have no word for "sex" or even "yes" (how, one wonders, is there an Irish people left on the earth if they cannot say "yes" to sex? There are many words for "sex," and Irish, like some other languages, just repeats the verb in a question to reply with "yes"); that the Moken people of Thailand have no word for "when"; that the Inuit had to come up with a word for "twilight" because of global warming, and so on.

The problem is that the harm of these myths goes beyond

the reputations of those who pass them on. In 1985, Ronald Reagan, about to begin a summit with Mikhail Gorbachev, mused about the differences between America and the Soviet Union, saying "I'm no linguist, but I've been told that in the Russian language there isn't even a word for 'freedom.' " There is one, of course: *svoboda*. Reagan, like Bryson, was dabbling in Whorfianism—in this case, the notion that the Russians had lacked freedom for so long that they did not have a word for it and presumably couldn't even talk about it. This, remember, was the leader of the free world, carrying this inane prejudice to his summit with Gorbachev.

One of the most common beliefs about other languages is that certain languages are "primitive." People in literate, wealthy societies often consider the languages of preliterate ones to be unable of conveying much beyond the most basic thoughts. The writing of the colonial era is filled with Western officers describing the "babbling" of the natives. And though no one is so rude to say things like that these days, this is the unspoken implication when a journalist reports on some newly discovered or rare language with "no words for" some basic phenomenon, such as time or sex or colors. The conclusion is tactfully left to the reader: these people are so primitive they can't even talk about life's basics.

The fact is usually just that those words haven't been discovered yet or that the "primitive" language simply expresses the concepts in different ways from the well-known Western languages. As linguists know, it is the popular imagination that is primitive. Not only is there no language in which you can't talk about time or sex, but also there is no such thing as a "primitive language" at all. Many such "babbling" tongues of preliterate or indigenous societies have rules of grammar that are mind-bogglingly complex—not to mention impressive—to any outsider who takes the time to look into them.

Take Tuyuca, spoken now by just under eight hundred people in Brazil and Colombia. Its speakers are poor, and are a prime example of the indigenous peoples taken as simple by colonizers and outsiders. Yet Tuyuca has a feature that linguists call evidentiality. In English, we can say simply, "The boy played soccer." But embedded in the Tuyuca verb is an ending that lets the listener know *how the speaker knew* that the boy played soccer. Did he see the boy playing? Did he hear him? Did he see evidence, such as muddy feet? Did he just assume it, since the boy loves soccer so much and has been gone for two hours? Tuyuca encodes this information directly into a verb suffix.

But are we back to mythologizing the exotic here? Surely the Tuyuca have some deep connection to the epistemological that Westerners lack. Perhaps they are very truthful people, or perhaps they were descended from a race of warrior-lawyers? Nonsense. Evidentiality is unusual, but many other languages, such as Turkish, have it as well. The Tuyuca surely think nothing of this feature of their language.

This brings us to one of the major points of this book: the world's languages—and language varieties such as accent and dialect—have far more in common than they have differences. Noam Chomsky, whose lifelong goal has been to describe the "universal grammar" underlying the world's languages, put it pithily when he said that human languages have far more in common with one another than any does with any other form of possible communication. If Martians came to Earth, they would conclude that we spoke one language, with local variations. It is possible to communicate beautifully, or boringly, in every language on Earth. But people don't like to believe this. They make self-aggrandizing myths instead.

As long as people mythologize language—whether "Our language is logical and beautiful" or "That language is primitive and bizarre"—they will try to control it. This takes several forms.

Dictators often proclaim one language in a country supreme and try to destroy others. Francisco Franco attempted to do this in Spain, for example, legislating Basque and Catalan from the public square. Josef Stalin, who never shed his own Georgian accent, flirted with Russification of minority areas in the old Soviet Union. China has tried to suppress its "dialects"—which are really separate languages—by pushing Mandarin, which it calls *putonghua,* or "common tongue."

Democracies are tempted to control language, too. Despite the overwhelming dominance of English in the United States, the U.S. Senate passed in 2006, à propos of no terrible crisis, a bill proclaiming English the country's "national" language—a status without which English had done just fine for 230 years. Quebec requires that English be banished to a distinctly second-tier status, with English on signs required to be half the size of the corresponding French text or smaller. France nervously asserts its national language over an international competitor, English, by limiting, for example, how much English can be used by businesses based in France. France also has a long history of suppressing its own native regional languages, such as Basque and Breton.

Not all attempts to control language are designed to promote one language entirely over another. Other policies are more subtle or benign. Irish children must learn the Irish language, called "Irish Gaelic" by some, in school. But only a small percentage of Irish still speak the language as their first, and all speak English as well. The vast majority will never use Irish after school, and those hundreds of class hours could be spent teaching science or mathematics, giving Ireland a competitive edge in the cutthroat global economy. The nationalist love for Irish, however, trumps mercenary calculations such as economic competitiveness. The language reminds the Irish of centuries of glorious history before Ireland's domination by England, serving as a link to the past, and—crucially—giving an Irishman the option of distinguishing himself linguistically with more than an accent in English.

The French employ another kind of language politics. The French government seeks to govern when and how the French language is spoken and written by its native speakers. Perhaps most famously, government ministries try to prevent infiltration of Americanisms by offering native French words instead. And the French have a distinctive institution, the venerable French Academy, to rule on questions of French usage. The idea seems strange to Americans or Britons—a government body determining how plurals should be formed? Or to rule officially on whether words denoting job titles (such as *ministre,* "minister") must always be masculine? The French, for their part, respect the Academy. But while this kind of thing delights and engages the French elite, the Academy and government ministries are, more often than not, cheerfully ignored. People the world over, even the French, tend just to speak the way they speak.

Sometimes government fiddling with language looks like mere practicality. For example, leaders might introduce a new alphabet—usually sold as simpler, more suitable, or more modern—in place of an old writing system. But this kind of decision isn't merely a technical one; it can have geostrategic implications. When the Central Asian republics of the former Soviet Union switched from the Cyrillic alphabet to the Roman one, they hinted at where they thought their future lay. Sometimes an alphabet isn't just an alphabet. Meanwhile, the Chinese hold on to their ancient writing system in part because it helps tie together the Chinese-speaking world. Writing phonetically—say, in the Roman alphabet—would reveal that what so many call Chinese "dialects" are as varied as the Romance languages. Recognizing China's real language situation punctures the useful political myth of a single, historic Chinese nation with only trivial internal diversity.

What these attempts to control language have in common is that they are all highly *political*—even when not advertised as such. The belief that language is powerful and one's own language is special, combined with the fear of others speaking differently (especially if you can't understand them), tempts politicians, and the bureaucrats, schoolteachers, and others who support them, to elevate one specific form of a language and denigrate others, and to mess with language itself. The consequences are often ugly.

In every such change there will be winners and losers. The subject is a sensitive one, and there are important decisions to be made. Are some languages or language varieties (such as dialects) really better than others? What would that mean, and how would we know? Should countries choose and promote a single official language? What are the costs and benefits of doing so? Do people have a right to watch TV and read newspapers in their minority languages? How about to be educated in them? Should government promote—or mandate—standard spelling, vocabulary, or grammar? How should countries educate young people in strategic foreign languages? Does immigration threaten the language of a host country? And what about the global stage: is the rise of English destroying other languages? Should tiny, disappearing languages (like Tuyuca) be kept alive, and what would be the reasonable cost of doing so?

A Brief History of Sticklers

In the Trenches with
the Grammar Grouches

Omit needless words! Omit needless words! Omit needless words!

—WILLIAM STRUNK, JR.

What do language pundits have in common with the wild-eyed crowds at certain political rallies or raucous sporting events? They have chosen a side. Fired by the thought that no one can express a thought clearly anymore, they see themselves on the side of right, light, and civilization. Young people who speak differently from the would-be guardians of proper language do drive the latter into a rage. The clumsy writing of high schoolers or college students causes spittle-flecked fury. Perhaps they see other ethnic groups speaking their native language differently than traditionalists do, and they are further provoked and annoyed. *Doesn't anyone know how to use the language anymore?*

In 2003, Lynne Truss published a little book that she admits she was stunned to see become a runaway bestseller. Fist published in Britain, it reached number one on *The New York Times*' list for nonfiction and stayed put for weeks. It has now sold more than 3 million copies worldwide, appeared in an illustrated edition and a children's edition, and became a publishing phenomenon so explosive it surprised Truss herself. Her subject? Punctuation.

Eats, Shoots & Leaves: The Zero Tolerance Approach to Punctuation takes its name from a joke about a panda who, like so many talking animals, walks into a bar. The bear orders food, eats it, draws a pistol, and unloads. To explain his behavior to the patrons as he saunters out, he tosses a "poorly-punctuated" wildlife manual over his shoulder, saying "I'm a panda. Look it up." The manual duly tells the reader that a panda is a small, furry bear that eats, shoots and leaves.

But to Truss, punctuation is no joke. Page after page, she unleashes not just irritation but fury on the decline of English punctuation and those who hasten it. She proudly calls herself a "stickler," and her thrilled readers could safely be called the same. What can possibly cause them such emotion over commas and periods?

The sticklers Truss appeals to in the book are distinguished by several features. One is anger out of proportion to the crime. They can't merely be distressed at the state of modern language use. They must say, "It makes me want to *scream* when I read 'TOMATOE'S ON SALE,' " or "Every time I hear 'between you and I' it's like nails on a blackboard." Truss herself turned her outrage knob to "blinding" by writing that those who misplace apostrophes "deserve to be struck by lightning, hacked up on the spot and buried in an unmarked grave."

All that rage must feel good on some level. After all, Truss was not the first to discover that greengrocers and sign painters are not the most adroit punctuators on earth. The insights in *Eats, Shoots & Leaves* are nothing new. How, then, did she sell so many books? One suspects it is her style, with nary a sentence failing to scream bloody murder or whip up a linguistic lynch mob. She doesn't do subtlety.

And if language rage feels good when you do it alone, when the usage police find one another, it is rage on uppers. The phrase "Sticklers, *Unite*!" is the unofficial motto of Truss's book. The novelist David Foster Wallace invented a fictional

Militant Grammarians of Massachusetts in one novel, a stickler union of sorts. In real life, the novelist's family used code name "SNOOT" to describe themselves, the usage militia.* The Society for the Promotion of Good Grammar (SPOGG), "for pen-toters appalled by wanton displays of Bad English," claims six thousand members. SPOGG features friendly blogs on its own website and sponsors National Grammar Day (March 4). Like most pleasant feelings, whatever feels good about language seething feels better when it's shared with others.

This epiphany—"I never *realized* that other people felt like I do"—points to one of the key features of the grammar and usage snob: the delicious feeling of seeing something that only a select few have ever seen before. The archetypal grammar grouch feels that

- English (or another language) is threatened as never before in its history.
- Language education is at an all-time low.
- Innovations, from pronunciation to vocabulary to grammar to slang, harm the language.
- Technology is aiding and abetting this mess.
- Before long, we will barely be able to communicate at all.
- The stickler is part of a hardy band of people who simply refuse to see standards lowered.

In other words, language "sticklers" thrill in a sense of *uniqueness:* their language is especially precious, it is especially threatened, and it is especially threatened *right now* as opposed to other times in history.

---

* As Wallace had it, the derivation was from "*Sprachgefühl* Necessitates Our Ongoing Tendance" or "Syntas Nudniks of Our Time," depending on whether the speaker was a SNOOT or not. *Sprachgefühl* is German for "language feel" or "sense for language."

This will probably come as a disappointment, then, to the sticklers reading this, but it nonetheless has to be said: generation after generation of grown-ups and sticklers have said the same thing, through every period in human history, for languages in every corner of the earth. If you look at the historical record, you will find that language has always been in decline. Which means, really, that it never has.

Language changes. The average language vigilante claims to know this and, if she has an English degree, will know it especially vividly from the history of literature. Of the first work known to be written in English, the epic *Beowulf,* barely a word will be immediately clear to the modern reader:

> Hwæt! We Gardena in geardagum,
> þeodcyninga, þrym gefrunon,
> hu ða æþelingas ellen fremedon.
> Oft Scyld Scefing sceaþena þreatum,

From that Old English of a thousand years ago, the situation had improved a bit three hundred years later. The text below, from Chaucer's *Canterbury Tales,* is recognizably English but still opaque to those who haven't studied the vocabulary and grammar of Middle English:

> Whan that the knyght had thus his tale ytoold
> In al the route nas ther yong ne oold
> That he ne seyde it was a noble storie
> And worthy for to drawen to memorie
> And namely the gentils everichon.

In those three centuries, English had changed so much that Chaucer would barely have been able to read *Beowulf,* if at all, and would probably not have been able to understand a spoken conversation with a Beowulf-era English-speaker either.

Another three centuries or so along, English had become this, from Shakespeare's *Coriolanus:*

> MENEUIS AGRIPPA: What work's my Countrimen in hand? Where go you with Bats and Clubs? The matter Speake I pray you.

> SECOND CITIZEN: Our busines isn't vnknowne to th' Senat, they 60 haue had inkling this fortnight what we intend to do, w now wee'l shew em in deeds: they say poore Suters haue strong breaths, they shal know we haue strong arms too.

We can just about make this out, but in this passage it's striking how distant it is. Modern editions of Shakespeare, with their changes of his spelling, capitalization, and punctuation, have helped generations of English teachers make Shakespeare seem contemporary to tenth-graders. Plus, when we watch *Romeo and Juliet* or *Hamlet* we know the stories and lines so well that we have no trouble following along. But a random passage from a less well-known play, unchanged by modern editing, shows more starkly how different the language is, and not only in spelling and punctuation: English had different pronouns (*thou, ye*); word endings (second-person verb ending—*est*, the third-person ending—*eth*); word order ("The matter Speake I pray you"); and the use or lack of auxiliary verbs ("Where go you?"). The pronunciation of Shakespeare's era would be quite strange to the modern ear, too: "deeds" would have been pronounced something like "dades."

When the United States came on the scene about two centuries later, the language was still in flux. At the time of the American Revolution, Benjamin Franklin thought all nouns should be capitalized. Noah Webster imposed spelling changes on a country that clearly did not think there was only one correct way to write a word. And Thomas Jefferson's apostrophes would have had Lynne Truss hacking him to pieces: "[W]hen we see or read of any atrocious deed, we are disgusted with it's deformity . . . we are pleased with the subsequent atonement, and view with emulation a soul candidly acknowleging it's fault and making a just reparation."

So language is changing constantly; printing and modern education have slowed it but have not stopped it. Given all this change, when, exactly, was language *perfect,* in the language pundit's mind? One has the feeling that the decline-mongers would feel rather sheepish hazarding any answer. The 1950s? The Edwardian era? The real answer, however rarely expressed, seems to be "when I learned it as a young person." I, for one, have zero doubt that when my generation is in its sixties, we will think that the kids can't talk anymore and education was really at its peak in the 1980s. But does anyone seriously claim to be able to show when, exactly, there was a "high point" of English and why that point and not others was the peak?

The fact is that scolds have been bewailing others' vocabulary, pronunciation, and grammar virtually since English was written down. The first printer in English, William Caxton, complained about English's diversity and change in a story he told around 1490:

> For we English men are so borne under the domination of the moon, which is never steadfast, but ever wavering, waxing one season and waning and decreasing another season. . . . [O]ne of them named Sheffield, a textile trader, came into a house and asked for food, and especially he asked for eggs [*eggys*], and the good woman answered that she could speak no French. And the merchant was angry, for he also could speak no French, but wanted eggs. And she did not understand him. And then at last another said that he wanted *eyren.* Then the good woman said that she understood him

well. Lo, what should a man in these days now write,
eggys or *eyren*? Certainly it is hard to please every man
by cause of diversity and change of language.

By the Elizabethan period a century later, a "standard" English based on the London dialect was being built, though
other dialects persisted around England. At the same time,
poets and playwrights played with still-fluid conventions.
Shakespeare violated virtually every rule that would later become a prescriptive shibboleth, gleefully splitting infinitives,
using "they" with a singular antecedent, verbing nouns, ending
sentences with prepositions, and so forth.

The new standard English, arising after Caxton and still
developing in Shakespeare's time, was based on the scribes of
London's Chancery, which produced government documents.
And with the growth of standard English, a growth in prescriptivist dictates could not be far off. The existence of an emerging
standard meant the beginning of linguistic self-consciousness:
the desire to speak "correctly," and the fear of being looked
down on.

Why is it "wrong" to end a sentence with a preposition?
Did you even notice that I just did it two sentences ago? Unless
you are a copy editor, you probably didn't. That's because this
is the natural way to frame that sentence. Who, upon seeing a
cake in the office break room, says, "For whom is this cake?"
instead of "Who's the cake for?" Where did this rule come
from?

The answer will surprise even most English teachers: John
Dryden, the seventeenth-century poet less well known as an
early, influential stickler. In a 1672 essay, he criticized his literary predecessor Ben Jonson for writing "The bodies that these
souls were frightened from." Why the prepositional bee in Dryden's syntactical bonnet? This pseudo-rule probably springs
from the same source many others do: the classical languages.
Dryden said he liked to compose in Latin and translate into En-

glish, as he valued the precision and clarity he believed Latin required of writers. The preposition-final construction is impossible in Latin. Hence: it is impossible in English. Confused by his logic? Linguists remain so to this day. But once Dryden proclaimed the rule, it made its way into the first generation of English usage books roughly a century later and thence into the minds of two hundred years of English teachers and copy editors.

The rule has no basis in clarity ("Who's that cake for?" is perfectly clear); history (it was made up from whole cloth); literary tradition (Shakespeare, Jane Austen, Samuel Johnson, Lord Byron, Henry Adams, Lewis Carroll, James Joyce, and dozens of other great writers have violated it); or purity (it isn't native to English but probably stolen from Latin; clause-final prepositions exist in English's cousin languages such as Danish and Icelandic). Many people know that the Dryden rule is nonsense. From the great usage-book writer Henry Fowler in the early twentieth century, usage experts began to caution readers to ignore it. *The New York Times* flouts it. The "rule" should be put to death, but it may never be. Even those who know it is ridiculous observe it for fear of annoying others.

Some of these invented rules managed to make their way into our lives, to plague us endlessly. But more often throughout history, prescriptivist grousing has utterly failed to stop language change. Jonathan Swift, writing about a century after Shakespeare, was the wickedest satirist of his generation. But when it came to language, the humor drained from him. In 1712, to the Earl of Oxford, he wrote:

[O]ur Language is extremely imperfect; that its daily Improvements are by no means in proportion to its daily Corruptions; and the Pretenders to polish and refine it, have chiefly multiplied Abuses and Absurdities; and, that in many Instances, it offends against every Part of Grammar.

To Swift, English had borrowed too much French. The young nobility were no longer getting a proper education. Spelling was slowly being altered to match pronunciation changes. He even wrote that "I would rather have trusted the Refinement of our Language, as far as it relates to Sound, to the Judgment of the Women, than of illiterate Court-Fops, half-witted Poets, and University-Boys." Women! Things must have been bad indeed.

One writing change annoyed Swift in particular:

> There is another Sett of Men who have contributed very very must to the spoiling of the English Tongue; I mean the Poets, from the Time of the Restoration. These Gentlemen . . . to save Time and Pains, introduced that barbarous Custom of abbreviating Words, to fit them to the Measure of their Verses; and this they have frequently done, so very injudiciously, as to form such harsh unharmonious Sounds, that none but a *Northern Ear* could endure: They have joined the most obdurate Consonants without one intervening Vowel, only to shorten a Syllable.

The offending examples? Swift offered "*Drudg'd, Disturb'd, Rebuk't, Fledg'd*, and a thousand others." He thought the *-ed* ending should be both spelled out and pronounced in every instance. Before Swift, it always had been, but by his time, there was some free variation, depending on what fit better into poetic meter, for example. Over time, though, the trend against pronouncing the *-ed* ending was too strong. Today, "disturbed," "rebuked," and so forth *must* be pronounced in the way Swift hated so much. Yesterday's abomination is today's rule.

The particular change involved in "disturbèd" becoming "disturb'd" is natural almost to the point of universality in the long run. Latin had *hominus;* modern French, its descendant, has *homme* (pronounced "um"). Classical Arabic has *kabir* and *saghir* (big and small); modern spoken Arabic has *kbir* and *sghir*. Time is hard on unstressed syllables, grinding them down as the pronounced *-ed* ending was. And so on through languages everywhere. It's as natural as life is short.

Like so many of his successors in the language-crank world today, though, Swift not only loathed this banal and common change; he ascribed it to moral failing:

> I am afraid, My Lord, that with all the real good Qualities of our Country, we are naturally not very Polite. This perpetual Disposition to shorten our Words, by retrenching the Vowels, is nothing else but a tendency to lapse into the Barbarity of those *Northern* Nations from whom we are descended, and whose Languages labour all under the same Defect.

Fast-forward three hundred years, and you can just hear Swift's successors complain that the teenage use of "like" signifies fuzzy thinking or that the rising intonation used by many teenagers ("So I really liked this *movie*? I saw it with *Brett*?") is a sign of shallowness. Not content to note a change or say they don't like how it sounds, the sticklers make snap judgments about others' souls.

Swift's preferred solution to sound change, grammatical evolution, and new vocabulary had already been tried elsewhere in Europe: the creation of a language academy. Like many others (including Dryden), he hoped that a body of eminent writers could render judgment on questions of usage; their reputations would be so great as to fix the language in place. Swift had a model in mind: the French and Italians had recently created their own academies (which we will meet in later chapters).

The later part of Swift's eighteenth century saw two figures emerge who would become the progenitors of two great traditions, though the labels "prescriptivist" and "descriptivist" did not exist yet. One was Samuel Johnson, the writer of the first great English dictionary; the other was Robert Lowth, the first bestselling English grammarian.

Today, Johnson is widely known and admired, while Lowth is barely known. Every student of the history of English learns that Johnson wrote a bestselling dictionary that set the standard for modern lexicography, even though his methods were sometimes unorthodox (he famously defined a lexicographer as "a harmless drudge"). Johnson also had the luxury of a talented biographer, a literary star in his own right, James Boswell.

Johnson recognized in his dictionary's preface that, contrary to Swift's hope, language could never be frozen in place, no matter how many great writers insisted on this or that usage. Johnson himself drew on the great writers—most of his dictionary entries cite just a handful of sources, including Shakespeare, Milton, and the King James Bible. But despite drawing on the greatest authorities possible, he wrote that his intention was "not to form, but register the language." He recognized explicitly that the language couldn't be frozen. Johnson therefore wouldn't be surprised today that spelling, punctuation, word usage, grammar, and punctuation have all changed quite a bit in the centuries since he wrote, even as his efforts helped slow down some of that change. Though it's true that Johnson sometimes seemed to feel that the language was in decline, he didn't rail against it with Swift's anger. Instead, he hoped the example of his dictionary would temper that change by providing a distinguished literary example.

Lowth was a different creature. He was educated at an elite school and studied at New College, Oxford, quickly distinguishing himself in religious scholarship. He published a new translation of the Old Testament book of Isaiah and ran in a circle of authors who were taking a new interest in the Middle Eastern languages (including the Hebrew of the Old Testament). Lowth and his fellow scholars would become a set of pre-Romantic Romantics, who looked to find the "genius" of languages that represented the spirit of their peoples. He would rise through the Church's ranks, through the position of bishop of Oxford, to become bishop of London, and would have become archbishop of Canterbury but for his ill health.

His work *A Short Introduction to English Grammar*, written while he was at Oxford, was an unlikely hit. It appeared anonymously in 1762, was subsequently reprinted every year or two until 1838, and influenced many grammarians after him. Some would even copy his rules word for word

Lowth's title page bears a quotation from Cicero, reading (tellingly, in Latin):

> Speaking Latin properly is indeed to be held in the highest regard—not just because of its own merits, but in fact because it has been neglected by the masses. For it is not so much noble to know Latin as it is disgraceful not to know it.

Lowth then redoubles the point. In his introduction, he asks "Does . . . the English language, as it is spoken by the politest part of the nation, and as it stands in the writings of the most approved authors, often [offend] against every part of grammar? Thus far, I am afraid, the charge is true. . . . Our best authors have committed gross mistakes, for want of a due knowledge of English grammar." Note that he even does his exemplar Cicero one better: not just the masses, but even "our best authors" commit "gross mistakes."

With this, Lowth lays the cornerstone of the prescriptivist tradition: that the rules are the rules, standing above actual practice. Who cares how "the politest part of the nation" speaks? Who cares what "our best authors" write? The rules are to be drawn from foreign languages, deduced from logic, or simply declared *ex nihilo*. The language was, thenceforth, to be shaped by sticklers and their grammars, not by the users (even the finest users) themselves.

Lowth's method was to instruct by "false syntax," taking examples from "our best authors' " offenses against proper grammar. The King James Bible, one might expect, could be exempt from this clergyman's criticism. The 1611 translation, by a committee of some of England's greatest scholars and writers, is still considered by many to be the finest volume of written English in history. But Lowth is unafraid to criticize even one of its best-known passages. The very first words of the Lord's Prayer contain a mistake, according to him: "Our father, which art in Heaven . . ." For Lowth, "which" can refer only to inanimate objects and "who" is required for persons (including the Supreme Being); it must be "*who* art in Heaven."

Shakespeare, too, falls short of Lowth's standards: "the lab'ring heart / who in the conflict that it holds with death, attracts the same for aidance 'gainst th enemy" (from *Henry VI*) should be "the heart *which*," writes Lowth. And on and on, with many other examples of bad English from the finest writer in the history of the language. Nor were the Bard and the Bible special targets. The good bishop also shows where John Addison, Milton, Alexander Pope, Dryden, Swift, John Locke, and the Anglican Church's liturgy offend against his rules.

Never did it occur to Lowth that the King James Bible and the works of Shakespeare were more than a hundred and fifty years old as he criticized them. Nor did it ever bother him, as he found "errors" one after another from the pens of the greatest writers, that perhaps they were right and he was wrong. For Lowth, the rules were simply obvious outgrowths of logic. There was no room for variation or change, because he was not describing the language as it exists but telling the language how it *should be*. The modern reader, meanwhile, is charmed by the things Lowth solemnly prescribes as proper English but that have now utterly fallen out of usage. For Lowth, "gat," "brake," "clave," "spake," "sware," "tare," "weare," "trode," and "crope" were the past-tense forms of "get," "break," "cleave," "speak," "swear," "tear," "wear," "tread," and "creep." He was successful but not invincible; those forms had already begun to disappear by his time.

Lowth repeated Dryden's proscription of the preposition at

the end of a sentence, "an idiom, which our language is strongly inclined to." It's not clear whether he was being funny in using the idiom itself in the act of prohibiting it. (Modern writers do this sometimes for humor, but Lowth doesn't do his own "false syntax," and he isn't intentionally funny elsewhere.) He recognizes that people end sentences with prepositions "in common conversation" but thinks that the practice should be banned from formal writing, singling out Locke for writing "We are still much at a loss, who civil power belongs to" and Shakespeare for "Who servest thou under?" (Also, that should be *whom.*)

Lowth pronounces another famous rule with a dubious logic: the ban on the double negative. The double negative was, even in Lowth's time, not common in educated standard English. But it was common in many dialects and in everyday English, and it had even been standard in earlier eras. Lowth proscribes it, however, with an appeal to a quasi-mathematical logic: "Two negatives in English destroy one another, or are equivalent to an affirmative." But there is no reason that this is necessarily so. Chaucer and Shakespeare used it. French uses two negative particles, *ne* and *pas* (*Je ne sais pas,* "I don't know"). Languages from Spanish to Russian require the negative pronoun to go with a negated verb (*No tengo nada,* "I don't have nothing," and *Nichevo ne znaiu,* "I don't know nothing"). But the double negative, already in decline in English by Lowth's time, was finished off (at least in polite circles) by his disapproval. Today, teachers can still be heard telling pupils that "I don't know nothing" means "I know something." Though most have never heard of Lowth, they are echoing his centuries-old, faulty logic.

Another kind of doubling would also attract his ire: double comparisons (including the double superlative). Shakespeare wrote of "the most unkindest cut of all" in *Julius Caesar,* and the King James translators of the Acts of the Apostles wrote "after the *most straitest* sect of our religion." Once again, the writers who used those phrases saw them, like the double negative, as an option, providing extra reinforcement. No, it's not logically possible to be straighter than the straightest, but poets (and ordinary speakers) often like to play with logic. It's one of the possibilities that language gives us. But for Lowth, the greatest writers of the language were wrong and the bishop of Oxford was right. Lowth's disapproval of the double comparative hastened its decline and death in modern English.

Lowth's tone and methods have several hallmarks. One, as we have seen, is intolerance for change: Lowth seemed surprised that Shakespeare wrote differently in 1600 than Lowth thought proper in 1762. A second Lowthian trait is an appeal to a kind of logic that resembles mathematics; that two negative words in a sentence must result in a positive meaning. (The possibility that they might reinforce each other eludes him.) Finally, Lowth, like many sticklers to follow him, was simply unwilling to accept variation as a fact of language. Though double negatives were common in many people's speech, for Lowth, there must be only one correct way. Poetic forms such as "most straitest" were to be shouted down. The rules were just the rules.

Though Lowth's own book was a bestseller, he multiplied his influence with his mark on another grammar-book writer, Lindley Murray. Born in America (the Murray Hill neighborhood in Manhattan bears his family's name), Murray moved to England in his later years, and the *English Grammar* he published there would quickly become a phenomenon in both countries. Published in 1795, it went through twenty-one editions in Britain and twice as many in America in just eleven years. His repetition of Lowth's rules helped carve many of them in stone. He reiterated the double-negative rule and corrected his predecessor on the sentence-ending preposition rule, saying that this was an idiom "*to which* our language is strongly inclined." He even made his example sentences morally as well as grammatically uplifting, saying (in the third person) that he wishes to promote in some degree, the cause of virtue, as well as of learning; and with this view, he has been studious, through the whole of the work, not only to avoid every example and illustration which might have an improper effect on the minds of youth, but also to introduce, on many occasions, such as have a moral and religious tendency.

In this, he was certainly not the first (remember Swift) nor the last (we'll get back to Lynne Truss) to mix up grammar and morality. A stickler hallmark is that those who speak or write differently can't be merely wrong; they must be depraved, too.

The nineteenth-century saw Lowth's and Murray's influence spread, through an explosion in books on grammar and usage that they heavily influenced. What began as a trickle in the mid-1700s was a tidal wave a century later. Britain was democratizing; the United States was a vulnerable young republic. Both began to promote universal education, believing that an educated citizenry was the strength of a nation. Unfortunately, this "education" often included the made-up grammar rules stemming from the likes of Lowth and Murray.

It was in the nineteenth century that another famous non-rule appeared. The first prohibition against the split infinitive occurs in an 1834 article by an author identified only as "P." After that, increasingly over the course of the nineteenth century, a "rule" banning split infinitives began ricocheting from grammar book to grammar book, until every self-conscious English-speaker "knew" that to put a word between "to" and a verb in its infinitive was barbaric.

The split-infinitive rule may represent mindless prescriptivism's greatest height. It was foreign. (It was almost certainly based on the inability to split infinitives in Latin and Greek, since they consist of one word only.) It had been routinely violated by the great writers in English; one 1931 study found split infinitives in English literature from every century, beginning with the fourteenth-century epic poem *Sir Gawain and the Green Knight,* through wrongdoers such as William Tyndale, Oliver Cromwell, Samuel Pepys, Daniel Defoe, John Donne, Benjamin Franklin, Samuel Johnson, Edmund Burke, Samuel Taylor Coleridge, Elizabeth Barrett Browning, and others.

Rewording split infinitives can introduce ambiguity: "He failed entirely to comprehend it" can mean he failed entirely, or he comprehended, but not entirely. Only putting "entirely" between "to" and "comprehend" can convey clearly "he comprehended most, but not all." True, sentences can be reworded to work around the problem ("He failed to comprehend everything"), but there is no reason to do so. While many prescriptive rules falsely claim to improve readability and clarity, this one is worse, introducing a problem that wasn't there in the first place. Yet as split infinitives in fact became more common, in nineteenth-century writing, condemnations of it grew equally strongly. The idea that "rules" were more important than history, elegance, or actual practice—a zombielike prescriptivism that mindlessly sought out so-called mistakes—held writers and speakers in terror of making them.

Beginning in the late nineteenth and early twentieth centuries, things began to change. Interest in the historical development of languages was overturning many old ideas. The philologist William Jones, in the late eighteenth century, had discovered the Indo-European language family. The realization that English and French were related to Persian and Sanskrit upended many cherished notions about the uniqueness of any given language. Knowing that languages so far apart shared an ancestor made people realize just what a contingent, mutable thing any one language was at any one time.

Perhaps as a result, the more thoughtful usage sticklers of

the twentieth century took a different tone from their predecessors. They used wit and persuasion, not bare pronouncements, as an aid to teaching people to write, rather than simply reciting mechanical rules. George Bernard Shaw typified this new kind of thinking. He was a linguistic genius who created the ultimate language snob, Henry Higgins. In *Pygmalion,* Higgins tells Eliza Doolittle that

> A woman who utters such depressing and disgusting sounds has no right to be anywhere—no right to live. Remember that you are a human being with a soul and the divine gift of articulate speech: that your native language is the language of Shakespeare and Milton and The Bible; and don't sit there crooning like a bilious pigeon.

But for the real-world Shaw, rules were a means to graceful expression, not an end in themselves. In a fury about one brainless prescriptivist, he wrote to a newspaper:

> If you do not immediately suppress the person who takes it upon himself to lay down the law almost every day in your columns on the subject of literary composition, I will give up the Chronicle. The man is a pedant, an ignoramus, an idiot and a self-advertising duffer. Your fatuous specialist is now beginning to rebuke "second-rate" newspapers for using such phrases as "to suddenly go" and "to boldly say." I ask you, Sir, to put this man out, without interfering with his perfect freedom of choice between "to suddenly go," "to go suddenly" and "suddenly to go." Set him adrift and try an intelligent Newfoundland dog in his place.

The most influential stickler of this new, thoughtful breed, however, was not a great literary figure like Shaw. Instead, it was an unlikely former schoolteacher and modestly successful essayist, who only in his last decades wrote the towering usage book that dominated the first half of the twentieth century.

Henry Watson Fowler, born in Kent, England, in 1858, taught at a private school into his middle age. But he was forced to forgo a promotion to housemaster at the school; he explained to his headmaster that he simply couldn't prepare the boys in his care for their confirmation into the Church of England. He later wrote, "Thirty years ago I thought religious belief true; twenty years ago doubtful; ten years ago false; & now it is (for me, of course) absurd." Unable to continue his first career, he moved to London, where he lived humbly, writing essays, until moving to the island of Guernsey to write with his younger brother Francis.

In 1906, the two put out a usage book, *The King's English,* that, according to *The Times* of London, "took the world by storm." Not a grammar book but a manual for better writing, it frowned on Americanisms, vogue new words, circumlocutions, and overuse of Latinate vocabulary. But it did all this in a punchy style that made the book, for those into that kind of thing, a page-turner.

Eight years later, Fowler and his brother enlisted in the army, lying about their ages, at the outbreak of the First World War. But they were given rear-echelon duty that both of them chafed against until they petitioned for release from service. Frank contracted tuberculosis and died; Henry was heartbroken.

As an old man and with some modest fame for the *King's English,* he wrote his greatest work; *A Dictionary of Modern English Usage,* now known to most simply as "Fowler's." In the alphabetically organized work, Fowler does everything from specify the pronunciation of words such as "pharaoh" to rule on the grammar and usage controversies of the day. On the split infinitive, his tone was typical:

The English-speaking world may be divided into (1) those who neither know nor care what a split infinitive is; (2) those who do not know, but care very much; (3) those who know and condemn; (4) those who know and approve; and (5) those who know and distinguish. Those who neither know nor care are the vast majority, and a happy folk, to be envied by most of the minority classes. . . . A real s.i. [split infinitive], though not desirable in itself, is preferable to either of two things, to real ambiguity, and to patent artificiality.

Elsewhere, Fowler equally demolishes other modern shibboleths. Under the headword "Fetishes," he scorns those who refuse to end sentences with prepositions. He derides the ban on "none" with a plural verb. ("None of us are happy" is fine with him. Most sticklers insist on "None of us is happy.") Under "Superstitions," he similarly dispatches those who will not begin a sentence with "and" or "but," describing the prohibition as an "ungrammatical piece of nonsense."

More than a printed and bound referee on usage controversies, the *Dictionary* also continues the work of *The King's English* in acerbically offering judgment on how to write better. Fowler's dislike of clichés and autopilot writing, for example, is clear in the entry on "hackneyed phrases":

> There are thousands for whom the only sound sleep is *the sleep of the just,* the light at dusk must always be *dim, religious;* all beliefs are *cherished,* all confidence is *implicit,* all ignorance *blissful,* all isolation *splendid,* all uncertainty *glorious,* all voids *aching.*

The clichés he goes on to condemn include some that today seem quaintly old-fashioned: "balm in Gilead," "consummation devoutly to be wished," "curate's egg," "in a Pickwickian sense," "neither fish, flesh, nor good red herring." His old-fashioned style is on display elsewhere too, for example writing that "Mahomet" is just fine, in response to those who would insist on the more accurate "Mohammed" or "Muhammad" for Islam's prophet. And he had apparently never met a female pedant: "Men," he writes, "are as much possessed by the didactic impulse as women by the maternal instinct."

So why the enduring appeal for such a fusty book? While feistily judgmental, Fowler was a realist. Language changes, he realized, as had his predecessor Johnson (and unlike Swift, who thought it could be stopped). Fowler mourns, for example, that *-monger* could once be appended to innocent words such as "cheese," "iron," and "fish" but had acquired a permanent taint of scandal with "war," "gossip," "whore," and the like. For Fowler it was an unwelcome development. But he saw no point in trying to reverse it; *-monger* could not be saved. Being aware of the flux of language, he himself would have been surprised to see every one of his judgments remaining valid a hundred years after he wrote *The King's English* and eighty after his *Dictionary*.

Fowler was painfully shy in person. But in his writing he combined confident self-awareness ("We have all of us, except the abnormally stupid, been pedantic humorists in our time") with an unapologetic habit for prescription. It was this mix of authority and humility that made his usage guide an unparalleled success. The dictionary is still in print, in a third edition, today. And Oxford University Press, its publisher, still gets letters of admiration, and sometimes queries, addressed to H. W. Fowler, who died in 1933.

Fowler was a particularly English type: old-fashioned, tobacco-stained, fond of cricket and of an early-morning swim in the bracingly cold waters of Yorkshire. His American equivalent, in fame though not in intellectual temperament, was an obscure Cornell professor named William Strunk, Jr., who required students in his English composition class to buy a little book that he had self-published.

Strunk's book was later edited by E. B. White, the novelist best known for *Charlotte's Web*. "Strunk and White," formally known as *The Elements of Style,* is far slimmer than Fowler's *Dictionary.* But on American shores, it is far bigger in the public imagination. *The Elements of Style* has been in print continually since 1959 and is estimated to have sold more than 10 million copies. In 2005 an illustrated edition was published. The book was set to music by a composer named Nico Muhly, and hundreds went to see it performed at the New York Public Library. Wendy Wasserstein borrowed the title for *Elements of Style,* a novel about New York's nervous days following the September 11 terror attacks. And in 2009, to mark its fiftieth anniversary, *Elements* was reissued in a leatherbound, gold-embossed edition.

What about a usage book makes it seem like a lifeline, a guide to the perplexed, a Bible? A clue is given by White: he tells us in the introduction that Will Strunk never seemed to entertain doubt. His commands were issued as if by a sergeant to his platoon: "Do not join independent clauses by a comma." "Do not break sentences in two." "Use the active voice." "Omit needless words." Many of *Elements*' readers, apprehensive about their language ability, craved authority. Strunk provided it to his Cornell students, and White passed it on to millions of readers.

But *Elements of Style* used this forcefulness in ways that were sometimes useful, sometimes odd. While Fowler had disdained obsession with the small things, Strunk often seems not to know what, exactly, is small. The first rule of his revered book? "Form the possessive singular of nouns by adding 's . . . whatever the final consonant"—except, for some reason unexplained by Strunk, ancient names such as Jesus and Moses. No justification is given for this exception for the ancients or for the rule at all. There it is, simply pronounced, leading *The Elements of Style*'s first page.

Surely a more important rule of composition, grammar, or style would begin any book being published in the twenty-first century: shirt-collar-grabbing stuff this is not. But that is the odd little book that is *Elements*. Its treasured commandments include leaving enough space at the top of a title page for editors' instructions to typesetters; using generous left-hand margins for notes; writing "August 9th" when the author is using the date but spelling it out in a quotation, as in "I come home on August ninth"; and many other trivia that have more to do with an idiosyncratic house format than with crucial rules of grammar, much less style.

Elsewhere, Strunk and White make other odd choices: "which" is said to be for "nonrestrictive" clauses, while "that" introduces "restrictive" clauses:

The lawnmower that is broken is over there.

versus

The lawnmower, which is broken, is over there.

The first is meant to specify which lawn mower (the broken one); the second presumes that the reader knows which lawn mower is being discussed and adds the fact that it is broken by the by.

This is given by Strunk and White as another of those rules that simply *is*, without need for justification. But commas, supported by context, actually do all of the crucial work here, so the rule is not needed for clarity. In speech, intonation would convey the same information as the commas. And as Strunk and White note, the restrictive "which" is common throughout English history: the King James translators and Shakespeare both use it. (Nonrestrictive "that" crops up too, mainly in nineteenth-century literature, but is less common.) White, furthermore, proves that restrictive "which" is just fine—by writing it more than once in his other works, such as in his own essay "Death of a Pig":

. . . the premature expiration of a pig is, I soon discovered, a departure which the community marks solemnly on its calendar.

Leaving grammar aside, Strunk and White condemn many word choices that grate on their ears. They seem to think that "claim" can't be used to assert the truth of a statement: Germany can *claim* Alsace-Lorraine, but a partygoing loudmouth can't *claim* he speaks French. This is typical of the kind of oddball rule that pops up in the book and probably originated with Strunk.

White adds a semifamous bugbear of his own. He, and generations of pedants after him, claim (sorry) that "hopefully" can be used to mean only "in a hopeful way" and not in a sentence such as "Hopefully I'll arrive on Tuesday." This is despite the existence of many other so-called "sentence adverbs," which work just like "hopefully":

Frankly, he's dissembling.

Honestly, he's a liar.

Seriously, he's a doofus.

All three would be absurdities if adverbs were required to refer to the grammatical subject. But obviously, they don't: they convey the writer's or speaker's own attitude. Most of these other sentence adverbs have never been condemned, but for some reason, *Elements* condemns "hopefully" with special force.

White's editor noticed that some of the little book's provisions seemed arbitrary. But White held his ground. For example, *Elements of Style* holds that "like" comes before nouns and pronouns. ("He smells like fish.") "As," by contrast, comes before phrases and clauses. ("He smells like fish, as you would expect from a fishmonger.") Never, so they thought, could you write "He smells like fish, *like* you would expect from a fishmonger." His editor thought this rule idiosyncratic to Strunk and White and wondered if it was really needed in the book. White clenched his jaw and held firm, and it was kept.

Having taken Strunk's pet peeves and added many of his own, delivering them with the voice of God, White was surprised at some of the reactions to the book when it was published. Who were these picky and annoying letter writers, pointing out "errors" that he had forgotten to condemn? He wrote a friend:

> Life as a textbook editor is not the rosy dream you laymen think it is. I get the gaa [*sic*] damnedest letters every day from outraged precisionists and comma snatchers, complaining every inch of the way.

One letter writer was worked up by a new and vogue usage, "to dress up." White politely responded that he thought it was just fine, saying that there was an important difference between "to dress" and "to dress up." But on what basis could White condemn "hopefully" while accepting the new extension of "to dress"? We never find out. Peeves are like that: my peeves are law, yours are unhealthy obsessions.

On writing style itself, Strunk and White issued two commands that are indeed usually best followed; the famous "Omit needless words!" and the instruction to use the active voice rather than the passive. But the form of the book itself—command after command, in contrast to Fowler's lofty mode of humorous and erudite persuasion—means that this advice has been passed down as holy injunction, rather than good guidance. (The influence of Strunk and White's inflexibility on the passive voice can be seen in the fact that many versions of Microsoft Word, a computer program that doesn't even understand language, automatically condemn the passive voice.) The fault isn't entirely Strunk's, for penning a hodgepodge of writing advice, grammar prejudices, and personal gripes for his students; nor White's, for adding a gloss and popularizing it. It is those who have treated *Elements of Style* like a sacred book, rather than the occasionally handy bit of idiosyncratic guidance that it is. People crave a hard linguistic hand, with no tolerance for variation. Strunk and White gave it to them.

There is really only one way to learn good writing: through good reading and extensive writing and revising. If students in college and high school are exposed to high-quality, well-edited writing year after year, some will develop into competent and even good writers. Many will not. But writing is, ultimately, an artistic *skill,* not the mechanistic application of rules, something that Fowler realized. Fowler's great redactor, Ernest Gowers, wrote of his hero that "the prime mover of his moralizing was not so much grammatical Grundyism as the instincts of a craftsman." However, for Strunk, baseless rules (which include never using "however" at the beginning of a sentence to mark a transition with some contrast, as this sentence does) needed to be shouted crisply. Perhaps Strunk thought that he knew when to break them but that all other writers had to be treated like incompetent freshmen. Though Strunk and White occasionally admit that language changes and rules can be broken, the forceful tone of their field manual has been better remembered than their occasional nods to flexibility and change.

And so we return to Lynne Truss. Fowler began the century with his careful, witty usage dictionary; Strunk passed the baton to White in midcentury, and advice became commands. By the turn of the twenty-first century, there was little new to be said about grammar, punctuation, or usage. So the best way to get attention was to pass on the old rules louder and more irately than ever before. And here we return to our theme: the politics behind the claim that language is going to hell in a handbasket on greased wheels these days.

How might we gather that Truss is concerned about more than just punctuation? The first thing we might look for is someone not overly shy about making statements that are flatly false. And sure enough, near the beginning of her furious little volume, she says that grammar and punctuation are "simply not taught in the majority of English schools." *if that was true wed expect that nearly everything written by people educated in england in the last few decades too look like this but it doesnt seem to be so* Mistakes may be more common than Truss would like, but to say that grammar and punctuation are "simply not taught" in most schools beggars belief.

A bit later on, Truss again enjoys the indulgence of the story that is simply too good to check: "There is a rumour that in parts of the Civil Service workers have been pragmatically instructed to omit apostrophes because no one knows how to use them anymore." This simply doesn't pass the laugh test. Sure, we get the weasel-worded introduction "There is a rumour," and of course some civil servants are incompetent writers. But the scene of a department head telling her staff, "Okay, everyone, it's time to stop using apostrophes—it's simply too much of a bother" is surely more urban legend than even rumor. Truss's own success in Britain as well as America reminds us that every office has at least one of her beloved sticklers, who would throw an almighty fit at any such injunction.

Truss goes on to describe her early days as a stickler in a passage that speaks volumes.

> While other girls were out with boyfriends on Sunday afternoons, getting their necks disfigured by love bites, I was at home with the wireless listening to an Ian Messiter quiz called *Many a Slip,* in which erudite and amusing contestants spotted grammatical errors in pieces of prose. It was a fantastic programme. I dream sometimes they have brought it back. Panelists such as Isobel Barnett and David Nixon would interrupt Roy Plomley with a buzz and say "tautology!" Around this same time, when other girls of my age were attending the Isle of Wight Festival and having abortions, I bought a copy

of Eric Partridge's *Usage and Abusage* and covered it in sticky-backed plastic so that it would last a lifetime. (It has.) Funny how I didn't think any of this was peculiar at the time, when it was behaviour with "Proto Stickler" written all over it.

What's going on here? "Tautology" isn't a grammar error; it's a logical one, with either unnecessary reinforcement in a phrase ("free gift," also called a pleonasm) or a statement written so that it can't be falsified, for example by definition or circular logic. Think of Yogi Berra's "You can observe a lot by watching."

This isn't nitpicking (although one could be forgiven for picking the nits off of the self-appointed world-beating nit-picker). It shows a major problem in many people's thinking about language errors: category error.

"Grammar," to the language specialist, is how words and sentences are built from meaningful components. It describes how nouns are made plural or verbs put into the past tense; how individual words can be bolted together into phrases, clauses, and sentences that obey the rules of syntax.

But for those to whom Lynne Truss is a hero, everything from spelling convention to word choice to logic is, somehow, "grammar." And in the popular imagination Truss typifies and electrifies, "grammar" always gives one and only one correct answer to any question. This is the distillation of Strunk's ethos: say it loud, show no doubt, and never, ever change your mind.

Admittedly, Truss says her book is about punctuation, not grammar. But from the "tautology" mistake, it seems she isn't quite sure what grammar is anyway or doesn't much care. The important thing she wants you to take away is that she cares obsessively for the Rules, whatever they are.

What about the political content of Truss's fury? It seems too obvious to be accidental that Truss mentions—not once but twice—sex and its consequences. She was learning punctuation while "other girls . . . were getting their necks disfigured by love bites" and reading Partridge while "other girls . . . were having abortions." When Truss mentions the years of her schooling—1966 to 1973—we finally see our culprit. It is the 1960s and all that went with it: free love, rebellion, drugs, protest, permissiveness, even the poor Isle of Wight Festival. It was the end of the sure and simple world of the 1950s, when the scariest thing around was Elvis's pelvis. It was unsettling even for those who enjoyed it. And for those who like certainty, it must have been pretty hard indeed.

Once life was simple, and there were *rules,* by God. Then the kids started putting flowers in their hair and occupying the universities. After that, the teachers got so scared that they threw out the rulebooks, started teaching "free writing," and saying "Express yourselves." Now nobody knows the bleeding difference between *its* and *it's*. The great majority of English schools simply do not teach grammar or punctuation.

The idea that there was once an age when people knew better crops up again and again in prescriptive rants. Truss betrays this with temporal phrases. "The disappearance of punc-

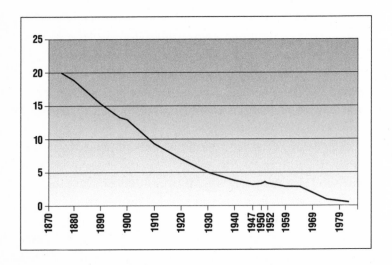

Illiteracy among the population 14 years of age and older in the United States.
Source: U.S. Census Bureau, at http://nces.ed.gov/naal/lit_history.asp.

tuation (including word spacing, capital letters and so on) indicates an *enormous shift* in our attitude to the written word, and nobody knows where it will end." (Emphasis added.) Truss doesn't spell out when exactly it was that people once worshiped the written word and punctuation was sacrosanct. But if this chapter has taught you anything, it is that no such period ever existed. To be sure, we can point to exam questions from turn-of-the-twentieth-century schools that seem to indicate that once every boy and girl got a frighteningly thorough education in grammar and writing. But this is misleading. At the turn of the twentieth century, few boys and girls actually got this education; many still lived in the countryside and skipped school to help their parents in the fields. Others, in the cities, dropped out to take factory jobs as soon as they were able. In both Britain and America, illiteracy is actually far lower today than in the past, not higher.

A hundred and forty years ago, one in five Americans was illiterate. Now less than one in a hundred is—and this fall began during a hundred years of "separate but equal" dismal schools for blacks in America. In Britain, illiteracy is rarer still. It may be true that formal grammar was taught more extensively in good schools in the past. But the notion that once upon a time, every schoolboy was an H. W. Fowler, every schoolgirl a perfectly punctuating Lynne Truss, but today no one can put two words together simply holds no water. Where is the former golden age of the written word?

But never, as the hack journalist says, let the facts get in the way of a good story. Truss and her followers, and their many predecessors over the centuries, want to enrage, not educate. Language is in terminal decline! Soon we will not be able to write at all, or perhaps even speak!

This isn't true, just as it wasn't when Swift said the same in 1712. But "declinism" sells; it sells political books, and it sells politically tinged language books. It is telling that Truss's follow-up book was not on educational reform or remedying

inequality. It was *Talk to the Hand,* on the decline of manners—
another *New York Times* bestseller.

Not only is declinism not new, as hundreds of years of examples show. It is not particular to the Anglophone world, either.
Not only have English and American schoolmarms worried
about "kids these days" for centuries. Similar concerns have
nagged speakers of languages around the world throughout
recorded history.

Cicero was the most famous grouch of the Latin age. He
said that standards of knowledge of Latin were "disgraceful."
He groused that nobody was pronouncing certain words correctly anymore. But even he knew he couldn't do anything
about it: "at some point, and it was late, since the truth was
wrenched out of me by the chatter in my ears, I relinquished to
the people the custom of speaking, I reserved the knowledge [of
correct grammar and pronunciation] to myself." Cicero was
right to worry; Latin was "declining," if you can call it that—
into modern French, Spanish, Portuguese, Italian, and the
other Romance languages.

Another theme that we've seen among declinists in the Anglophone world also crops up globally. This is the notion that
generations ago, even simple folk spoke or wrote better than
the most cultivated people today. While today's grouches
worry that no one knows how to distinguish "who" and
"whom," endings that mark case (like "whom," which signifies an object rather than a subject) often disappear from languages over time. To the sticklers, this common process always
looks like disintegration from an earlier, happier time when
everyone knew the endings. Change is always disintegration.
Jacob Grimm (1785–1863), known by most for his work with
his brother collecting fairy tales, was actually a philologist. He
was no Germanic grammar grouch, as he understood that language changed naturally. But even he regretted that German

had lost so many grammatical endings, writing nostalgically that

> In reading carefully the old Teutonic sources, I was every day discovering forms and perfections that we generally envy the Greeks and Romans when we consider the present condition of our language. . . . Six hundred years ago every rustic knew, that is to say practiced daily, perfections and niceties in the German language of which the best grammarians nowadays do not even dream.

But one nostalgic's "perfections and niceties" of an earlier age are simply another's outdated, unnecessary endings of a bygone era. German had no "golden age," at least not any more than English did. Language just changed.

Declinism isn't limited to the speakers of classical or "sophisticated" European languages. Nonwritten languages change even faster than those with a written tradition. Printing and writing, dictionaries and grammar books slow—though they can't stop—language change. So oral cultures might have even more reason to worry about "kids these days" than cultures with a written heritage. Wolof, a widespread West African language used by many nonnatives to communicate when they don't share a native language, may be losing some of its sixteen genders. (You might have thought German was complicated with three, but many languages have far more obligatory noun classes than the European languages do. Though they have little to do with sex, linguists call these genders, a word related to "genre.") Because of the large numbers of nonnatives who can't learn all sixteen genders, many "kids these days" hear, and thus learn, Wolof without them. This doesn't mean that Wolof is in decline. And in fact, in nonliterate societies, you hear less declinism than in literate ones. But linguists nonetheless do report hearing parents complain about the language of the kids, whether by ordinary change, mixture with another language, or some other garden-variety phenomenon.

This isn't as common as it is in more literate societies, of course. The existence of written grammars—not to mention modern systems of education that pound those grammars into students' heads—creates a class of people with a strong incentive to showcase their education by complaining that they've mastered difficult rules others can't seem to grasp. But the fact that field linguists even occasionally find related, stickler-like attitudes among nonliterate societies too should give the modern American or British declinist some perspective. Every language is always changing; it simply can't be true that they are all in decline.

One of the nastiest things to do in an argument is impugn another's motives and to claim you know what someone else *really* means. So let me finish this with a tip of the hat to the many sticklers I have disagreed sharply with in this chapter.

Fowler's magisterial rulings speak not only for their author's erudition but for his passion. His willingness to slaughter sacred cows such as the split-infinitive rule should be emulated by every self-appointed grammar curmudgeon. Strunk's rather more wild-eyed ways—especially the insistence on keeping his advice so terse that it did not allow for thoughtful discussion—shows us a man who saw a language he loves mauled by too many college students. (And this a hundred years ago, further demolishing the notion of some kind of past golden age of linguistic perfection.) E. B. White was a fine writer who was right to occasionally violate the edicts he ordered others to follow in *Elements of Style*. Even Truss's zesty writing, when she stays away from violent revenge fantasies, makes it perfectly clear that she enjoys putting words on a page. As for Bishop Lowth, who bequeathed us some of the most unkillable stupidities of English grammar teaching, I struggle to find many kind words for him. I suppose he did produce a fine translation of Isaiah, and I hope his Hebrew grammar instincts were better than his English ones.

The point of all this is to put prescriptivism—from the elegant Fowler to the hyperventilating Truss—into some perspective, historical and global. What is today English is the descendant of a dialect almost randomly chosen; had King Alfred the Great not moved his capital to London, we would be writing in an unrecognizably different Wessex-derived dialect today. Today's English writing conventions were made up piecemeal over centuries. Those rules change, just as "silly" no longer means "innocent" as it did centuries ago. Educational standards may drop, and slightly fewer people may be skilled at using the written conventions of the standard dialect than at some point in the past. But then again, most people will never be skilled writers anyway, ever, for the main reason that they don't need to be. Elegant use of written English simply isn't needed for most people's daily lives. As Truss noticed in school, there are, after all, sex, music, and a whole host of other things to spend time on. It is people who are decent writers themselves who, strangely, discover that mastery of written mechanics is the ultimate coin of human worth.

And yes, there is a political content to this idea too. It is the politics of an aggrieved conservatism, standing against youth, minorities, and change. We have seen declinism across the centuries and across cultures. But for today's declinists, the point of departure seems particularly sudden and stark. It is usually only hinted at but sometimes said quite explicitly that the world was better before the 1960s. That happens to correspond with challenges to authority of all kinds: the liberation of women, the rise of youth culture, and sexual autonomy for most people, something many conservatives have still not gotten their heads around. It is also the era of the civil rights movement in America, the beginnings of nonwhite immigration to Britain, and whole hosts of things that polite people don't criticize directly.

When criticism of these ultimately positive upheavals

didn't seem the right thing to do, those who were unsettled found innocent victims to defend. The music just didn't sound like *music* anymore. Drugs were addling a promising generation. Crime was beginning to turn "downtown" into "the inner city." And the language itself was increasingly mangled, as teachers were afraid to teach and kids were emboldened to refuse to learn.

For racial minorities, language played a cruel role in their incomplete emancipation. Minority groups have always struggled hardest to master the standard language. Either they suffered hundreds of years of the most depraved discrimination (blacks in America) or they come from foreign-language backgrounds and poverty, are stuck in poor schools, and are the victims of racism upon arrival.

Standard languages are both a tool for and a weapon against these groups. Those minority-group members who learn the standard are praised as "articulate," are seen as successfully integrated, and have a fast track to the top. Everyone loves an underdog success story. But those who don't master the standard—because they speak a different home dialect (many black Americans), go to bad schools (most racial minorities in the West), or come from a different language background (recent immigrants and their kids)—have a hard road already. And racism against them is too easily hidden behind, and justified by, the criticism that "they just don't know how to speak correctly." If we recognize that they simply come from different dialect or language communities, this problem takes on a different hue: the task of teaching people who have slipped off the social ladder to get their feet back on the rungs—through standard English.

So by all means, learn and cherish the rules of standard written English. It has a great history and binds together disparate groups in a society. This book is written in it, by someone who loves language too. But it's useful because it *works,* not because its arbitrary rules are somehow sacrosanct. Some rules are silly. Some vary over time. Some vary by place. Some are matters of house style. And some are disputed.

Of the rules that remain, those that are widely accepted as part of the standard language, some are obvious. (No child above the age of four needs to be taught that the past tense of "I am" is "I was.") Some are not. (Many educated people can't use "whom," and it may be passing out of the language.) And in the case of punctuation and mechanics, the rules are mainly not even grammar, strictly speaking. Punctuation is there to make writing *easier to read*, not to appease angry language gods.

Sometimes even Truss seems to agree:

> What happens when [punctuation] isn't used? Well, if punctuation is the stitching of language, language comes apart, obviously, and all the buttons fall off. If punctuation provides the traffic signals, words bang into each other and everyone ends up in Minehead. And if you take the courtesy analogy, a sentence no longer holds the door open for you to walk in, but drops in your face as you approach.

That's more like it: bad punctuation as loose stitching, bungled traffic signals, or, perhaps the best metaphor, discourtesy. The conventions of any language, and especially the written conventions, are not a matter of good versus evil, the saved and the damned, or Christ and Antichrist on the plain of Megiddo. They are simply conventions, and useful ones at that. Lynne Truss seems, in her less operatic moments, to know this. But such a reasonable tone wouldn't have sold quite so many books.

Another Way to Love Language

The Insights of Linguistics

The '60s attitude in education that grammar "doesn't allow us to express our inner souls," that grammar is in fact a class warfare tool used by the ruling elite to oppress the lumpen proletariat, may have placed the English language beyond redemption. This suits some linguists fine.

—CHRISTOPHER ORLET, "Our Inarticulate Future," *The Weekly Standard*

Why are linguists so hell-bent on placing the English language beyond redemption? Is the discipline of linguistics, or the school of "descriptivism," ruining our linguistic savvy, our ability to communicate? Who are these linguists, anyway, and why do they hate our language so much? Is it possible that people who have chosen to dedicate their entire lives to studying language—the professional linguists Christopher Orlet disdains in the quotation above—love language, too, and. if so, how could they see it so differently from the way the sticklers do?

In 2006, Louann Brizendine published a book that tapped straight into readers' intellectual id. And no, "intellectual id" is not an oxymoron. There are some things that people seem desperately eager to believe, and they're delighted to find those things "confirmed" by a piece of scholarly-seeming work. Brizendine's *The Female Brain* was just such a hit.

In the book Brizendine claimed, among other things, that women spoke 20,000 words a day, while men utter just 7,000. It was all part of her larger thesis that women's brains work differently from men's. And it was just what many people—especially henpecked husbands, I suspect—wanted to hear. The British *Daily Mail* wrote, "It is something one half of the population has long suspected—and the other half always vocally denied." A journalist blogging at *The Washington Post* wrote, "Women talk too much, and men only think about sex . . . you need a Ph.D. to figure that out?" (Brizendine has an M.D.) The claim was touted prominently on the book jacket and was an Internet sensation.

Something didn't sound right to Mark Liberman, a linguist at the University of Pennsylvania, though. Women speaking three times as much as men? Though his field is phonetics, Liberman also keeps a popular blog, Language Log, where he and about a dozen other linguists regularly post on general-interest language topics that crop up in the news.

Had Brizendine done some new research? Or had Liberman missed some past research that found this huge disparity in men's and women's speech? He looked in the back of Brizendine's book—one-third of the text is footnotes, lending it a weighty air—and found only one reference for the 20,000-word claim: a self-help book called *Talk Language: How to Use Conversation for Profit and Pleasure,* by Alan Pease and Allan Garner. Pease and Garner had not done any original fact-finding research on the subject themselves, nor did they cite anyone who had.

Liberman dug around further. Had anybody else done the research on how much women and men talk? Sure enough, he found that they had. Unsurprisingly, there's a huge amount of variation in talkativeness. Some people, male or female, never shut up, and some rarely talk at all. But as for average differences between the sexes, Liberman found that studies found either no difference at all or a small one—in favor of men. Yes, according to some studies, men talk (on average) slightly more than women. Liberman has not yet found any study showing women talking significantly more, though he's asked his blog's readers to send him any, promising to publish the results. None has shown up.

Confronted with this, Brizendine hedged. She claimed that the Pease and Garner self-help book in her footnotes was meant to be "further reading," not a scholarly citation. She claimed an unfair backlash against her ideas: "It's very politically incorrect to say there are any gender differences." She backtracked to say that women produced more "communication events"—gestures, facial expressions, and whatnot—than men. But in the end she promised to take the bit about female logorrhea out of future editions of the book. Well she might. A study published in *Science* the next year, 2007, was the first to track a large number of people (210 women, 186 men) throughout the day in both the United States and Mexico. Both sexes used about 16,000 words a day, though on average, in this study, the women used 3.5 percent more words, a statistically trivial difference. Brizendine had said women talk 185 percent more than men.

Of course, Brizendine's dud "fact" was already out of the gate, racing around blogs and book reviews. As the book went into multiple translations, foreigners latched on as fast as English speakers have. ("Warum gebrauchen Frauen 20 000 Wörter am Tag, während Männer nur 7000?," as *Das Weibliche Gehirn*'s German publisher touted the claim on Germany's Amazon.de.) It is likely that, despite Liberman's efforts, it will become one of the early twenty-first century's favorite factoids, something that everyone "knows."

Liberman was at it again in May 2009. First George Will, the conservative newspaper columnist, then Stanley Fish, a professor of English with a perch at *The New York Times,* and finally Mary Kate Cary, a former speechwriter for George H. W. Bush, all published columns or blog posts noting that the new Obama presidency was looking unduly egocentric. Specifically, all three claimed that they were starting to hear the word "I" coming out of Barack Obama's mouth more often than seemed proper for a man whose unofficial campaign slogan had been "Yes *we* can." It was supposed to be about the movement, not the man.

Liberman did something that had never occurred to Will, Fish, or Cary: he checked the easily available public record. He looked at the first press conferences given by Obama and his two predecessors. The word "I" comprised 4.5 percent of the words George Bush used in his first two press conferences; Bill Clinton's rate had been 3.9 percent. Of Obama's words in his first press conference, just 2.9 percent were "I." When Cary piled on with her column about how her old boss, the first president Bush, had been far too genteel to prefer the word "I," Liberman went on to show that the elder Bush, too, used it far more often than Obama had. It seems that Obama is unusually I-shy for a modern president.

But Liberman has only a blog, albeit one that gets about 10,000 visits a day; the other three wrote in *The Washington Post, The New York Times,* and the website of *U.S. News & World Report.* No points for guessing which version of the "facts" more people will read and remember. Liberman may not change the public perception, but he patiently chugs on, fact-checking the columnists and pundits' claims of language, motivated by the sometimes naive-looking belief that the truth matters and that in language it is easily discoverable, right there on the record, if only people care enough to actually look.

To get a better idea of what linguists actually do, I thought it was a good idea to observe one in his native habitat. Liberman meets me in his office at the Linguistic Data Consortium, an independent research outfit attached to the University of Pennsylvania. The LDC was set up with funding from the Pentagon's famed Defense Advanced Research Projects Agency (DARPA). On my brief tour around, few people look up from their work. A young woman transcribes an audio file into written Chinese. An Indian programmer and a Tunisian partner work on a computer program that will automatically analyze any Arabic word of a text: click on a word, and the program will tell you the part of speech, case (subject, object, possessor, etc.) or conjugation, attached pronouns and prepositions, proper pronunciation (short vowels are not written in Arabic), and so forth. Reading in Arabic is difficult because many of these things are clear only from context. Humans can use their common sense. The program uses a sophisticated statistical analysis of the words around it to decide whether *ktbt* should be read as *katabtu,* "I wrote," *katabat,* "she wrote," *katabta,* "you [male] wrote," or *katabti,* "you [female] wrote." The program could eventually prove useful in improving the still-rocky quality of computer translation, a field where breakthroughs to higher quality without human assistance seem always five years away.

All around the LDC, hard drives are scattered like bags of chips around a sophomore dorm room. Stacks of CD-ROMs and DVDs a yard high sit next to machines that will mass-produce copies of the LDC's products for use by other research outfits. In the computer room, servers lie in horizontal stacks in tall racks, while the fans that cool them create a surprisingly loud hum. Eight or nine small screens show live television in Arabic, Chinese, and other languages.

Liberman explains the genesis of the LDC, going into more detail than a casual visitor needs but showing the pride of its director. DARPA is famous for funding blue-sky research into technologies so far ahead of the curve that its projects either fail spectacularly or create technological great leaps forward that the market would never deliver. DARPA's interest in linguistics is obvious; machine translation and "defined-item recognition" (such as finding the name "Osama bin Laden" on blogs and television broadcasts and in wiretaps) are clearly in-

teresting to the Pentagon. But the center does no classified research; by the terms of its grant, the LDC must share its work.

Over the course of lunch, I find Liberman open-minded
about everything we discuss, though he is plenty opinionated.
When the famous debate over Whorfianism (which we'll return
to in chapter 4) comes up, he makes a mini-case against it, then
refers me to some scholars who support it. He speaks so slowly
that when I listen to my tape and play it on fast speed, I sound
like an auctioneer and he sounds normal. In his writings on
Language Log, he slowly unwinds thoughts until he has
trawled around and gathered enough information to support
what he wants to say. The overwhelming impression is that of
a man who is relentlessly *empirical:* he doesn't form an opinion
first and then scour for facts that support it. As with the Brizendine and Obama-"I" episodes, he looks at the facts first, does
the math where appropriate, and determines what truths the
facts support.

For those with conservative attitudes to language, this careful
empiricism might come as some surprise. The usage wars that
have pitted sticklers, or "prescriptivists," against professional
language scholars, almost all "descriptivists," have had both
an epistemological and a political cast. The sticklers we met in
the last chapter want to tell people how to speak and write.
Linguists want to discover how people *do* speak and write and
deduce "rules" from observation or description. For sticklers,
this is an intellectual mess.

Take Mark Halpern, a computer programmer by trade
who has also written about language for the *The Atlantic* and
The Vocabula Review and published a book in 2008 called
Language and Human Nature. Halpern has mixed it up with
Liberman on Language Log; when Liberman gently mocked
Language and Human Nature, Halpern sent in a long reply
that Liberman duly posted on the blog. The two men are good
examples of their respective sides of the debate.

Halpern is not the most small-minded or angriest stickler. He acknowledges that some prescriptivist rules are silly and that language change has been the norm throughout history. He doesn't even self-apply the label "prescriptivist," but he is nonetheless a proud "linguistic activist." Language changes through processes that linguists give dry names and tend to describe, not condemn. "Reanalysis" refers to the process by which a mass of certain small round cooked vegetables was once known as "pease" (a mass like "oatmeal" or "porridge") and later was reanalyzed as the plural of a singular noun, "pea." "Semantic shift" refers to how words (for example) often move down-market; "lady" once referred to a female of noble birth but now applies to any female. Linguists tend to note these things and explain. But Halpern scornfully calls those same things "simple ignorance," "social climbing," or "semantic inflation."

Linguists, he feels, aren't really scientists, methodical observers. Instead, he smells an agenda: Halpern liberally (or should that be "conservatively"?) heaps the label "progressive" on linguists. In Halpern's mental caricature, linguists think nobody should condemn anyone for fear of hurting their feelings; linguists approve of any and all language production, including "mistakes," and this is because they are in league with the other softheaded left-wingers who make up the academy. Linguistics is bound up with postmodernism and the denial of the existence of objective facts. This enables "linguistic decadence," which paves the way for atrocities such as anti-Semitism and communism to be wrapped in healthy-looking labels such as virile nationalism or communitarian spirit. When people no longer pay proper attention to language, Halpern argues, they are more likely to be suckered by politicians.

Halpern's writings make clear that he is a political conservative. His criticism of academics as seeking to destroy the very notion of objectivity is an old saw of the political Right. Oddly enough, though, this view of linguists as destroyers of healthy objective thinking is not limited to one-half of the political spectrum.

David Foster Wallace closely mimicked Halpern's critique in a 2001 article in *Harper's* entitled "Tense Present: Democracy, English, and the Wars over Usage," an article widely read and quoted because of its author's dazzling writing in the novel *Infinite Jest,* and his essays and short stories. Wallace was clearly not a political conservative himself, but he makes many of the same mistakes Halpern does when he talks about linguists and linguistics.

Wallace, who admitted to being a usage stickler himself, from a proud family of the same, argued many of the same things that this book does: that language controversies are political ones too, and that identity politics lies at the heart of the project to promote a language standard.

Wallace taught composition at the University of Illinois at Bloomington, an experience that taught him that minority students—coming, as they usually did, with a different language or a distinct dialect such as Black English*—needed standard English even more than whites. His sensitivity to this makes him stand out among sticklers, as does his self-awareness:

> we SNOOTs know when and how to hyphenate phrasal adjectives and to keep participles from dangling, and we know that we know, and we know how very few other Americans know this stuff or even care, and we judge them accordingly,

When Wallace says this, he's not paying himself a not-so-subtle compliment, like Truss. He uses "judge" here to mean no healthy thing. Sensitivity to the political content of sticklerism pervades the essay.

But Wallace nonetheless wheels around to make the case for standard English by relying on utterly misguided arguments

---

* Linguists also call this Black Vernacular English (BVE) or African-American Vernacular English (AAVE), but I see no reason not to use the shorter term.

about what linguists actually are and what "descriptivism" is. He was thus right in only half of his political argument. The famously hip Generation X novelist sounds just like Halpern, the far older writer and proud conservative, when he caricatures linguists and "descriptivists" as part of the progressive, liberal, post-1960s can't-we-all-just-get-along brigade. But he makes error after error along the way. He wrongly identifies the 1961 publication of *Webster's Third New International Dictionary* as the "Fort Sumter" moment of descriptivism. Though based on descriptivist principles, it included monitory notes such as "chiefly dialectal" or "nonstandard" when listing stickler-bait words such as "heighth" and "irregardless." (Somehow Wallace missed these yellow flags, writing that "heighth" and "irregardless" are listed "without monitory labels.") In fact, the 1961 publication of *Webster's Third* built on insights that had been gathering in linguistics for decades, and descriptive practice could be seen in venerable previous dictionaries such as the *Oxford English Dictionary*.

Worse, Wallace somehow confuses linguistics with the humanities. The guiding principles of those two modern disciplines are utterly different. Yes, English and comparative literature departments focus heavily on race, class, gender, colonialism, paradigms, and the like. Wallace doesn't seem to have talked to many colleagues in the linguistics department, though, because very few linguists spend their research time thinking along the lines Wallace condemns.

Perhaps the low point of the Wallace essay comes when he writes:

> Descriptivism so quickly and thoroughly took over English education in this country that just about everybody who started junior high after c. 1970 has been taught to write Descriptively—via "freewriting," "brainstorming," "journaling," a view of writing as self-exploratory and -expressive rather than as communicative, an abandon-

ment of systematic grammar, usage, semantics, rhetoric, etymology.

Wallace has a point here, but it has nothing to do with linguistics. It seems he really means to attack the progressive education movement, which sought (with decent intentions but often misguidedly) to increase the focus on how much students enjoy education. Make it entertaining and personal, and students will learn. But linguists had virtually nothing to do with throwing out the rules of grammar and usage in favor of "freewriting" or "journaling." Wallace was not a journalist, but he would have done well to pick up the phone and call a linguist: if he had chosen a random member of the Linguistic Society of America, he would have been a lot more likely to find someone like Mark Liberman than some softheaded proponent of making kids feel good through "freewriting." In the same sentence, Wallace describes linguists as "doctrinaire positivists" (true of linguists, in that they think scientific truth is discoverable) and having "their intellectual roots . . . firmly in the U.S. sixties" (untrue, at least as far as most of their scholarship goes).

So if they're not really wooly 1960s let's-all-get-along types, how do linguists actually think? Talking about his discipline, Liberman makes a useful comparison to economics. At one end of the spectrum in both fields are the highly data-driven types, the quants whose number crunching and use of computers mean articles filled with formulae utterly forbidding to the outsider. At the other end of both disciplines are the theorists. In economics, this means those who try to come up with elegant (if jargon-laden) explanations for why economies behave as they do, while rarely getting into the data. The same is true of theoretical linguists, who do most of their writing from their studies, trying to figure out how the guts of human language, especially its syntax, work. Much of this field centers around debates about Noam Chomsky, who upended linguistics beginning in the 1950s. Many modern debates still pit passionately pro- and anti-Chomsky camps against each other.

But Chomsky's linguistics does not spring from his politics. For decades, he has been a scathing left-wing critic of American foreign policy in Southeast Asia, Latin America, and the Middle East. But those who might expect that this would lead to antiauthoritarian permissivism in his linguistic work will be disappointed. A typical passage reads not like the postcolonial theorist Edward Said or the postmodern critic Michel Foucault, but like this:

(64)

   a. this book is too interesting to put down without having finished

   b. this book is too interesting [O [PRO to put t down without PRO having finished e]]

The structure (64b) is an instance of (57) with α=O; that is, t is the trace of the empty operator O moved to COMP in the syntax, and e is the parasitic gap licensed by the variable t. If there were no such operator O, the structure would be barred for the reasons already discussed: e would be an NP-traced A-bound by *this book* (structurally analogous to (59b), in which α locally A-binds t and e), rather than being assigned the status of a parasitic gap, as it is.

I don't know what this means, but I take comfort that several linguists tell me they wouldn't, either. For linguists who like to leave campus, this is one of those things you forget after settling into a nontheoretical field after graduate school.

Liberman, as an applied phonetician who began his career at Bell Labs, is one of those who keeps a foot outside the academy. He says that Chomsky once told him that it wouldn't matter a whit to have descriptive grammars of all the world's languages (and that one might as well survey the location of every blade of grass on MIT's campus). For a data-monger like Liberman, the prospect of so much raw information would be drool-inducing.

But whether theoretical or data-crunching, linguists have beliefs about how language works that are as sharply held as that of any Lowth, Fowler, or Truss. And they are just as frustrated when they see others saying things that to them are just plain wrong. Why did Liberman spend so much time debunking Louann Brizendine's "fact" of 20,000 words a day for women against 7,000 for men? Because getting the facts right is important, and the claimed "fact" is used to buttress a theory with important social implications—that women's brains differ significantly from men's. Liberman doesn't disagree that women's brains might well be different; he just objected to seeing bogus information from his field wielded to prove it. If fun facts are fun only when they're true, important facts are important only when they're true.

Linguistics does not have its roots, as Wallace thought, in the 1960s. It goes back much further than that, and perhaps the best introduction to the discipline is a look at one of its most famous subfields, historical linguistics. Historical linguists have been responsible for some of the field's most breathtaking intellectual achievements, including the reconstruction of languages that have not been spoken for thousands of years and were never written down.

The ancient Greeks and Romans thought a lot about language, putting their thinking to use mainly in developing rhetoric, logic, and poetics. They did little studying of how their languages had come to be, however. Elsewhere, the Indians took their Sanskrit language more seriously than possibly any culture in the world, believing that the exact form of its sacred texts gave access to the divine. The scholar Panini, from what is now Pakistan, composed a grammar of Sanskrit that

consisted of almost four thousand rules, one of the most extensive grammars of any language ever published—and this in the
fourth century B.C.

After Panini and the classical era, things would largely go
downhill in thinking about language. The Arabs made useful
and interesting studies of Arabic but rarely looked abroad.
(They were largely codifiers of classical rules, highly successful
prescriptivists in their time—one of the roots of the Arabic
"diglossia," as we will see later.) Christians, meanwhile, believing the literal truth of the Babel story, sought to discover the
original human language. Some thought it to be Hebrew; others tried to classify the world's languages in groups named after
the sons of Noah. One scholar, Johannes Goropius Becanus,
thought that the world's first language was his own language,
Flemish. (The Language Log bloggers, including Liberman,
named an award for Becanus, the "Becky," for outstandingly
ill-informed linguistic pontificating. Its first recipient was
Brizendine.)

But modern historical linguistics would have to wait almost
two millennia to come into its own. It had not a Fort Sumter moment but a Christopher Columbus moment. William Jones, a
lawyer, had been a British colonial official in Calcutta. But he
was also an amateur linguist, and when he returned to London
he gave a lecture that spawned a thousand voyages of linguistic
study after him. Having studied the classical European languages
and then Sanskrit in India, he noticed something striking:

> The Sanskrit language, whatever be its antiquity, is of a
> wonderful structure; more perfect than the Greek, more
> copious than the Latin, and more refined than either, yet
> bearing to both of them a stronger affinity, both in the
> roots of verbs and in the forms of grammar, than could
> possibly have been produced by accident; so strong in-
> deed that no philologer could examine them all three,
> without believing them to have sprung from some com-
> mon source, which perhaps no longer exists: there is a

similar reason, though not quite so forcible, for suppos-
ing that both the Gothic and the Celtic, though blended
with a very different idiom, had the same origin with the
Sanskrit; and that the old Persian might be added to the
same family.

Language may not be in decline, but they don't make British
civil servants like they used to. The lawyer and amateur linguist
had just taken the biggest step yet in the invention of modern
linguistics. Greek and Latin *pater* ("father") looked too much
like Sanskrit *pitar, mater* too much like Sanskrit *matar;* Jones
found so many such correspondences that they simply couldn't
be attributed to chance.

As with Columbus's discovery of America, Jones may not
have gotten there first. Others before him had noted the similarities among Latin, Greek, and Persian, for example. But it
was Jones's public announcement that changed the world. Further investigation would show that Hindi, Punjabi, Kashmiri,
and other north Indian languages, plus Persian, some of the
languages spoken in the Caucasus and Central Asia, and virtually all the European languages, were related. (Of the European
languages, a very few, including Basque, Finnish, Hungarian,
and Estonian, did not form part of the family.) As relatives, the
newly discovered huge new family needed a common ancestor.
This language, painstakingly reconstructed in ensuing years,
came to be known as Proto-Indo-European.

Jones's discovery and the quotation above are as well known
to linguists as Thomas Jefferson's opening of the Declaration of
Independence is known to American schoolchildren. The discovery of Indo-European led to an explosion of interest in languages and their histories. The first modern scientific linguists
began to investigate just how the modern languages had emerged.

If Jones's speech formed a foundational text for linguistics,
one of its first early lawgivers was Jacob Grimm—perhaps the
James Madison of the discipline. In his work, he began to develop one of the tools of modern language science: the laws of

language change. Grimm proved that languages don't change randomly due to speakers' laziness; they change *systematically*. Grimm noticed, in piecing together modern German words with their Gothic ancestors and with Greek, that certain sounds in one almost always corresponded with a related sound in another. Where Greek had *p*, Germanic would tend to have *f*, as Greek *pous* ("foot"), which became German *Fuss*. Other Germanic languages share the *p*-to-*f* shift: Gothic *fotus*, Icelandic *fótur*, Danish *fod*, Swedish *fot*, and of course English "foot." Other languages kept the *p* sound, like Latin (*ped-*). We see them today in "pedestrian" and "podiatry," derived from Latin and Greek into English.

Grimm found many other systematic changes, such as Greek *b* to Old Germanic *p* to modern German *f*, and tied them together in what linguists now know as Grimm's law. Other scholars have refined the original "law," improving on its details, and extended that work to the other Indo-European languages, finding equally systematic changes to the ones Grimm had discovered. German and Danish scholars jumped especially eagerly into the new research.

The discovery first of the huge Indo-European family, and then of systematic changes over time, made it impossible to see language the same way again. While the books of Lindley Murray and Robert Lowth were selling millions of copies by simply pronouncing ex cathedra rules—"Two negatives destroy each other"—Jones, Grimm, and their companions and followers were investigating dozens of languages across thousands of years. They were discovering rules of phonetic and grammatical mutation, finding both regularity and huge variety. The laws the early linguists discovered even allowed them to reconstruct, to a certain extent, words and stems of the Proto-Indo-European language itself, though that language had never been written down. One German scholar, August Schleicher, went so far as to write a short fable in what he said was Indo-European. Of course, true knowledge of the exact language—which was more probably a bundle of dialects and not a single standard language—isn't possible, and Schleicher's effort is enjoyable for his audacity if not to be trusted for accuracy.* (Other scholars have updated it as scholarship has advanced.) Today, joining together with archaeologists and historians, historical linguists continue to try to locate the original Indo-Europeans in time and space. Some posit Turkey as their home, while others make the case for southern Russia.

Whatever their disagreements, though, all historical linguists know of Jones's speech and Grimm's law, and the incredible intellectual achievements that followed. That Irish, French, Hindi, and Armenian sprang from a common source is not a curious fact but a commonplace one to the historical linguist. After having those stories drilled into their heads in the first year of graduate school, it is far harder for the modern linguist to look at any language today, whether English or Sinhalese, and see anything but a snapshot of a general, constantly mutating phenomenon called "language" at a particular place and time. While the stickler might see the misuse and gradual disappearance of "whom" as proof that education and society have been flushed down the toilet, most linguists—even though they will almost certainly use "whom" in their written work themselves—see the pronoun's replacement with "who" as merely another step in English's gradual shedding of case endings. In

---

* It is "Avis, jasmin varnā na ā ast, dadarka akvams, tam, vāgham garum vaghantam, tam, bhāram magham, tam, manum āku bharantam. Avis akvabhjams ā vavakat: kard aghnutai mai vidanti manum akvams agantam. Akvāsas ā vavakant: krudhi avai, kard aghnutai vividvant-svas: manus patis varnām avisāms karnauti svabhjam gharmam vastram avibhjams ka varnā na asti. Tat kukruvants avis agram ā bhugat." The English is "[On a hill,] a sheep that had no wool saw horses, one of them pulling a heavy wagon, one carrying a big load, and one carrying a man quickly. The sheep said to the horses: 'My heart pains me, seeing a man driving horses.' The horses said: 'Listen, sheep, our hearts pain us when we see this: a man, the master, makes the wool of the sheep into a warm garment for himself. And the sheep has no wool.' Having heard this, the sheep fled into the plain."

the era of *Beowulf,* English nouns had endings that showed what role they played in the sentence, as Latin did. But nearly all of them disappeared by the time of Shakespeare, and a linguist would see the death of "whom" as simply the conclusion of the process.

John McWhorter, an expert in language history and change, compares language to a lava lamp. For him, as for most linguists, it doesn't make much sense to get red in the face because the globs of goo, like language's words and rules, simply won't stay put. (Of course, it *does* make sense, but not on linguistic grounds. Prescriptive rage feels pretty good for many people.)

All this doesn't mean that linguists want to throw out the teaching of standard grammar rules to schoolchildren, for example. But knowing what linguists know about eons of linguistic history and change really puts things into perspective: any "rule" that makes the average stickler want to commit assault with a red pen seems terribly temporary and contingent to the linguist. Studying a dozen languages or a thousand years of history will do that. The sticklers, though they grudgingly acknowledge that language changes, could do with a bit of the same perspective.

Historical comparative linguistics, which for a long time went by the name "philology," is just the first and perhaps the most famous subfield of modern linguistics. For about a century (roughly the nineteenth), that was almost all there was. Ferdinand de Saussure, the brilliant Swiss linguist, was first known for his historical work. He hypothesized consonants, "sonant coefficients" (later known as laryngeals), in Indo-European. These sounds articulated at the back of the throat—consonants like a rasping *h* or a quick stop of the airflow with the glottis— must have once existed in Proto-Indo-European, he reckoned. There was no other explanation for variations in vowels in Indo-European's successor languages. Of course there was no direct evidence, as Proto-Indo-European had never been written down. But Saussure was proven right, decades later, by the discovery of Hittite texts, which included laryngeals.

Saussure's theoretical work is more famous, however, leading to the rise of linguistic "structuralism." He posited that *langue,* the system of a language, and *parole,* its external manifestation, were two sides of the same thing; one could no more separate them than one could cut just the obverse and not the reverse of a piece of paper. Linguists, to that point, had been focusing on individual words, sounds, and grammar points and their histories. Saussure got linguists thinking about how all the pieces all hung together, contingent on one another, a structure. Saussure's research led, through a series of intermediary theorists and half a century of advances, to Noam Chomsky.

Before Chomsky, psychologists, not linguists, had published the most prominent theories of how our brains and tongues work together. A dominant school was the "behaviorism" of B. F. Skinner, a psychologist (but not a language expert). Skinner posited that human language was little more than a sophisticated version of the stimulus and response he had observed in other animals. Behaviors were learned through rewards and punishments. Rats could not only learn to press a lever for food; they could progressively learn more complicated tasks if rewarded properly.

Skinner posited that the human animal also responded to stimuli. A child, responding to his mother's praise, gradually learned to say the words that would elicit it, Skinner wrote in the 1959 book *Verbal Behavior.* Language was a fancy version of the same process that made a rat press a bar:

> Behavior alters the environment through mechanical action, and its properties or dimensions are often related in a simple way to the effects produced. When a man walks toward an object, he usually finds himself closer to it; if he reaches for it, physical contact is likely to follow; and if he grasps and lifts it, or pushes or pulls it, the

object frequently changes position in appropriate directions. All this follows from simple geometrical and mechanical principles.

Much of the time, however, a man acts only indirectly upon the environment. . . . Instead of going to a drinking fountain, a thirsty man may simply "ask for a glass of water"—that is, may engage in behavior which produces a certain pattern of sounds which in turn induces someone to bring him a glass of water. . . . The consequences of such behavior are mediated by a train of events no less physical or inevitable than direct mechanical action, but clearly more difficult to describe.

Though Skinner did not say that humans were no different from rats, the extension of his earlier work is clear: he wrote that "the results [of his work] have been surprisingly free of species restrictions."

Chomsky would have none of it, writing a devastating review of Skinner's book that killed the behaviorist view of language with one stone to the temple. (In 1959 Chomsky himself was not yet Goliath.) Chomsky pointed out that while certain linguistic reactions to a stimulus were predictable, others were nothing of the sort.

A typical example of stimulus control for Skinner would be the response to a piece of music with the utterance *Mozart* or to a painting with the response *Dutch*. These responses are asserted to be "under the control of extremely subtle properties" of the physical object or event (108). Suppose instead of saying Dutch we had said *Clashes with the wallpaper, I thought you liked abstract work, Never saw it before, Tilted, Hanging too low, Beautiful, Hideous, Remember our camping trip last summer?*, or whatever else might come into our minds when looking at a picture.

Skinner offers "response strength" as evidence that the stimuli are connected to responses; a rat repeatedly and urgently pressing a bar would indicate a tight connection between behavior and reward. In trying to extend the concept to language, Skinner writes that "if we are shown a prized work of art and exclaim *Beautiful!*, the speed and energy of the response will not be lost on the owner." Chomsky drily replies that "It does not appear totally obvious that in this case the way to impress the owner is to shriek *Beautiful* in a loud, high-pitched voice, repeatedly, and with no delay." No, not obvious at all.

Having killed behaviorism with this kind of dry wit, and having also published his revolutionary 1957 book *Syntactic Structures,* Chomsky launched linguists on the task of trying to construct "grammars" of languages. These were not books that should be beaten into the heads of young children to correct their habits. Chomsky instead defined a "grammar" as a set of rules that could produce all plausible sentences in a language but none of the implausible ones. As Chomsky wrote in *Syntactic Structures, Colorless green ideas sleep furiously,* while nonsensical, was grammatical. All of the pieces fit together as adjectives, nouns, verbs, and adverbs should. *Tired young children sleep marvelously* has the exact same form. By contrast, Chomsky noted that *Furiously sleep ideas green colorless* is both nonsensical *and* ungrammatical. And *The child seems sleeping,* though sensible, isn't grammatical. The pieces don't fit together. Crucially, virtually any normal speaker would make the same judgments about the three statements. A grammatical sentence can be false, badly written, or illogical. An ungrammatical string of words can be true, beautiful, or powerful. Grammar simply isn't the same thing as rhetoric, logic, mechanics, or style.

Since Chomsky's late-1950s publications, linguists have largely concerned themselves with discovering exactly what rules that people use are and how they work in the human mind. This has been an enormous and intensive research project—but one that those outside linguistics have had little clue about. David Foster Wallace, in his caricature of descriptivism, wrote:

> The very language in which today's socialist, feminist, minority, gay, and environmentalist movements frame their sides of political debates is informed by the Descriptivist belief that traditional English is conceived and perpetuated by Privileged WASP Males and is thus inherently capitalist, sexist, racist, xenophobic, homophobic, elitist: unfair.

This notion—that linguists, as descriptivists, want to throw out the rules because they are "inherently capitalist, sexist, racist, xenophobic, homophobic, elitist, [and] unfair" would come as a surprise to Geoff Pullum, one of the many linguists who, since Chomsky, have been trying to figure out how language really does work in the human mind. Pullum, an expert in English grammar at the University of Edinburgh, is no "Let's overthrow the man, man" hippie. He is a very different, and rare, breed: the pissed-off, curmudgeonly descriptivist.

Language rants are usually the domain of the sticklers. But Pullum, who blogs along with Mark Liberman at Language Log, has had it. When he sees someone making what he thinks are foolish claims, he isn't professorial or even G-rated. In one typical post, he goes through and demolishes a list of copyediting shibboleths—that, for example, "have to" and "need to," or "note" and "notice," mean starkly different things and mustn't be confused. Finishing up, he writes:

> The things mentioned above are not debatable, they are facts about English that can easily be checked, and it is about time copy editors were told to stop wasting millions of hours on pointlessly correcting them when they were correct in the first place. God dammit, I can feel the veins standing out in my neck. I need to step outside for a while and kick something.

"Facts about English"? What is a descriptivist, in Wallace's caricature, doing talking about "facts" about a language if descriptivists think that the rules of standard English are just a
racist, homophobic (etc.) tool of oppression? Doesn't "descriptivism" mean that if a native speaker says something, it is ipso
facto okay?

This is "utterly insane," says Pullum. Of course English has
rules: in fact, he lays them out in an 1,860-page book, *The
Cambridge Grammar of the English Language,* which he coau-
thored with an Australian syntactician, Rodney Huddleston.
Descriptivists like Pullum do believe people can misuse those
rules; when they do, they miscommunicate or just sound silly.

But linguists imagine rules very differently than do Wal-
lace-style grouchy grammarians, deriving them from observation of some of the billions of words spoken each day and
analyses of the trillions that have been written down (and that
are, today, conveniently searchable by computer). Linguists
might observe native speakers undetected, record them in casual conversation, ask them what sounds grammatical to them,
or observe what educated people write. If a sentence strikes the
vast majority of speakers of a language as well formed, it is
well formed.

This doesn't rule out variation, say, by dialect or region.
"His team is in trouble" is grammatical in standard American
English. "His team are in trouble" is grammatical in Britain.
And linguists would say, "His team in trouble" is grammatical
in Black English—it is perfectly comprehensible and, crucially,
native speakers of the dialect will not bat an eye at it. But "The
team am in trouble," even if comprehensible, is grammatical in
no dialect of English. Descriptivists draw their rules from native speakers, but that doesn't mean anything goes. Grammar
rules should generate sentences that the large majority of
speakers of a given (dialect of a) language would accept as correct. Pullum's nearly two thousand pages of rules in *The Cambridge Grammar* so happen to focus on modern standard
English. But just such a grammar could also be written about

Black English or the English of southeastern England at the time of Shakespeare.

Pullum has special vitriol for *Elements of Style,* which he calls "E. B. White's disgusting and hypocritical revision of William Strunk's little hodgepodge of bad grammar advice and stylistic banalities" or elsewhere simply a "horrid little notebook of nonsense." Pullum catches E. B. White using a "which" to introduce a restrictive clause in the second paragraph of *Stuart Little,* something White himself prohibits in *Elements*. But Pullum notes that it is no good pointing this out to the self-appointed language guardians. When you tell prescriptivists that they have just violated their own rule, they simply say they erred and promise to do better next time. When you point out that dozens of great writers violate the same rule, they retreat to "Everybody makes mistakes sometimes." They never imagine that the rule itself may be bogus.

This myth is the opposite of "everything is correct," and Pullum calls it "nothing is relevant." The Rules exist on some plane of their own, and no amount of empirical evidence—say, repeated examples from professionally edited works of indisputably great writers—matters. For Pullum and the majority of linguists who are like him in this regard, if great writers break a rule frequently and naturally in writing, everyone else follows suit in speech, and doing so creates no confusion, that rule is illegitimate, a waste of everyone's time. *The Cambridge Grammar* thus calls prescriptivism with no recourse to evidence as mere "universalizing of one person's taste."

What does the modern descriptivist syntactician look like when he formulates his own rules? These rules are a mix of logic, the linguist's intuition about what a native speaker would consider acceptable, and examples taken from large bodies of written or transcribed language. Using a mix of data and his own judgments (both are needed, since people can make real-time mistakes, but a linguist's intuitions can be wrong too), the linguist seeks to tease out the rules.

For example, if you knock on someone's door and the person on the other side says, "Who is it?," the stickler's correct response is "It is I." The thinking is that "it" is a subject pronoun, and "is" means "the first part of this sentence and the last must be grammatically equivalent, because 'is' makes two things the same." That means that since "It" is the *subject,* the complement must be "I," a *subject* pronoun, and not "me," which is used as the *object* of verbs, prepositions, and so forth.

In pure prescriptivist form, the rule is simply the rule. It must not vary, for formality or by grammatical context. It is probably based on Latin grammar, where "predicate" and "predicand" (as they're known in the jargon) match in case. But this is by no means required by universal logic. French uses alternate pronouns: the nominative is *je,* but "It is I" translates not as *C'est je* but *C'est moi.* The Scandinavian languages, cousins to English, do much the same: *Det er mig* in Danish, for example.

As Pullum and his coauthor, Huddleston, have it, the case of *I* or its equivalents can alternate between their subject forms (*I, he, she, they*) and their object forms (*me, him, her, them*) in English.

Consider these examples:

a. It is *I* who love you.   b. It's *me* who loves you.

c. It is *I* she loves.   d. It's *me* she loves.

e. Yes, it is *she*!   f. Yes, it's *her*.

g. This is *he*.   h. This is *him*.

i. The only one who objected was *I*.   j. The only one who objected was *me*.

k. This one here is *I* at the age of twelve.   l. This one here is *me* at the age of twelve.

For Pullum and Huddleston, the difference between (a) and (b) is simply one of formal versus informal register. (a) is formal

but would ring oddly in many contexts; (b) is neutral to informal. Those who might insist that the rules are the rules and
must never vary would have to insist on (c) as well, which is so
stuffy or archaic as to be ridiculous in the early twenty-first
century. In (k), a plausible scenario in which the speaker is
showing an old photo, the prescriptive rule leads to a sentence
that isn't merely stuffy but probably unacceptable to most
speakers. At the very least, someone who spoke like that would
be considered very odd and probably not invited to many parties. If the "rule" produces sentences the vast majority of people wouldn't say and would reject if others said them, the rule
is, by (descriptivists') definition, no rule, or it needs modifica-
tion.

Several objections might occur to the stickler. One is that
the rules should simply be standard and clear. If you allow for
variation, children will not be able to learn them. But in this
case, the descriptivist reply is that there is indeed a rule: both
nominative and accusative are acceptable in most cases and differ by formality. To the accusation that having two choices is
intolerable because consistency must be ironclad, the linguist
would simply point to many other optional variations in English: "It's" versus "It is," for example. No rule requires that
"It is" be contracted, or kept apart. Both are available and
serve different needs, usually different levels of formality.

One more thing needs to be said about how linguists think
as opposed to traditional sticklers. The self-appointed stickler
usually holds the written language far above the spoken in its
purported logic, clarity, elegance, and style. Spoken language,
with its far more errors, false starts, and variation by time,
place, exhaustion, and presence of alcohol, seems by comparison debased and debauched.

For the linguist, the focus is almost the other way around.
All typical, healthy adults speak, and spoken language has been
in existence for tens if not hundreds of thousands of years.
Writing is a newcomer by comparison. Spoken language may
be a natural faculty wired in the brain, which needs input only

during formative years to become the amazing machine that is the adult language-producing box. Writing is an artificial modern skill that must be taught for years when children are older, and (as the stickler knows) the results often fail to impress. Sociolinguists more often study how people talk in different situations, not how they write. Comparative linguists doing fieldwork spend much of their time learning languages that are fascinatingly rich and usually hugely complicated—but have no writing system at all.

This isn't to say that linguists don't care about writing. Historical linguists such as Jacob Grimm obviously relied on older writings. Syntacticians such as Pullum pore through written works to see if theoretical or rare formations can be found and, if so, how often. But the notion that the written word is the "true" one and the spoken word "false" makes little sense from the linguist's chair. Everybody speaks, but not everyone reads. Just a few hundred of the world's six thousand languages are written down. And few of the world's people write on a regular basis. Even in the literate world, the average person is a fluent speaker and a fairly clumsy writer.

Is it possible to bridge the gap between prescriptive and descriptive? There is absolutely no reason why not; Pullum and Huddleston, for example, explicitly declare that their *Cambridge Grammar* is descriptive only but say that a writer seeking usage advice is well advised to find a good style manual. (Just not *The Elements of Style*.) Linguists just don't see that as their job. David Foster Wallace mocked linguists' pretensions to descriptive scientific accuracy, saying that it would be like an ethics textbook that described how people behaved, rather than how they should. But linguistics isn't ethics; it's not the humanities either. It's more like economics or political science, in which methods range from highly theoretical to highly quantitative.

And the popular grammar crank's complaint against descriptivists, that they don't believe in the rules (or that they are creations of the oppressive white capitalist Man), as shown by the above, is so far off the mark that the linguists have only themselves to blame for not getting the word out better about what they do. Chomsky, a feisty left-winger in politics, has spent half a century discovering grammar rules but has never connected his politics and his linguistics by writing a book aimed at conservative misunderstandings of language.

The idea that language has no rules does exist in linguistics, but it is an exotic minority position that most reject. Geoffrey Sampson, of the University of Sussex, put forth that position in an article called "Grammar Without Grammaticality": "I believe that the concept of 'ungrammatical' or 'ill-formed' word-sequences is a delusion." Pullum responded with the exact opposite position: that nearly any string of words is ungrammatical. Take ten common English words; they can be combined in 3,628,800 different ten-word strings ($10 \times 9 \times 8 \times 7 \times 6 \times 5 \times 4 \times 3 \times 2 \times 1$). Almost none of those 3 million–plus strings will be accepted as sentences by an English speaker. In this light, producing a grammatical sentence is a miraculous thing indeed.

There are many other huge disagreements among modern syntacticians. Chomsky first promoted a vision in which the brain changes a meaning-based structure ("deep structure") into the actual form of words used by a speaker ("surface structure") through a process he called "transformation." He has since abandoned transformational grammar, but others have continued work in a transformational vein.

Research into syntax—constructing grammars for the world's languages—is now split not only between pro- and anti-Chomsky researchers, but between those who follow his older work and those who support his new "minimalist program." The new program has tried to strip down the number of rules considerably and even argues that the feature of "recursion" is the only unique feature of human language (as distinct from other forms of language such as whale music, bee dances, and so on). Recursion is the ability to fit one kind of syntactic unit into another of the same type; "the cat" is a noun phrase, and "the cat in the hat" is a noun phrase that has noun phrases ("the hat" and "the cat") within it. But though once upon a time everyone in linguistics seemed to be responding to the dominant "classical" Chomskyan paradigm, today the minimalist program has put the titan himself into a smaller, more controversial camp, against, for example, his fellow "innatist" (a believer that some elements of grammar are wired in the brain), Steven Pinker.

All this should dispel the notion that descriptivists don't believe in rules. But they see their role as discovering, not pronouncing, them. Some (like Pullum) use real-world evidence. Others (like Chomsky) construct artificial examples to illustrate their points. But what neither does is sit in a chair saying "This is how it is, by Jove, and anyone who doesn't know this rule is a fool." Remember our analogy of linguistics to social science. A political scientist or an economist who says "Vote Democrat" or "Progressive taxation is unfair" is not doing academic work. She has every right to say that, but this is the stuff of an op-ed, not a peer-reviewed journal. And linguists see their job much the same way. Saying "That is annoying and incorrect" isn't what they're after; "This is informal, and many usage books recommend against it" is more their style. Pullum is the rare one who will add "but you should feel free to tell them where they can shove it."

Syntax is at the more theoretical end of the linguistic spectrum, though; as mentioned, there are many syntacticians who spend their day going through bodies of text for real-world examples of this or that construction. But linguistics also has subfields that are far more directly empirical, two of which are relevant to the sticklers-versus-linguists debate.

The first is psycholinguistics. The field itself grew out of Chomsky's revolution against behavioralism. When Chomsky posited that many language structures are innate, psycholinguists redoubled their efforts trying to figure out how the brain processed language. Many of their efforts are not of interest here. But their methods are: psycholinguistics offers a test of many prescriptivist notions.

The Elements of Style by Strunk and White, for example, says that

> The pronoun *this,* referring to the complete sense of a preceding sentence or clause, can't always carry the load and so may produce an imprecise statement.
>
> > Visiting dignitaries watched yesterday as ground was broken for the new high-energy physics laboratory with a blowout safety wall. This is the first visible evidence of the university's plans for modernization and expansion.
>
> In the left-hand example above, *this* does not immediately make clear what the first visible evidence is.

As usual, no evidence is offered that "this" really doesn't carry the load. We are told to believe that this sentence is harder to understand—here, at least, Strunk and White are telling you to think of your reader's comprehension, not merely yelling at you. But they offer no support for this pronouncement; the reader is meant to merely take Strunk and White's word for it.

As it happens, though, these kinds of things can often be tested in a laboratory. One simple method, for example, available to modern researchers is the minute tracking of eyeballs as readers scan a page of text. A vague or unclear passage will make readers stop tracking through the text. (Test subjects are sometimes told that they will be asked questions about the text afterward, so that they try to comprehend it.) If the eyeballs pause on the "this" in a construction like the one Strunk and White proscribe, it may indeed be vague or problematic. (That wouldn't make it improper *grammar,* meaning the pieces of the sentence don't add up. It's very easy to write a grammatical sentence that people would have to stop again and again to read. It simply means that avoiding it would make better writing.) As it happens, there is just such a test under way: the sexily named Anaphora Resolution and Underspecification research program at the Universities of Essex and Glasgow. (The program is also studying whether computers can parse the sentences in question.) When wondering whether a certain construction is acceptable, Strunk and White *pronounce;* linguists *research*.

Sometimes their research might give comfort to prescriptivists. Sex-indefinite singular pronouns have been a source of a long-running descriptivist battle. "Everyone has finished their dinner" is a stickler no-no. It uses "they," a plural pronoun, to refer back to "everyone," which is grammatically singular. (Even if it is semantically plural, we say "Everyone is," not "everyone are.") Linguists say that the sex-indefinite singular "they" goes back in English writing to the King James Bible, among other places: "They set forward, **every one** after **their** families, according to the house of **their** fathers" (Numbers 2:34). And of course virtually everyone but the most Wahabbist stickler uses "they" in plain conversation. The band Jane's Addiction sang "Everybody has their own opinion" because in a punk-influenced rock song, "Everyone has his own opinion" would sound silly and "Everyone has his or her opinion"— both prescriptivist and politically correct—would sound idiotic. Strunk and White, naturally, counsel simply "his," asserting that it stands for both sexes, and that "his and her" is stylistically ugly.

As it happens, the Anaphora Resolution and Underspecification program has data. Two groups read slightly different texts. One group got the unremarkable

> Mr Jones was looking for the station. He saw some people on the other side of the road, so he crossed over and asked them politely where the station was. It was in a different part of town.

Others got this (emphasis added):

> Mr Jones was looking for the station. He saw **some people** on the other side of the road, so he crossed over and asked **her** politely where the station was. It was in a different part of town.

Compared to the first group, readers in the second group took, on average, an extra tenth of a second to process this before moving on with their eyeballs.

Other subjects were given this:

> Mr Jones was looking for the station. He saw **someone** on the other side of the road, so he crossed over and asked **them** politely where the station was. It was in a different part of town.

Here, readers paused about an extra twentieth of a second. It seems that upon finding "them," they wondered briefly where the plural antecedent was. But they quickly moved on, twice as fast as those in the first example above, who paused at a genuine oddity.

The point, again, is this: if a prescriptivist says something is illogical or confusing, this claim can be tested. Some tests would show the sticklers wrong, but some might prove them right. David Foster Wallace considered the scientific study of language to be "Unbelievably Naïve Positivism." Unfortunately, he never seemed to look into what he was talking about; linguists can't know everything about every speaker's language, but they certainly can discover quite a bit.

If Noam Chomsky doesn't care much for real-world data, the fact that he is the world's best-known linguist doesn't mean that he is representative of the whole clan. At the other end of the spectrum are those who constantly seek out how language is actually being used day to day. Among them are sociolinguists, perhaps those most relevant to the subject of this book. Chomsky studies language in the abstract; sociolinguists study how it is used on the streets and in the fields of the real world.

Do you find New York accents annoying? As a southerner living in Brooklyn, I have to confess that sometimes they grate on my ears. William Labov, perhaps the world's foremost sociolinguist, discovered an interesting fact: New Yorkers don't like their accents either.

Or at least they act as though they don't. The accent we associate with New York is actually a working-class accent (and, contrary to popular belief, it doesn't differ much from Brooklyn to the Bronx to the other boroughs). There was once also a high-class New York accent—think Franklin Roosevelt saying "We have nothing to feahhh but feahhh itself"—but it is rare today.

Among the features of the working-class New York accent are the dropping of *r* sounds after vowels, the replacement of the *th* sound, as in "third," with *t;* the replacement of the *th* sound, as in "then," with *d;* and so on. I once actually asked someone for the location of a bar which, improbably enough, happened to be located at "toity-toid and toid."

To test the prestige or lack of it for these sounds (rather than just asserting that they're lower class), Labov went to three New York City department stores for his 1966 doctoral research. Saks, Macy's, and S. Klein were high to low status, respectively. Asking for a department he knew to be located on the fourth floor, he surreptitiously recorded the answers of the employees.

The results neatly confirmed his suspicion: an employee's accent became more "New York" as he traveled down the socioeconomic ladder. Employees were most likely to drop the *r* sound in both "fourth and "floor" in S. Klein, the low-end store, more than 90 percent of the time. (The *r* is slightly more likely to drop in "floor" than in "fourth," incidentally.) In

Macy's, employees dropped the *r* in "floor" 73 percent of the time. In Saks, the number was 70 percent *r*-lessness.

Another interesting finding is the attitude the employees showed when Labov pretended he couldn't hear them and asked them to repeat themselves. When they did, they were speaking carefully, and lo, they avoided the lower-class pronunciation and became far more likely to pronounce the *r*. Another Labov study showed that in casual speech, the *r*s were dropped almost all the time. But when subjects read words aloud from a list, *r* pronunciation shot up. How much attention a subject is paying—quick unmonitored speech, careful speech, reading from a page—makes a big difference and inspires linguists to come up with ingenious experiments to tease things out.

Did Labov show that *r*-dropping is a laziness? When they repeated themselves or read from a page, Labov's New Yorkers were less likely to drop the *r*s. But that doesn't mean pronouncing the *r* is "careful" or "educated" and hence correct, while dropping it is "ignorant" or "lazy." The social dynamics are much more interesting than that. In surveys, New Yorkers rate *r*-dropping as undesirable, even as they do it themselves. And intriguingly, Labov found that the lower middle classes pronounced their *r*s even more carefully than the upper middle class in formal settings (as when reading aloud). He guessed that these socially vulnerable but hopeful people *hypercorrect* when put on the spot, anxious not to seem lower class than they are.

Why, then, does anyone drop *r*s? Labov posits "covert prestige": the working classes' way of showing solidarity and pride. It isn't only the upper classes or sticklers that monitor their language. Members of any group—not just academics or pedants but sports announcers, rappers, and construction workers—signal who they are and who they want to be associated with by how they talk. The persistence of *r*-dropping among New Yorkers, despite the pressures to climb socially, shows that climbing the social ladder is not all that matters. Working-class New Yorkers (and many others) are caught between social ambition and solidarity with the class they come from.

Most people imagine languages as codified, straightforward, and pure. The rules are written in grammar books, the meanings of words are in dictionaries, and every sound has a correct pronunciation. Linguists, obviously, don't think that way. And sociolinguists try to figure out in what ways these things, like Labov's *r*s, vary socially: by region, class, gender, social situation, and many other factors.

Dialectology is a big part of sociolinguistics. Most languages have clear and stable subvarieties. (What counts as a "dialect" and what a "language" isn't linguistically clear cut itself and usually political, as will become more apparent in later chapters.) Since dialects are often ignored if not flat-out denied by the keepers of the pure language, it often falls to the sociolinguists to describe how they are used.

As you would expect, they don't find sloppiness or laziness when they describe (for example) southern English, Cajun French, Swiss German, Damascus Arabic, or other nonstandard varieties. They find dialects or languages with stable grammar and pronunciation—not as stable as those of the written standard languages (which have the advantage of a large body of written literature), but highly coherent nonetheless. As Labov put it, "a decade of work outside the university as an industrial chemist had convinced me that the everyday world was stubborn but consistently so." Where others saw a mess, he saw order.

Take what sociolinguists call "code switching": moving back and forth between two languages or distinct dialects in a single conversation. For example, in the New York subway I often hear examples like this one from Labov:

> Por eso cada, you know it's nothing to be proud of, porque yo no estoy proud of it, as a matter of fact I hate it, pero viene Vierne y Sabado yo estoy, tu me ve hacia mi, sola with a, aqui solita, a veces que Frankie me deja, you know a stick or something, y yo aqui solita, queces Judy no sabe y yo estoy haci, viendo television, but I rather, y cuando estoy con gente yo me . . . borracha porque me siento mas, happy, mas free, you know, pero si yo estoy con mucha gente yo no estoy, you know, high, more or less, I couldn't get along with anybody.

What looks like a jumble to an onlooker is more systematic and more interesting. Studies of code switching show regularities. For example, some code switchers do so only between sentences. But others do so almost freely within sentences. It turns out that though the latter looks more jumbled, as in the passage above, it is actually most common among those who speak both languages well and who have more positive feelings towards their bicultural identity.

Studies of code switching have shown that the switch from one language to another often involves emotional moments: describing a stressful experience, for example. In the case of this New York mix, Spanish may be to show solidarity (the mentions of mutual acquaintances are in Spanish). But the speaker switches, after a long stretch of Spanish, to English for "happy" and "free" ("I feel more happy, more free, you know"). This might be because the English words "happy" and "free" might carry different emotional freight—as distinctly American wishes—than their Spanish equivalents *feliz/contenta* and *libre* would. What other country on Earth put "the pursuit of happiness" in its founding document?

Other language phenomena that look messy or random are also predictable and systematic ways of seeking solidarity. One example is a behavior many Americans have guiltily confessed to me: that when they travel to (say) Scotland or Ireland, before long they find themselves half imitating the local accent, and maybe its rhythm and vocabulary too. Most people who do this think that they are uniquely chameleonic and feel slavish and foolish in changing their own accent to sound like the natives. In fact, like many other things, sociolinguists have seen this all around the world and given it a name: accommodation. If you think about it, you probably speak more quietly when talking to someone who speaks unusually softly. If you're talking with someone who runs a hundred miles an hour conversationally, the chances are good that you speed up too. The desire to show solidarity with conversation partners motivates these changes of speed or volume. The traveler's accent shifts are no different. And choice of speaking style and vocabulary can be another way of getting closer. As a teacher, I have noticed that I get more colloquial and relaxed when talking to my students; I want to feel as though I'm joining the group temporarily.

But accommodation has its flip side: intentional distancing. I am more formal and stiff on purpose when dressing down students or expressing disappointment. I want them to know that I am the teacher and they have to listen to what I say because of our teacher-student relationship. The same kind of distancing may be going on when a boss raises his voice at a whimpering subordinate. The message is that we're *not* the same: I can be loud and you must be quiet.

How language choices like this hang together with identity and politics is particularly clear in the case of what linguists call "diglossia." In the classic diglossic situation, two varieties of a language, such as standard French and Haitian creole French, exist alongside each other in a single society. Each variety has its own fixed functions—one a "high," prestigious variety, and one a "low," or colloquial, one. Using the wrong variety in the wrong situation would be socially inappropriate, almost on the level of delivering the BBC's nightly news in broad Scots. Their functions are quite different.

Children learn the low variety as a native language; in

diglossic cultures, it is the language of home, the family, the streets and marketplaces, friendship, and solidarity. By contrast, the high variety is spoken by few or none as a first language. It must be taught in school. The high variety is used for public speaking, formal lectures and higher education, television broadcasts, sermons, liturgies, and writing. (Often the low variety has no standard written form.)

Diglossic pairs include Swiss German and standard German; colloquial Arabic (in many regional guises) and classical/standard Arabic; Haitian creole French and standard French; and two varieties of Greek called *dhimotiki* (demotic) and *katharévousa*. An important point to remember is that the "low" varieties are socially but not linguistically low. They are no run-down gutter cants. They are highly regular languages; linguists can and do write grammars of, for example, modern Palestinian Arabic. But in the typical diglossic situation, most people think the low variety isn't the "real" language. The real language is the (high) language, which must be taught, essentially as a foreign language, to children who have never used it before they begin school.

Attitudes toward the low varieties vary. In Switzerland, standard German gives German-speakers access to the economy, writing, television, and culture of a big international arena, including neighboring Germany and Austria, which with 90 million people dwarf the 4 million German-speakers of Switzerland. But Swiss German is a token of pride, separating the Swiss from their neighbors. Personal ads in newspapers are often taken out in Swiss (called *Schwyzerdütsch*, among other things, by the natives). And since it varies from place to place in Switzerland, one's own variety of Swiss can signal allegiance to a particular region or town. The Swiss, in other words, have no problem with their diglossia, and there is certainly nothing lower class about speaking it.

Slightly more mixed feelings prevail in Haiti regarding the relationship between standard French and their own, by now highly regular, creole variety. Knowledge of standard French is crucial for access to power in government or business. But French is also the language of a former colonial power, and Haitians are proud of the Creole, with a few exceptions. (Some in the upper rungs of society disclaim knowledge of the Creole but can be heard to speak it fluently nonetheless.) Creole makes you Haitian.

In Greece, the relationship between demotic (low) and *katharévousa* (high, closer to classical Greek) is even more obviously political. In the twentieth century, with people speaking varieties of demotic as the native language, politicians made an effort to regularize and spread the formal use of the low variety. But the conservative pushback was fierce: a translation of the Bible into demotic Greek sparked riots in 1921. When a group of colonels took control of Greece in a 1967 military coup, they halted the official spread of demotic.

The restoration of democracy restored demotic (which shares, incidentally, the same linguistic root, *demos,* "people"). *Katharévousa,* once known as a pragmatic compromise between ancient and modern Greek, was now associated with authoritarian politics. Demotic has basically won the day. A Greek student of mine, Maria, typifies the shift. Her grandmother read a book of Greek mythology, written in *katharévousa,* to her mother. But Maria's mother spot-translated it into demotic when she read it to her. Maria, like most young Greeks, can understand written *katharévousa* but cannot speak it.

The victory of demotic has not resolved Greeks' language anxiety, however. There is a general opinion that Greek is in decline. Maria, though she doesn't speak it, describes *katharévousa* in terms that are common to speakers of the "low" variety when talking about the "high" one: that it is more complex, expressive, and beautiful. In Maria's words, it is "a complex mathematical problem meets a paintbrush with vibrant colors." (The "complexity" refers to the fact that low varieties have fewer word endings, which have eroded with time.) At the same time, she is democratic about her demotic, expressing frustration that the most important hour of the week for many Greeks, church, is *katharévousa*-only. Since the New Testament was originally written in a form of ancient Greek closer to *katharévousa,* it may be understandable that Greeks would want to hang on to it. But this also means that many parishioners have little idea what is being said to them.

Even though demotic has won out, political angst still plays into language attitudes in Greece. Greece joined the polyglot European Union in 1981 but has failed to thrive through trade, aid, and integration as many other countries have. It has fallen economically behind many of its European partners. Words and phrases from *katharévousa,* nowadays sometimes mixed into demotic, remind Greeks of a time of national glory and Greek domination of the neighborhood. There will always be those who think that if the language hadn't been let go, Greece would still be a power to reckon with.

If that nostalgia goes for Greek, it goes triply for Arabic. After the advent of Islam in the seventh century, the Arabic language roared out of its home in the Arabian Peninsula, spreading north, east, and west like a fire across dry brush. With the prophet Muhammad's conversion of enormous territories to Islam came the spread of the language of the Qur'an, which he said had been dictated to him by the archangel Gabriel. The exact words of the Qur'an were so sacred that learning to read it in Arabic was the only way to access the religion itself. Today, there are twenty-two members of the Arab League, with a combined population of over 300 million (though not all are Arabic-speakers).

But the Arabic language should stand as a caution to sticklers. The veneration of the Qur'an (and also the *hadith,* or sayings of the Prophet), had the effect of canonizing, and freezing, one form of Arabic. Medieval grammarians made detailed studies of its properties while Europe remained in the dark ages. Poetry and even storytelling flourished. Arabic was the language of science, the reason *alkali, alcohol, algebra,* and many other English words come from Arabic.

But Arabic, like every other language on Earth, despite the existence of a prestigious written standard, went on changing in the mouths of its speakers. And having spread from Morocco to Iraq, over a territory bigger than any modern country but Russia, it changed not in one stream but many. Today's linguistic situation in the Arab world isn't just diglossic but "polyglossic"—that is, incredibly varied. Though most Arabs don't like to admit it, today, spoken Arabic is not a "dialect" of classical Arabic. It has become a different language in widely varying forms, classed by linguists into North African, Egyptian, Gulf, Levantine, and Iraqi, each with many subdialects.

Sometimes classical Arabic, also called *fusha* (pronounced "fus-ha"), resembles the colloquial, especially when the vocabulary is somewhat elevated:

> Classical: *Hiyya mu'allima fii jaami'at Dimashq.*
> Syrian colloquial: *Hiyye m'allme b'jaami'at Dimashq.*
> (She is a teacher at Damascus University.)

But elsewhere it is clear, even in simple sentences, just how far Arabic has moved in 1,300 years:

> Classical: *Ra'aytu ar-rajul ma'a ibnihi. Yathhabaani ila as-suq al'aan.*
> Palestinian colloquial: *Shuft az-zalame ma' walado. Biruhu 'a as-su' halla'.*
> (I saw the man with his son. They're going to the market now.)

In the first full-length Arabic conversation I ever had, with two young Egyptians I met in South Africa who didn't speak English, I could speak only *fusha* (not yet having begun learning a modern colloquial Arabic dialect). They tried to respond in kind. But it was a clumsy exchange on both sides. They mixed in not only typically Egyptian pronunciations (such as *gadiid* for *jadiid*, "new") but "wrong" ones in *fusha* that came from their dialect, such as *munazama* for *munadhama* ("organization"). Though I struggled to remember some vocabulary, in other ways my *fusha* was better than theirs. (On the other hand, a sociolinguist might say my overall performance was much worse; *fusha* is utterly inappropriate for late-night hotel-bar drinks. I must have sounded something like a professor lecturing to them.)

Furthermore, "Arabic"-speakers from one region can have serious trouble speaking to Arabs from another. A Moroccan and a Lebanese will lose much subtlety and confidence in understanding if they try to talk to each other in their home dialects. If they have trouble and need to talk about a difficult technical topic (such as engineering or computer science), they will often switch to English or French rather than *fusha*. Meanwhile, a Moroccan from the countryside and his uneducated Lebanese counterpart would hardly be able to carry on a conversation at all.

Talking about this is awkward, and Arabs are often at pains to stress that really they do speak the same language and it's a shame more people don't speak "better Arabic." They are in denial that classical Arabic has no native speakers, and they are in a messy situation with few ground rules. This denial has political roots and heavy implications. Many Arabs recognize that they speak differently from one another, but they still strongly identify with an "Arab nation." Mastery of *fusha* Arabic, including literacy and familiarity with classical texts, remains a gateway to social prestige.

At the same time, the modern colloquial Arabics have been put to political use too. Remember Labov's lower-class "covert prestige." Just as Bill Clinton could turn up his southern accent when in front of the right kind of crowd, Gamal Abdel Nasser, the revolutionary president of Egypt from 1952 to 1970, mixed Egyptian colloquial into his speeches to Egyptians. While he was president of the short-lived United Arab Republic, which merged Egypt and Syria, however, he never used Egyptian colloquial in his speeches in Damascus; he was not fluent in Syrian colloquial, and during this pan-Arabist heyday he wanted to seem Arab, not Egyptian, to the Syrian crowds.

The ongoing use of *fusha* for education has repercussions. Mohamed Maamouri, a Tunisian who works at the Linguistic Data Consortium with Mark Liberman, argues that teaching children in *fusha,* essentially a foreign language, hampers literacy and learning and psychologically distances them from the culture of the written word. Illiteracy is 40 percent in the Arab League states; among women it reaches 50 percent. And even those who can read feel cut off from the content that reading gives access to. Maamouri relates the impressions of Khaled, a typical sixteen-year-old in Tunis:

> Since he chose to specialize in Sciences, most of his subjects are taught in French: all the scientific subjects are taught in French. This has been the case since the first year of secondary school. Before then, all of his classes were taught in Fusha. Khaled doesn't like Fusha and thinks he can do without it. With his friends, he speaks mostly Arbi [Tunisian colloquial], with a little French thrown in. Nobody speaks in Fusha, it sounds too weird and forced. The only classes he has in Fusha are liberal arts classes, like history, religion and social studies. These classes bore him. The teachers are too traditional, and have no sense of humor.
>
> Khaled understands most of what [his cousin] Sourour [who grew up in Saudi Arabia] says when she speaks in Arabic, but she does not understand Arbi. He has to use Fusha or French in order to speak to her. They finally settle on a mixture of the two, because her French is not as good as his.

Arabs are told that the language they grow up speaking isn't a "real" language and the "real" language is one that they learn in school, not made for fun or creativity. This alienation from the written language has obvious consequences for the development of journalism, political activism, and other forms of democracy-building that rely on the written word. But Maamouri laments that there is no one with the political clout in the Arabic world to push through reforms that might ameliorate the situation.

One option might be to simplify the grammar of *fusha*—the case endings are notoriously difficult but also largely unnecessary—while also mixing in words that are found in many of the colloquials. Such a "middle Arabic" would be closer to today's living languages than to the distant, aloof *fusha* that springs from the Qur'an. Such "middle Arabics" already exist in an ad-hoc way, for example in informal writing online. This makes sense; online writing is often spontaneous, which calls for colloquial, but it is still written and so draws on the only standard written variety, *fusha*. Codifying middle Arabic would create a useful, but somewhat artificial, language. And artificial languages—from wholly invented ones such as Esperanto to the pandialectal "New Norwegian" invented as a vehicle for Norwegian nationalism—have a poor track record. They can become written languages and will always have their adherents for political reasons. But they belong to no one. In any case, doing this with Arabic today remains unlikely. Distancing Arabic from its roots implies distancing modern Arabs from a cherished religious, military and cultural history. And no coherent vision of modern Arab life has yet emerged to replace those past glories.

These are just a few of the issues that sociolinguists deal with. For other, "purer" linguists who work with the Saussurean system, sociolinguists may seem interdisciplinary vagrants with messy data. For the sociolinguists, sitting in the library and concocting example sentences, rather than getting out and listening to people talk, seems as detached from the real world as describing the chemistry of sugar fermentation is from tasting wines.

What linguists—theoreticians and field researchers—have in common is a search for facts that can support robust, testable theories. They are not in the business of overturning paradigms of capitalism, patriarchy, and colonialism. Of course, many linguists are politically left-wing, but so are most academics. And some linguists' work has explicitly political content: sociolinguists, in particular, deal heavily with issues of class, social mobility, and power and how language interacts with them.

By that same token, as seekers after social facts, they also discover that a prestige variety of a language—whether standard English or Arabic *fusha*—has a social value. People treasure these languages for their literary heritage and for the way they bind communities together. Ultimately, it seems, most people like belonging to a community and a legacy, and written standard languages provide both.

But variation from that norm—whether a person grows up speaking Swiss German or Black English—is just that: variation. Black English is no more "broken-down English" than Swiss German is "broken-down German." And as Bill Labov's *r*-dropping experiments found, sometimes people cling tightly to the way they talk even when they know it deviates from the prestigious form—the working classes value a sense of community, too. Variation is a linguistic fact of life and one that a true lover of language should study in all its fantastic variety—not seek to eradicate through a homogenizing, orthodox sticklerism that has little to do with history, logic, and beauty and much to do with power, status, and control.

More Equal than Others

How All Languages Can
Express Almost Everything

"The limits of my language mean the limits of my world."
—LUDWIG WITTGENSTEIN

In a video that became a brief Internet sensation in 2008, a black journalist walks toward the camera slowly, microphone in hand, intoning in standard, serious reporterese:

> What really happened on that Thursday here at Augusta High School that led to Chris Woods's death?

Suddenly, he doubles over in disgust and whirls almost 180 degrees around, spitting. A bug has flown into his mouth. The next few words to come out are not so standard. His accent changes completely as he says

> The fuck is that? Shit! . . . I'm dyin' in this fuckin' country-ass fucked-up town. Shit flyin' in my mouth. Da fuck! I can' see, pollen . . . les' get da fuck out this country motherfucker.

I've probably watched the video fifty times, and it makes me laugh every time. I've quoted the video so often that a friend suggested I call this book *Shit Flyin' in My Mouth*.

But I don't like the title the video is given on YouTube: "Ghetto Reporter." The comments below the video are revealing:

> i love how is voice is so pro in the beggining then the real side of him shows!

> I love how he talks white, but after the bug flies in his mouth, he talks ghetto!

> it is funny how he goes like HICCUM [the spitting sound] when he gets bug in his mouth fucking nigger! haha lolz

You don't have to be a racist to find the juxtaposition of Broadcast Standard and (highly) extemporaneous Black English funny. Comedy depends on putting incongruous things side by side. But the comments reveal that many viewers saw more than funny incongruity. For them, the black reporter had managed to put on a veneer of respectability, but it was so shallow that it fell away instantly upon surprise, revealing the thuggish "ghetto" beneath.

I saw something different. My wife, who is from Denmark, speaks an incredibly fluent English that never fails to surprise me. Ninety-eight percent of her speech in a given week is in English. But as soon as she stubs her toe on our bed frame, she always says the same thing: *For Satan!*, cursing in Danish. Don't be confused by the surface similarity with English; *for* means in Danish what it means in English, and Satan is spelled the same way, but this isn't a cute equivalent of "The devil!" *For Satan* is one of the rougher curses in Danish, about as taboo as what many English speakers would say upon a good hard toe-smashing: *Shit!* or *Fuck!*

What happens to my wife is the same thing that happened to the "ghetto reporter": upon a sharp and nasty surprise, they switch immediately into their home language—or in the reporter's case, dialect. The reporter, Isiah Carey, isn't "ghetto" with a veneer of respectability. He is a speaker of Black English from Baton Rouge, Louisiana, who has learned formal standard

English in the course of a career that would win him several journalism awards. The fly incident shows him not to be barely civilized but *bidialectal*. A few other videos of Carey horsing around between takes have made it to YouTube under the series title "Roving Reporter Etiquette Lessons." They show him comfortably switching back and forth between Black and standard English. One video shows him professionally finishing a take, pausing for a few seconds, and then growling at a dog that's been yapping nearby, "I'm gon' kick yo' ass." No linguist would lift an eyebrow at this; remember "code switching" from the last chapter. Surprise or emotion almost invariably make people switch to their first language or dialect, as predictable as swearing.

The idea that the reporter is doing the same thing in something called "Black English" that my wife is doing in Danish would rub a lot of sticklers the wrong way, though. Danish is the language of Kierkegaard and Niels Bohr; the way the reporter swears makes sticklers think of black thugs and the crisis of education among America's black youth. In other words, the notion that Black English is a standard dialect, a native language with grammatical and phonological rules, on par with Danish, seems borderline insane.

But linguists have long known that Black English isn't a broken-down version of "real" English. It isn't being made up by speakers who don't care about grammar. It has a grammar, in the Chomskyan sense of a set of rules that produce acceptable sentences. Violate them, and you'll sound odd. For example, the verb "to be" must be left out of many sentences in the present tense: *She my sister.* But when it is used, it preserves a distinction (linguists call it "aspect") that doesn't even exist in standard English: *He sick* means he's sick right now, while *He be sick* means he's sick usually or frequently. Other grammar features are double negatives (*Ain't nobody gonna do that*) and greater use of "do" as an auxiliary (*I done told you a thousand times*). Phonetic features include the "-in" ending on verbs (*shit flyin in my mouth*).

Some of these are regular features of other languages, too. We have seen double negatives in other European languages. Pronouncing the "-ing" ending as "-in" used to be the high-class pronunciation in Britain. And "do" has an idiosyncratic function in standard English, too: why do we use it to form questions, turning "You have a car?" into "Do you have a car?" Black English (which shares this feature, and others, with southern white English) just extends this "do support" a bit further.

Another distracting factor is that many black Americans don't speak black dialect, either because they never learned it or never use it: think Condoleezza Rice. But many speak both Black English and standard English, and comfortably switch between one at home and among black friends, and the other at work with white colleagues. And code switching isn't (pardon the pun) just black and white; there are intermediate varieties that use some but not all features of Black English. One speaker can move between them in a single conversation. This tempts the conclusion that sometimes black people speak "carefully" and sometimes "lazily."

Americans' familiarity with dialect continua is also poor. The average speaker of a European language is familiar with different "versions" of his language: Sicilian Italian, Plattdeutsch ("low German"), two standard versions of Norwegian (Nynorsk and Bokmål), and so on. Many of the Europeans who speak these dialects are proud of them. They recognize High German or Florentine Italian as de facto standards. Some have feelings of inferiority about their speech, derided as "slang," "jargon," "argot," or "patois" by speakers of the prestige dialect. But plenty of others would never dream of seeing their nonstandard varieties as degraded or lazy. No proud Sicilian American would accept that his grandmother speaks "ghetto Italian"; different, yes, ghetto, no. Plenty of Jewish Americans are proud of Yiddish and would never let it be called "ghetto German" either. Nor would most Americans dream of calling this "ghetto English":

But, Mousie, thou art no thy lane,
In proving foresight may be vain:
The best-laid schemes o' mice an' men
Gang aft a-gley,
An' lea'e us nought but grief an' pain,

The author is, of course, Robert Burns, the poet beloved for his use of Scots English. Many Americans of Scottish heritage drink a dram in his honor on January 25, Burns's birthday. His poetry in dialect helped bring honor to a people looked down on for centuries by the dominant English. Scots are just one example of a group proudly embracing their nonstandard dialect.

Yet the controversy over "Ebonics" showed just how willing many Americans are to frown on one English dialect in particular, Black English. In 1997 Oakland's school board decided to recognize, and use as a teaching aid, the "primary language" of most black students, which they called Ebonics. It was a word that almost no one had ever heard before. (It had been coined, with hardly anyone noticing, in the 1970s.) But within weeks of the 1997 Oakland school decision, the whole country was talking—and laughing—about it.

Oakland's heart was in the right place. The school board drew upon a hazy understanding of dialectal linguistics to argue that black kids come from a different linguistic background and that recognizing this would help them learn standard English faster.

But the board made major mistakes of both substance and marketing. Probably the worst was "Ebonics" itself, a goofy name that lent itself to immediate parody. The school board also shouldn't have referred to it as a "language"; though "dialect" and "language" have no clear-cut definitions, virtually all linguists would call Ebonics a dialect or variety of English. The word "language" exaggerated how different "Ebonics" really is. A third stumble, both political and linguistic, was the board's clumsy reach for a proud Afrocentric heritage, claiming that Ebonics drew on a past in the linguistic forms of West African languages—a highly debatable, probably untrue assertion that was anyway unnecessary to their case.

And perhaps that case did not even need to be made; some linguists argued that Oakland would have been better off focusing on improving its dismal inner-city schools generally, not on giving black kids an exoticized, partially invented "foreign"-language background as an explanation for bad performance. But those writers also based their claims on evidence, not a political rejection of Black English as a valid variety. John McWhorter, a black linguist then teaching at Berkeley, pointed to studies showing Ebonics-like teaching approaches as unsuccessful. Others disagreed: the Linguistic Society of America noted that in Sweden, teaching kids standard Swedish through approaches that recognized their nonstandard Swedish dialectal starting points had been shown to be effective. Similar approaches had shown the same elsewhere. The LSA thus said that the Oakland school board's general thrust was "linguistically and pedagogically sound." The point is that the linguists, even if inclined to the political left and friendly to the Ebonics approach, thought of this as a suitable question for data gathering and study, not a theological first-principles approach that Ebonics simply had to be wrong.

Not that the linguists were listened to: *The New York Times,* which published several editorials and op-eds criticizing Ebonics, rejected several op-eds from linguists making the case for Oakland's approach. The debate in the real world showed not only a divorce from the linguist's data-driven approach; most people didn't know what Ebonics was about at all. What Oakland had proposed was teaching black kids to recode, or translate, their Black English *into standard English.* But this crucial point was utterly lost on the public. Instead, what filtered through to the average, busy news reader were the big, bold headlines reading:

Oakland Schools Sanction "Ebonics" (*Chicago Tribune*)

Black English Recognized for Schools (*The Philadelphia Inquirer*)

Oakland Schools to Teach Black English (*Miami Herald*)

The words "sanction," "recognized," and especially "teach" gave a false impression that thousands of jokesters were only too quick to seize: that black kids, having been recognized as too dumb to learn in real English, would be taught algebra and literature entirely in Ebonics. The college humor magazine that I worked on at Tulane was a typical example. We wrote that

> Like George Shaw's strong-headed Eliza, the black youth of America should be taught the value of communicating properly, for therein lies their best leg up from poverty. Perhaps a modern adaptation of the lessons of Pygmalion would help to do so: *My Fair Sista Sista,* a musical comedy in which young flower girl Moiesha Doolittle repents her attitude of "Just step off, Henry Higgins. Just step off," and learns that young ladies shouldn't say "The rain in Spain be fallin mainly in the hood, nigga."

We, like so many others eager to get a good line in, didn't realize that "teaching the black youth of America the value of communicating properly" is exactly what Oakland was trying to do (if you replace "properly" with something less value-laden, such as "in standard English.")

Essentially, the problem Oakland was dealing with is the same one seen among Arabic speakers today. Children arrive at school being told that the language they have been speaking all their lives so far is debased and without value and they must immediately begin learning the "real" language. The effect on their motivation and connection to reading doesn't need to be guessed at (though it can be, correctly): it produces apathetic readers who feel that writing culture is not for them.

James Baldwin, the black novelist (who wrote, yes, in standard English), put it this way in a 1979 article:

> A child cannot be taught by anyone who despises him, and a child cannot afford to be fooled. A child cannot be taught by anyone whose demand, essentially, is that the child repudiate his experience, and all that gives him sustenance, and enter a limbo in which he will no longer be black, and in which he knows that he can never become white.

Baldwin's prognosis may seem too gloomy today, but the kernel of truth remains. Blacks have always been America's most beaten-down minority. At the same time, they have been told that the route to success in America was via education. The Ebonics movement wanted to give black kids a crucial tool, standard English, without telling them that their Black English was wrong, it was merely different and would have to give way to standard English in academic life. But the outrage over Ebonics proved that learning "white" English wasn't enough; from the conservative schoolmaster's point of view, Black English had to be shamed out of black children.

The Ebonics controversy taught linguists that they had badly, or at best incompletely, put their ideas across to the general public. Several of those ideas should have played a bigger role in the Ebonics story. One is that all language varieties are highly regular. Linguists have yet to discover a language with no rules, which speakers simply make up as they see fit. This can happen, briefly, when two peoples come into contact with each other and don't share a language. But if that improvised language persists for long enough to be learned by children, it becomes standard and predictable. In the linguist's terminology, the improvised "pidgin" becomes the regularized "creole."

Another tenet taken as an article of faith by most linguists is the fundamental equality of languages. Virtually every language—and every dialect, including Ebonics—has the capacity to express virtually any thought. True, they may need specialized vocabulary for, say, talking about subatomic particles or hydrochlorofluorocarbons. But this is actually fairly easy. Most languages can accept new words without much trouble. The point is that all languages have the structural features they need to be great languages capable of expressing the most sophisticated thought.

This is, without doubt, going to be a long, hard sell for the linguists. People have very-high-stakes relationships with their languages. They frequently believe them to be uniquely expressive, logical, or beautiful. And they are frequently tempted by myths about the deficiencies of other languages they don't know.

Why do linguists think that most any language can do anything, while the Lynne Trusses of the world see linguistic incompetence all around them? Mainly because linguists and sticklers focus on different things. Sticklers focus largely on writing and see how most people don't master the formal grammar or use the higher-level vocabulary of their language well. (They also, as we saw in chapter 2, often just make up new rules with no basis and then insist that mastery of those rules is the most basic sign of intelligence.) Linguists focus on speech and see how even small children, the uneducated, and, yes, speakers of frowned-upon languages and dialects can create an astonishing—infinite, even—number of novel utterances in a variety of situations, making themselves perfectly understood. To the declinists and sticklers, most people are idiots. To a linguist, mastery of the unbelievably complicated rules of language is so commonplace that it's no surprise most people forget just what a miracle it is, in any language.

The belief that all languages are basically equal hangs together with—though it isn't identical to—the belief that language is an innate human phenomenon. The "innateness" thesis is by no means accepted by all linguists. But it is accepted by many, including some of the field's most famous names. Noam Chomsky posited, near the beginning of his soon-to-skyrocket career, that there must be a specialized part of the brain, a "language organ," that is primed, waiting only for input, to learn the rules of any given human language. This is possible only because all languages—not just "Berlitz" languages such as Chinese and Spanish but every other one from Aari to Zyphe—are more like one another than any of them is to any other kind of language. Chomsky called these features "Universal Grammar" and set out to find them.

The matter is still one of great debate. But when linguists see a story like that of Nicaraguan Sign Language, it reaffirms the belief almost all of them share that humans have an incredible—not a shamefully inadequate—capacity for language.

Nicaragua, like most poor countries, did not have well-developed support systems for deaf children. They were merely left to grow up as best they could, in small and scattered schools. They did not (as they did in richer countries) meet and form larger deaf communities and thus create families consisting of all or mainly deaf members communicating through sign language. In fact, there was no sign language for them at all. Deaf Nicaraguans, thus, were language-deprived.

In 1977, though, the first sizable school for disabled children (including deaf children) was built in Managua, a pet project of Hope Portocarrero, the wife of the then dictator Anastasio Somoza. Teachers tried to normalize the deaf students by teaching them to lip-read and speak Spanish. Signing, as a result, was discouraged, but students were allowed to gesture to each other when out of the classroom. The school's work was interrupted by the Sandinista revolution in 1979 but reestablished when the leftist Sandinistas had taken control.

At first, the deaf children at the school, in their prime language-learning years (roughly the decade before puberty), had made ad-hoc pantomiming gestures. But over several years, these gestures developed remarkably. First the students began to approximate each other's gestures, causing standard signs to emerge. These remained rudimentary until the next generation, when a new batch of young children came to the school and learned the system as their first language. This transformed Nicaraguan Sign Language from a pidgin to a creole. It now had utterly regular rules, capable of expressing anything any spoken language can express, and a body of native speakers who would transmit NSL to new generations. Fascinated linguists have had the chance, for the first time in history, to watch a language being born, literally, from nothing. One recent study showed that it is children still in their language-learning prime who innovate new features of the language like "spatial modulation." (This involves making a series of signs in a particular unusual position—for instance, to the speaker's left—to indicate that a string of verbs all refer to the same subject.) If children are the innovators—their learning of NSL made it a true language, and they are refining it—then even if "innateness" does not exist, the human brain's language capacity is nonetheless truly extraordinary.

NSL was a stunning and unique piece of evidence for the human language ability. But for linguists, it was not entirely surprising. Many other new languages have been created in modern memory: "normal" creoles, such as Saramaccan (a Portuguese-English creole used in Suriname) to Tok Pisin (an English creole that is the official and most widely used language of Papua New Guinea). The "pidgin" origin may tempt the conclusion that these, too, are broken-down languages, but they have highly sophisticated grammars. Like Black English aspect-marking "he sick" and "he be sick," many creoles make fine distinctions English does not.

But to test the alternative hypothesis, how would we know if one language was "better"—more sophisticated, more expressive, more logical—than another? Or one language cruder, less expressive than another?

Sticklers often deride language changes because they erode

distinctions that were previously there. Using "infer" for "imply" robs the language of a neat verb, "infer," which doesn't have another ready synonym. "Awesome," "terrific," and "fantastic" once had clear connections to awe, terror, and fantasy, but have since been bleached into bland synonyms for "really good."

Linguists give several answers. New words often step in ("awe-inspiring" now means what "awesome" used to). Context and additional words often provide the correct meaning of vague words or phrases ("I don't mean 'ha-ha' funny but 'weird' funny"). The stickler reply is that this is unnecessary and impoverishing; a language that requires the support of context and extra words to make fine distinctions is an impoverished one.

Mark Halpern, the opponent of modern linguistics we met in the last chapter, sees a danger in increasing vagueness of language when words' meanings shift or old words acquire second meanings: "When I shout 'Fire!' it is rather important that those addressed know immediately whether I mean 'Run for your lives!' or 'Pull the trigger!' " Never mind that it is virtually impossible to imagine a real-world situation in which this ambiguity is possible.* Is Halpern right that a "good" language is one in which single words are packed with so much meaning that other words, grammar, and context aren't required? If he is, then his native language and mine, English, is among the world's worst languages.

Examples abound. The English verb is almost totally uninflected in the present tense; it merely adds "-s" to the third-person singular. (I speak, you speak, he speaks.) The Arabic present-tense verb has eleven distinct forms (a couple of forms do double-duty):

---

* Okay, two mafiosi are in a crowded theater; the boss tells his lieutenant to shoot their mark, but when he shouts "Fire," the theatergoers stampede out, killing the two gangsters. The mark, miraculously, survives.

aktubu	"I write"
taktubu	"you [masculine singular] write"
taktubiina	"you [feminine singular] write"
yaktubu	"he writes"
taktubu	"she writes"
taktubaani	"you two write"
yaktubaani	"they two write"
taktubaani	"they two [feminine] write"
naktubu	"we write"
taktubuuna	"you [masculine plural] write"
taktubna	"you [feminine plural] write"
yaktubuuna	"they [masculine] write"
yaktubna	"they [feminine] write"

As is common in languages with rich conjugational endings, the pronoun isn't required, since the ending alone shows whether the verb means "he writes" or "they write." "Yaktubu" is a full sentence. English, by contrast, requires the support of a pronoun. But does this really make English impoverished and vague? Would Halpern and the rest of the "No vagueness!" battalions concede the crude inferiority of the English verb to its Arabic counterpart?

And speaking of pronouns, English is poor in that department too. Arabic has two "theys," letting us know if the group is male or mixed (*hum*), or all-female (*hunna*). Arabic also distinguishes two (*huma*) from more than two (*hum/hunna*). But Arabic is itself impoverished compared to Kwaio, spoken in the Solomon Islands, which distinguishes not only singular, dual, and plural but singular, dual, paucal (a few), and plural (many). And it distinguishes "we" (you and me) from "we" (me and those with me, but not you). This handy distinction would head off many social awkwardnesses in English:

COOL KID: Uh, we're going to the movie.

AWKWARD, OBLIVIOUS CLASSMATE: Great, I'll grab my jacket!

COOL KID: [Groan.]

But somehow we English-speakers get by with just seven pronouns to Kwaio's fifteen.

Case, like verbs and pronouns, is little marked in English. "He" is distinguished from "him," but ordinary nouns are not marked, and no one seems to know how to use "whom" anymore. English lost a case-marking system that existed in the *Beowulf* era. And case marking can be handy: it allows for flexibility in word order, which can be usefully manipulated for emphasis: the Russian

Starogo muzhshchinu ubyla molodaja zhenshchina
Old   man   killed young   woman

means "A young woman killed an old man," not the opposite. The case marking on both the old man and the young woman tells us who killed whom and allows us to put the surprising element, the identity of the killer, in the attention-grabbing spot at the end of the sentence. But mighty Russia must envy its tiny neighbor: Estonian has fourteen cases to Russia's six. One word can convey "like the book," "with the book," "onto the book," "out of the book," and many others.

English looks simplistic in many other ways, too; it has no genders. Swahili has twelve. Tuyuca, mentioned earlier, has "evidentiality," requiring the speaker to attach a verb suffix to verbs in a declarative sentence showing how the speaker knows what he is saying is true. English lacks that.

Then again, English has features that many languages lack. Black English is like Russian in usually leaving out "to be" in simple present-tense sentences:

He my brother.   *On moi brat.*

English has both a definite and an indefinite article ("a"/"an" and "the"), putting it into a category with only about 20 percent of the world's languages. It distinguishes "I speak," "I am speaking," and "I do speak" in the present, which most languages don't do. (Ask any English learner how annoying this is to master.) And although orthography isn't related to grammatical complexity, English has the most difficult alphabetic spelling in the world.

English is an "analytic" language. It has moved away from using suffixes and toward word order and auxiliary words (such as prepositions) to convey meaning. This change isn't good, bad, or indifferent; it is just change. Other languages, such as Chinese and virtually all creoles, are more analytic still. Meanwhile, the "synthetic" languages lean heavily on word endings, from the ordinary (marking nominative versus accusative case) to the exotic (evidentiality, for example).

But all this counting up of complexities misses the point. Fetishizing the differences between languages—who makes finer-grained distinctions between this and that with word endings and who uses context or helping words—misses the forest for the (admittedly fascinating) trees. Every language can do pretty much everything, even if, contra the sticklers, grammatical endings change or disappear over time; even if words lose a specific meaning in favor of a more general one; even if straightforward mistakes catch on until nobody knows the original meaning of a word anymore. English speakers suffer no confusion from the fact that we no longer use the case endings on nouns that prevailed in *Beowulf*; we won't suffer if we lose "whom" either. The same can be said of Spanish and French, which shed Latin's case endings. Or the spoken colloquial Arabics, which get along with a fraction of the word endings found in the Qur'an. This kind of thing happens in every language, yet *no language has ever declined* in intelligibility. It's just not a thing that languages do.

But doesn't careful attention to language equal careful attention to facts and logic? Here the sticklers have an important point. As a teacher, I can verify that woolly and vague thoughts are usually badly expressed, and students with something vivid and interesting to say usually find a way to write them or say them well.

But the connection between thought, logic, and language doesn't run clearly in the direction many sticklers think it does. And to address this point, we must address the famous—some would say notorious—Sapir-Whorf theory of language.

Briefly, Edward Sapir was an American linguist who studied American Indian languages, and Benjamin Lee Whorf, though not a professional linguist, extended and popularized Sapir's ideas. In Sapir's often-quoted words,

> Human beings do not live in the objective world alone, nor alone in the world of social activity as ordinarily understood, but are very much at the mercy of the particular language which has become the medium of expression of their society. It is quite an illusion to imagine that one adjusts to reality essentially without the use of language and that language is merely an incidental means of solving specific problems of communication or reflection. The fact of the matter is that the "real world" is to a large extent unconsciously built up on the language habits of the group. . . . We see and hear and otherwise experience very largely as we do because the language habits of our community presuppose certain choices.

Whorf expanded this idea—that a person's access to reality is conditioned by the language he speaks. Whorf himself became so known for this that the Sapir-Whorf Hypothesis is often simply known as "Whorfianism": other writings of Sapir indicate that he wouldn't have gone as far as Whorf did. Famously, Whorf argued that, for example, the Hopi Indians of the American Southwest did not use the segmented, linear words for time common to the Indo-European languages. As a result, Whorf thought, the Hopi did not conceive of time in the same way that Westerners did.

It is an appealing notion, stimulating two popular beliefs that recur throughout this book: that language is fearsomely powerful and that languages differ exotically from one another (that is, they have different fearsome powers, and some languages are more powerful than others). If language is powerful enough to affect thought itself and languages differ vastly, then peoples themselves must be even more different than they seem on the surface.

The chief problem with Whorfianism is that it is, at least in its strong form, not true. Whorf presented not a single sentence of Hopi in his work. More detailed research on that language would take decades later to appear, in the 1970s and 1980s. It showed that the Hopi did indeed have time words like Westerners did, albeit in a different form. Other research confirmed that the Hopi were perfectly capable of thinking about time in the same way Westerners did. Whorf's modern defenders note that his claims were exaggerated by his followers. He died young, having not completed much of his work and thus leaving his ideas open to misinterpretation.

Fair to the man himself or not, "Whorfianism" is now a byword for misguided thinking among many linguists. It isn't hard to debunk the strong version of it. It is quite easy to think of a concept that you lack a word for. This was the thinking behind, for example, *The Atlantic*'s lighthearted back-page column "Word Fugitives," which used to invite readers to send in newly coined words for common problems and situations that don't have one. December 2008, for example, featured

> a term for the "irresistible impulse" to rearrange the dishes in a dishwasher that someone else has loaded. According to zillions of readers, that's *obsessive compulsive dishorder*. Another zillion, give or take, pegged it as *redishtribution*—or *dishorderly conduct*, *redishtricting*, *dishrespect*, or *dish jockeying*.

If strong Whorfianism were true, how could people formulate the concept without the framing it in language first? How would legitimate new words emerge? It's obvious that once we need to refer to something often enough, we find it useful to coin a word for it, so language and thought are clearly bound together. But isn't it clear that the thought precedes the word?

Weaker versions of Whorfianism, however, may be true. The existence of certain traits in a language might *incline* speakers one way or another, rather than restricting or strongly defining what they can or can't think. Lera Boroditsky of Stanford University has braved many linguists' disdain of Whorfianism to do some research on the subject. She has argued, for example, that Mandarin-speakers think of time as a vertical line, whereas English-speakers think of it as a horizontal line. Whereas we say "last month," they say "down month." And if you ask a Mandarin-speaker, pointing to a spot in front of him, "This is today. Where is tomorrow?" he will be more likely to point *above* that spot. English speakers will point in front of it (i.e., farther away from the speaker).

But is this strong Whorfianism or merely an interesting difference in metaphorizing? Time is not space, and so when we are forced to use space metaphors to describe time, it's hardly surprising that if we use an up–down metaphor in speech ("up month" and "down month"), we'll use a vertical motion in physical pointing, with the same going for horizontal metaphors and horizontal movement. Those looking for fascinating differences between speakers of different languages will need a bit more.

Boroditsky gets more concrete when she looks at several languages closer to home. German and Spanish both assign all nouns a gender. (German has masculine, feminine, and neuter, while Spanish has only masculine and feminine.) Mostly these genders are arbitrary. But since they have a surface relationship to sex differences, Mark Twain once noted with amusement that "in German, a young lady has no sex, but a turnip has."

(*Mädchen* is neuter, while *Steckrübe* is feminine.) In many languages, even living things don't always always have the same grammatical gender as their natural gender would suggest.

Genders may be arbitrary, but Boroditsky found that they can still affect how people think about things. To test this, she collected a set of words that were masculine in Spanish but feminine in German or vice versa. "Key," for example, is masculine in German (*der Schlüssel*), and when asked to describe a key, Germans were more likely to choose words such as "hard," "heavy," "metal," and "useful." Spaniards, who use a feminine word for "key" (*la llave*), were more likely to associate it with "golden," "tiny," "lovely," and "intricate." But this is not German toughness; when Germans have a feminine word, such as "bridge" (*die Brücke*), they are more likely to describe it as "beautiful," "elegant," and "peaceful." Spaniards, who use a masculine word (*el puente*), choose words such as "strong," "sturdy," and "towering." More interesting still is that this testing of Germans and Spaniards was done in English. Once a key was associated with masculinity, the prejudice persisted across Germans' minds even in a foreign language. Boroditsky also found that German painters tend to paint death as a male figure—unsurprisingly, as death is masculine in German. Russian painters make death female, as does their language.

In perhaps her most tantalizing piece of research, Boroditsky found that the Kuuk Thaayorre of Australia have no words for "left" or "right," "front" or "back," all words related to the position of the speaker. Rather, the Kuuk Thaayorre refer always and only to fixed cardinal directions. So they will say, for example, "You have an ant on your southwest leg" and "Move your cup a little to the north-northeast." When they greet, instead of "Hello," they ask, "Where are you going?" and the reply will be something like "South, in the middle distance." Boroditsky marvels that they stay constantly oriented. When she asks a roomful of Stanford or MIT professors to close their eyes and point southeast, few of them can. But the average five-year-old Kuuk Thaayorre–speaker can do so. And this isn't merely because their living conditions—geography, lifestyle, and so on—require staying oriented. Boroditsky points out that groups living near the Kuuk Thaayorre, in nearly identical conditions but without this feature in their languages, also lack the ability to stay constantly oriented.

Boroditsky's work puts her in a camp of neo-Whorfians. She strongly believes that different languages train the mind in different ways. Boroditsky rejects the notion—prominently expounded by Noam Chomsky, Steven Pinker, and others—that human language is fundamentally a single phenomenon, with interesting surface variations but much deeper universals.

But the neo-Whorfians argue that language steers—it does not govern—what we perceive and think. Some languages, such as Chinese, have no word for "brother," only "older brother" and "younger brother." These languages surely force people to pay more attention to birth order. But this is far from saying that languages without this distinction pay no attention to birth order.

And when it comes to the equality of languages, Boroditsky feistily agrees with the universalists: there is simply no such thing as a "better" or "worse" language. English, by most measures of "complexity," is simple. Yet few of its defenders would argue that its lack of extravagant grammar leaves its speakers unable to think with complexity and subtlety. The academic debate over Whorfianism and universals will go on, often among psychologists and philosophers as well as linguists.

While linguists debate exactly what Whorf really meant and whether findings such as Boroditsky's should revise their traditional disdain for certain Whorfian claims, in a furious and controversial academic debate, many, perhaps even most, outside the academic community unthinkingly accept a form of Whorfianism even though they have never heard the man's name.

There are two versions of pop Whorfianism out there, both

misguided and both political. The first is, alas, represented best by one of the finest writers in twentieth-century English letters, George Orwell.

Orwell, born Eric Blair, called himself a "democratic Socialist" (always capitalized thus in his writing). Though a man of the left who volunteered with the Republicans in Spain, he was stridently anti-Soviet and anti-Communist, modeling his most famous character, Big Brother, after Stalin. Left or right, he hated any kind of totalitarianism.

At the end of his 1948 novel *Nineteen Eighty-four,* Orwell added an appendix on "Newspeak," the propaganda-laced language designed by the totalitarian state of Oceania. Newspeak was to gradually replace English (Oldspeak), and it was described as the only language that shrank in vocabulary and expressiveness every year. Every concept would have only two valences, positive and negative, and thoughts such as "freedom" and "rebellion" would eventually vanish from the lexicon entirely.

This was a form of pop Whorfianism. In Orwell's conception of Newspeak, if you couldn't put a name on something, you couldn't think it. This is clear when he writes:

> The purpose of Newspeak was not only to provide a medium of expression for the world-view and mental habits proper to the devotees of Ingsoc [English Socialism], but to make all other modes of thought impossible. It was intended that when Newspeak had been adopted once and for all and Oldspeak forgotten, a heretical thought—that is, a thought diverging from the principles of Ingsoc—should be literally unthinkable, at least so far as thought is dependent on words. . . . A person growing up with Newspeak as his sole language would no more know that *equal* had once had the secondary meaning of "politically equal," or that *free* had once meant "intellectually free," than for instance, a person who had never heard of chess would be aware of the sec-

ondary meanings attaching to *queen* and *rook*. There would be many crimes and errors which it would be beyond his power to commit, simply because they were nameless and therefore unimaginable.

In one phrase, "at least so far as thought is dependent on words," Orwell begged the question. Thought isn't dependent on words. At most, even if more research confirms what Lera Boroditsky suspects, language and thought interact far more subtly and interestingly than the one-way street—"thought is dependent on words"—that Orwell proposed.

And even if—to take a science-fiction book a tad too seriously—Oceania succeeded in banning all the undesirable words overnight, they would never truly disappear. They would almost certainly be reinvented. After all, Nicaraguan deaf children did it beginning with no language whatsoever. And as we will see in a future chapter, the re-creators of modern Hebrew took the limited stock of words in the Bible and the Talmud and created a modern language with words for everything from "telephone" to "clitoris." Language is simply far too vital, and too fired by its own internal logic, for any state ever to chase out "undesirable" words for good. We need them, and if we didn't have them we'd quickly create them, again and again if necessary.

The more serious version of Orwell's Whorfianism preceded *Nineteen Eighty-four:* his celebrated 1946 essay "Politics and the English Language." In it, Orwell offered six memorable rules of writing, quite near the beginning of the essay, rules that would have made Strunk and White proud. And it has to be said that they are rules that, if borne in mind by the apprentice writer, will improve most prose.

(i)   Never use a metaphor, simile, or other figure of speech which you are used to seeing in print.

(ii) Never use a long word where a short one will do.

(iii) If it is possible to cut a word out, always cut it out.

(iv) Never use the passive where you can use the active.

(v) Never use a foreign phrase, a scientific word, or a jargon word if you can think of an everyday English equivalent.

(vi) Break any of these rules sooner than say anything outright barbarous.

For Orwell, this had political consequences. In an earlier essay, "Why I Write," he described in himself (quite accurately) one of the characteristics that made him a good writer: "a power of facing unpleasant facts." For him, this was connected intimately with vigorous, clear writing. Lazy writing—euphemism, cliché, and dead metaphor—all led to lazy thinking. This lazy thinking, in turn, made both writers and readers susceptible to political manipulation. Those who don't pay attention to the abuse of a euphemism such as "pacification" for "gunning down rebellious villagers" are making Big Brother's job easier. A lazy writer who didn't try to look freshly at the world around him every day and find arresting new language to talk about it surrendered the weapons of the struggle—words—unilaterally.

But Orwell, pointed and brilliant thinker that he was, fell into the same trap as so many of his fellow language grouches. The first sentence of the essay begins "Most people who bother with the matter at all would admit that the English language is in a bad way." He was right that legions of people who think about English think it's "in a bad way." But he, the great facer of unpleasant facts, was fortunately not describing a fact but instead just indulging our friend the age-old, worldwide habit of declinism. Remember that Swift thought that English had reached a near-terminal decline in 1712. The Fowler brothers complained of hazy imagery, foreignisms, and jargon in 1906's

The King's English, published when Orwell was three. Henry Fowler repeated many of the same complaints in 1926's *Dictionary of Modern English Usage,* when Orwell was a young imperial policeman in Burma. Lynne Truss says the same today. The English of Orwell's 1946 was not "in a bad way," unless the English of 1712, 1906, 1926, all were too, and today's as well.

Beyond succumbing to the old temptation of linguistic declinism, Orwell made a conceptual mistake. He may never have heard of Whorf, but somewhere he got the idea that language precedes thought. To be sure, he said that writers should "let the meaning choose the word, and not the other way around." But elsewhere in "Politics and the English Language" he wrote that "if thought corrupts language, language can also corrupt thought," as if the ruined state of "the English language," whatever that would mean, was making people dumber.

Once again, with emphasis: the language, including its grammar, pronunciation, vocabulary, and common phraseology, is not mainly responsible for the content of people's thoughts. If people were spouting a lot of political poppycock in Orwell's time, that is because that was an ugly time in global politics, not because English or any other language had gone downhill. How, for example, did he think Hitler and Stalin had come to power, in nations that possessed two of the world's greatest written traditions? How on the other hand, if English was so debased, had Britain and the United States found the steel to defeat the axis? Orwell, a keen student of both fascism and communism, should have known that it wasn't the state of German or Russian that had weakened Germany and Russia for dictatorship; it was the impoverishment and humiliation of the people, who believed the nonsense fed them because they were angry and afraid, not because their language was softened up. Orwell, a great writer, can be forgiven for thinking language is the most important thing on earth. But sometimes people just let themselves be misled, and language has nothing to do with it.

Take a modern piece of linguistic-political legerdemain. Is the problem with the following sentence linguistic?

> The British Government has learned that Saddam Hussein recently sought significant quantities of uranium from Africa.

These sixteen words don't violate any of Orwell's rules. They are clear English—he might have preferred something less fancy than "significant quantities," but all in all, they are straightforward enough. Millions believed them. The problem with this statement, spoken by George W. Bush while making the case for the war in Iraq in 2003, is that it was deliberately misleading: using the verb "learned" made it sound as if the British government were certain that Saddam had sought uranium in Africa. In fact, Britain's intelligence services only suspected it, with a degree of uncertainty intrinsic to intelligence work. Bush's listeners believed it, but not because they didn't know how the verb "learned" works. They wanted that war, and they trusted Bush to give them good information—and those eager to believe Bush included many bright people who would never dream of leaving a modifier dangling. The problem of political credulity, whatever its provenance, isn't primarily a problem of language.

But when people are losing political arguments, it's too easy to blame the language itself. This isn't limited to the right or the left. For example, George Lakoff, a left-wing linguist at the University of California at Berkeley, thinks Democrats have lost many of the modern political battles because they are "out-framed" by Republicans, who get their preferred terminology for things repeated (and internalized) by voters. Lakoff has made a one-man industry of convincing Democrats to reframe things like "taxes" as "membership dues," a battle he has yet to win.

From the right, meanwhile, Mark Halpern, the stickler and

Orwell admirer, hopes to stop the cultural rot he sees coming from the left by promoting his brand of sticklerism, because

> becoming sensitive to mere solecisms increases one's sensitivity to language in general, and is a big step in learning to detect and resist dishonest and tendentious language.

This is partly true, but not in the way Halpern thinks. *Of course* being sensitive to language makes people more likely to detect and resist dishonest language. This isn't because language has some mythical power to make people smarter. Being sensitive to science is a big step in learning to detect and resist dishonest language. Being sensitive to history is a big step. Being sensitive to political philosophy, logic, economics, and even mathematics is a big step, because all of these things are *learning,* and knowledge creates aware and critical citizens. There is nothing magical about language in this regard. Knowing the difference between "infer" and "imply" is no more likely to create a skeptical, bullshit-detecting citizen than knowing the atomic weight of uranium or the capital of Niger. Smart people of all types don't tend to be hoodwinked so easily.

Halpern is right that Americans (and most other nationalities) are paying too much attention to the wrong things much of the time. Everyone could spend more time with a book and less with *The Biggest Loser* on television. But he is wrong in his pseudo-Whorfian notion that paying attention to traditional grammar rules and usage shibboleths gives you a kind of talismanic defense against dishonesty. In fact, blindly memorizing rules is just the opposite of the kind of flexibility, empiricism, and fingertip-feel that a characterizes a mind resistant to dangerous dogmas. Halpern is joining a long lineup of people who have begun with decent ideas ("Pay attention to language use") and recruited them to silly political ends: learn prescriptivist rules, or the terrorists and communists will win.

--- -- -- -- -- --

Orwell is an example of political Whorfianism within one language: speak and write proper English, and your political acumen will improve. A related phenomenon is Whorfianism between languages and dialects. We've already seen the dismissal of Black English as incapable of being a vehicle for higher thought. We see the same around the world. Most people today are usually too polite to dismiss the expressiveness of other languages. But they do still have a habit of seeing one—nearly always the prestige variety of their own language—as more equal than others.

The French, linguistic nationalists par excellence, are famous for sharing this kind of nationalistic Whorfianism. In 2007 a group of French activists made an outrageous push to have their language recognized as the sole legal language of the European Union. The effort went nowhere. Since the EU's founding, all national official languages had the right to be declared official EU languages.* The notion behind official equality is a sound one. How are (say) Finns to connect with "their" European Union if their native Finnish is not an official language? The twenty-three-language situation is unwieldy but politically necessary.

Where, then, did the French get the preposterous idea of making French the sole legal language? The culprit, again, is pop Whorfianism. Maurice Druon, the "perpetual secretary" of the French Academy until his death in 2009, (he retired in 2000, but Academy membership is permanent), said that, of course, "all languages are equal." But he went on to contradict this completely by saying that

---

* The Irish waited a few decades before insisting that Irish be made an EU language. The Luxembourgers, rather more sensibly, have never insisted on making their third official language, the little-known Letzeburgesch, official at the EU level.

The Italian language is the language of song, German is good for philosophy and English for poetry. French is best at precision, it has a rigor to it. It is the safest language for legal purposes. . . . The language of Montesquieu is unbeatable.

Oddly, the French were supported by a former Romanian prime minister and a former Polish foreign minister. Belief in the superiority of a language for this or that task is usually but not always limited to one's own language.

It's hard to believe that any adult could take these notions seriously, but many people do. The superiority of German for philosophy, in particular, is something I've heard from serious Americans, too. I'm not sure, though, where Druon got the idea that English is best for poetry. France and Germany certainly have their share of great poets. Perhaps he was being devilish; saying a language is good for poetry could be a way of saying it is pretty but not so serious.

In 2008, the French National Assembly (the main house of parliament) considered a brief addition to the constitution: "The regional languages are part of the patrimony of France." The statement, not only harmless but obvious, resulted in an outcry. This is because French has a near-mythical status as the very spirit of the French nation. In arguing against the proposal, one opponent of the proposal, Jean-Claude Monneret, wielded this argument:

> Not all languages have the same dignity. Even if one is a linguist—as I am—and convinced of the necessary pluralism and survival of all languages, one can't put on the same level a great language of culture and an impoverished dialect. Is there a Rousseau in Occitan, a Tocqueville in Basque, a Balzac in ch'ti, to allude to

a recent film, a Stendhal in Breton, a Montesquieu in Catalan?

"Impoverished dialect" is strong language for someone who claims to support the regional languages. But Monneret seemed to find it self-evident that Catalan, Basque, and the others were not "dignified" because they had not produced a Rousseau or a Tocqueville.

Could this possibly be because those languages are not up to the task? Certainly not. The reason French has its Tocquevilles and English its Miltons and German its Goethes is because French, German, and English were *big* languages, undeniably: the main languages of some of the most powerful nations in the world. And the English, French, and German we know today are what they are because, largely, of historical accident. Had Martin Luther come from Hamburg, he might have translated the Bible into something more like Niederdeutsch ("low German" from the northern flatlands, closer to Dutch), and that, not Hochdeutsch ("high," now standard, German) would be the prestigious language of everyone from Schiller to Wittgenstein. The same might be said for the southeastern dialect that became standard English or the Île-de-France French that became standard French. Their supremacy is political, not linguistic.

But Monneret has a point. Once language does become a standard, a self-fulfilling prophecy begins. As the prestige language of the state, the standard becomes the vehicle of education and learning. This produces a body of literature in the standard for the simple reason that even if Montesquieu or Rousseau had spoken Basque as their first language, they would have had to be unambitious, cantankerously contrarian, or highly regionally nationalistic to write in Basque. Nobody would have read their work outside the region. So Monneret's argument is correct but uninteresting: *of course* the great authors he mentioned wrote in standard French. This tells us nothing about the qualities of the language itself and more about the number of people who can, and would, read a great novel in Basque.

That self-fulfilling prophecy, however, muddies our picture of linguistic equality. Once there comes into being a body of literature in a language, a literary style follows. Lexicographers compile dictionaries, keeping rare words and stylistically useful synonyms alive. So a prestige language may have more resources for a writer to draw on than another. And that is what makes those languages' admirers think that they are superior to any other: the flexibility and refinement of vocabulary, in particular, are enticing.

Many people share this idea that a language is "sophisticated" to the extent that it has a large vocabulary. In this view, language is simply a store of words—the thicker the dictionary, the better the language. The kind of person who believes this usually delights in etymology or the collection of linguistic curios, rare words that no one ever uses in natural conversation. Does anyone really ever say, "I have triskaidekaphobia" instead of "I have a fear of the number thirteen?" The most obvious showing off here is of the speaker's vocabulary—see how many words I know? But below the surface is a pride in the treasury of words itself. See how many delightful and rare words my language has?

This thinking—"language as a storehouse of words"—misleads in a number of ways. Some languages, of course, seem to have more words than English, because they routinely coin single words where English uses a combination of two or more. German is famous for this. Foreign learners, like Mark Twain writing in "The Awful German Language," gnash their teeth (or laugh) over words like *Unabhängigkeitserklärungen* ("declarations of independence") and *Waffenstillstandsunterhandlungen* ("cease-fire negotiations"). But the fact that German coins long words while English uses a phrase (which functions grammatically just like German's compounds) doesn't mean, in any real sense, that German has a richer vocabulary. It means little more than that Germans have less recourse to the space bar than English-speakers do. Other "agglutinating" languages, whether Turkish or Inuit, can cram together so many different meaningful pieces ("morphemes," in the linguist's argot) that the stock of words is virtually infinite. But that doesn't make Turkish or Inuit richer than English.

That said, languages can, in fact, have more or less rich vocabularies. This usually means one of two different things. One is that languages that have had a great deal of contact with other languages will absorb foreign words and (in the happiest circumstance) keep their own. This will result in sometimes useful synonyms; think of the English groupings that come from the conquest of England by the Normans and the Vikings. This is how we have *kingly* (Anglo-Saxon), *royal* (French), and *regal* (Latin). This gives writers, especially (since they can choose their words at leisure) a stylistic flexibility that languages less rich in near synonyms lack.

The other way in which the European languages really are richer than the average isolated language of New Guinea is their technical vocabulary. Since the modern sciences by and large come from Europe and North America, the vocabulary of chemistry, physics, and so on tends to be drawn from the European languages, particularly English (though English originally drew them from Latin or Greek).

This, again, is true but uninteresting. Of course English is replete with technical terms while Kuuk Thaayorre is not. But this isn't a comment on the strengths of English or the weakness of Kuuk Thaayorre. It is a comment on the success of Anglophone scientists and the relative dearth of Australian aboriginal Nobel Prize winners.

Meanwhile, lack of scientific vocabulary need not hold a language back. There are two options for making up the shortfall. A country seeking to elevate its national language to a status where it can be used (say) for university teaching and research need only mint words. It can either bring them over from the original European language, making allowance for the native sound system (Arabic did this with *fiziya'*, physics), or by coining a word from native roots (Arabic *ahyia'*, "biology" from *hayaa*, "life"). Sometimes both happen: the "official" word for "computer" is *hasoub*, from a native root. But most Arabs simply say, and sometimes write, *kombyuter*. Hungarian, Hebrew, and Turkish are just some of the languages that have been artificially, but successfully, enriched by this mixture of borrowing and native invention. It takes time and expertise, but it is a relatively straightforward process for most languages.

So the real test of a language isn't whether it allows its speakers to discuss any technical matter under the sun. Most people can't discuss the finer points of cosmology or particle physics in any language. The question we should ask, before declaring one language or dialect inferior, is whether it is capable of expressing the full range of human thought; not whether it has a thick enough dictionary but whether it has a structure that can accommodate these demands as long as the needed words are either available, borrowed, or invented.

If we look to grammar, we find that some languages have myriad affixes that make distinctions that would rarely occur to an English-speaker. But we have seen—despite sticklers' complaints that languages can lose their ability to make important distinctions if they are used "carelessly"—that languages that lack inflection are no less sophisticated or supple.

English is one such language; though it certainly has its complexities, it is fair to say that it is simpler than most of its Germanic cousins. Yet it is the most successful language on Earth. Mandarin Chinese is another. Though the writing system is absurdly complicated, this is a historical oddity; the modern spoken language is in fact far simpler than the other "dialects" of Chinese (actually languages, a debate taken up in chapter 6). In word endings, number of tones, number of overall sounds, and many other areas, Mandarin is the simplest of its family, simpler, too, than the classical Chinese that it replaced in the republican era at the beginning of the twentieth century. Yet Mandarin has been plenty successful, used by more people than any other language on Earth and serving as the official language of a rising political and economic power to boot.

In fact, John McWhorter argues that successful languages tend to be simplified by their success. To put it more exactly, languages such as English, Mandarin, and Arabic, because they have been learned by many millions of people as a *second* language over the course of their history, have shed inflections in favor of "analytic" structures. Twelve genders, as in Swahili, or fifteen cases, as in Estonian, put a huge load on an adult second-language learner. Languages don't spread *because* they are simple and flexible (as some think true of English). The causation runs the other way around. They are forced to be simpler and more flexible when they spread. English was simplified—the stickler would say "dumbed down"—by its history of contact: between the Anglo-Saxons and the Celts, Vikings, and Norman French they came into contact with. And it seems to happen to other languages too: a statistical analysis of thousands of languages found that languages spoken by large numbers of people have relatively simpler grammar, in particular the prefixes, suffixes, and so forth that distinguish, say, Latin from English. Languages shake off bits and pieces as they grow and spread.

Sticklerism and nationalism are thus, though they so often go together, a bad fit. There is no way to seriously proclaim the overall superiority of this language or variety over that one. We can merely say that some languages have been elaborated—their grammar formalized, their vocabulary stored up—in such a way that makes certain kinds of literary and scientific writing easier. Other languages can be banged into shape for these same tasks. But we often see languages getting simpler as they succeed. More people use, and change, the rules. Sticklers may not like it, but shedding unnecessary bits of grammatical baggage may be necessary for a language to spread in the very long run. Success has its price.

5

Welcome to X. Now speak Xish

Language and Nationalism

We have created Italy. Now we have to create Italians.

—MASSIMO D'AZEGLIO (Italian statesman, 1798–1866)

If you could go back in time to the shores of Iberia in about A.D. 1200, you would encounter (provided you didn't land in the parts of the south still ruled by Arabic-speaking Muslims) people who spoke a Romance language related to vulgar Latin. If you had studied, say, the Latin Bible translation of Saint Jerome from the early fifth century, you might be able to make out a good number of words people were using.

Pretend that you have learned the local language fairly well. If you then moved inland and observed the inhabitants of the next town, you'd find nearly the same language. But you'd also notice a few differences. Maybe all the words that contained a sound like *th* now had an *s* sound where *th* had been or used *ei* where the previous town had used *eh*. From town to town you'd see more changes along those same lines.

People from regions near one another would understand one another, but people from two towns far enough apart wouldn't. At one point on your journey, you might see people speaking a language recognizably related to Old Spanish. Farther on, you might see something like Old French. You could

continue in much the same way down into Italy and across to
Sicily, never encountering a sharp language break. At most, at
a river crossing or mountain pass, you might find the differences slightly more abrupt.

The point is that at that time in history, it was almost never
obvious what was a local pronunciation, what was a dialect,
and what was a language. There were no neat border crossings,
with flags and uniformed customs officers, telling you when
Spanish ended and French began. People just spoke as they
spoke, usually sounding something like the people near them.
Modern-day maps like to show where speakers of this or that
language live, perhaps with French-speakers colored red or
German-speakers blue. But a map of medieval Europe with a
dot for each speaker would show a mess, with a great deal of
overlap. There would be no "red," just reddish hues from
brownish red to orange-red to hot pink, representing the different Romance dialects spoken in Italy, Spain, Portugal, and
France. Our Germanic "blue" might be greenish in the area
that became the Netherlands and purplish in the area that became Bavaria. Linguists speak of a "Romance continuum" or a
"Slavic continuum" to describe this primordial state of affairs.
There were no "languages" as we think of them today, codified
in dictionaries and grammar books. Everything was dialect.

How did we get from muddy continua to crisp borders?
How did the hazy and shifting mess of dots get sorted into rigid
containers, all the red dots in this one, all the blue dots in that
one? What happened to change our thinking from "Everything
is a dialect" to "There is one proper French (or English or German)"?

In short, the nation-state happened. Or more specifically,
waves of nation-state building happened. The varying attitudes
we see today toward language can, to a surprising extent, be
traced to how and when a nation-state was built.

Americans tend to use "nation" as a synonym for "country." But political scientists and historians, as well as many
Europeans, tend to use the term for a much more specific

phenomenon: a group of people who feel they belong together, whether they have a country of their own or not. Nations tend to share several things: a sense of common history, a religion, cultural customs, some geographic continuity, and, of course, a language. And though all of these can be powerful, the two most powerful of all tend to be religion and language. Where people share the same faith and the same speech, they tend to consider themselves a nation.

"Nationalism" is the political ideal that emerged as the nations of Europe became self-aware. In short, it is the idea that every nation should have a state and every state, just one nation. As nationalist thinking grew, beginning in the seventeenth and eighteenth centuries, the old blurry linguistic borders became inconvenient for nationalists. To build nations strong enough to win themselves a state, the people of a would-be nation needed to be welded together with a clear sense of community. Speaking a minority dialect or refusing to assimilate to a standard wouldn't do.

States First: The First European Powers

The first great nation-states of Europe didn't emerge from bottom-up nationalism. They were built through the conquest of large territories by feudal kings and lords. Feudalism was a pyramidal system in which (to simplify quite a bit) the king stood above lords, lords stood above local minilords, and minilords owned the land on which peasants worked. Serfs rendered labor to their lords and were protected. Vassals—those lower in the pyramid—rendered military service and taxes to the lords above them in exchange for their land. Lords raised forces for their king when a major war had to be fought. Everyone had a place, and those on top didn't much care whether those below them all spoke the same way, so long as the bills were paid in money, goods, or military service.

Of this era, three great states emerged, each in its own way: England, Spain, and France. England was a Germanic Anglo-

Saxon-speaking land repeatedly invaded by Vikings, who left settlers (and linguistic heritage) in the north of the country. Then came the invasion that made the modern country: the Norman Conquest of 1066. England was, for several centuries, a Germanic-speaking country ruled by French-speaking foreigners. Early Norman kings spoke no English, and it would be about three centuries before English triumphed at the highest level and English kings spoke their subjects' language as their own. By that time, of course, English had been heavily influenced by French.

Spain was almost entirely conquered by the Moors in an invasion beginning in A.D. 711. Of the modern territory of Spain, only the northern fringes remained in Christian hands. But a slow reconquest by Christian forces gradually pushed the Moorish tide back, over centuries, until the reconquest was completed with the 1492 fall of Granada. The heart of the new Spain was Castile, which had been the biggest of the Spanish kingdoms, united with Aragon, another kingdom, through the marriage of the storied "Catholic monarchs," Isabella of Castile and Ferdinand of Aragon. From the last years of Islamic Iberia through the rise of unified Spain, the Castilian Romance dialect gradually became "Spanish."

The territory and language of France, similarly, radiated out from a core: the Île-de-France, or Island of France, the territory around Paris. The kings in Paris controlled some lands directly and others through dukes, counts, and other assorted nobles. Gradually, though, the latter were folded directly into the French state through war or inheritance. The French we know today was but one of many Romance dialects in the territory of France. It just happened to be that of the capital region.

All of this state building required armies, and armies required taxation. Taxation required records, of land and population, and so records were kept—in the language of the capital. "Chancery English," the emerging standard of record keeping in London, is partially synonymous with Late Middle

English. Many Spanish-speakers today still call their language *castellano,* "Castilian," and not *español,* a reminder that "Spanish" is one of many older Spanishes. And "Francien," the dialect of the Île-de-France, was little more than the first among equals for centuries. It competed with other "langue d'oïl" languages in the north (so called for *oïl,* their word for "yes"). The langue d'oïl faced robust competition from the "langue d'oc" region in the south, where medieval troubadors worked in Provençal (also called Occitan, which used *oc* for yes).

It would take centuries—essentially an internal cultural conquest—for these languages to dominate their own countries. Spain was politically unified after 1492 but remained linguistically heterodox. King Charles I, who was also Charles V of the far-flung Holy Roman empire, was said to boast, perhaps apocryphally, "I speak Spanish to God, Italian to women, French to men, and German to my horse." This was hardly surprising, though, as his territory included parts of the modern Netherlands, Italy, Germany, Romania, Czech Republic, Hungary, Austria, and others. In Iberia itself, linguistically distinct Portugal broke away after a short-lived union. Empire, not nation-state, was the order of the day. Even within Spain, most regions were unified around Castilian over the ensuing centuries, but Galicia, Catalonia, and the Basque Country continued to hold on to Galician, Catalan, and Basque.

Paris-based kings also took centuries to complete their hold over modern France. Even so, by the time of the 1789 French Revolution a census showed that just a fraction of the people spoke standard French. Provençal/Occitan, Basque, and Catalan persisted in the south, Alsatian in the east, Picard in the North, and the Celtic language of Breton in the west—a situation considered intolerable to the revolutionaries. Henri Grégoire, an unusual Catholic bishop who enthusiastically supported the Revolution, was dismayed to find how many Frenchmen spoke "degenerate" languages, or "patois," as he called them. "These crude idioms perpetuate the childhood of the reason and the old age of prejudices," he wrote in his "Report on the necessity and the means to annihilate the patois and universalize the use of the French language."

And though the modern United Kingdom took its form with the 1707 Act of Union bringing England and Scotland together, languages other than standard English carried on a vibrant life. A distinctly Scottish English, Scots (of Burns's "gang aft a'gley"), dominated Scotland. Gaelic, related to Irish, Breton, Manx, and Cornish, persisted in the highlands and Scottish Islands: in 1755, the British census showed 300,000 people—a quarter of Scotland's population—to be monolingual in Gaelic. In Ireland, English became the majority language only in the mid–nineteenth century, when the Irish-speaking population was devastated by the potato famine and emigration: the 1841 census showed 4 million Irish-speakers in a total Irish population of 8 million. And finally, Welsh persisted in Wales, though that country had been unified with England since the English king crowned his son "Prince of Wales" in 1301. The Welsh language was particularly strong in the mountains and the coastal regions distant from England's heart; as so often elsewhere, forbidding geography was the best friend of a small language.

So by the dawn of the modern age, only one of two pieces was in place for modern linguistic nationalism. No great European state was homogeneous—the idea would have seemed odd to the rulers themselves. But standard languages had emerged, even if they were largely limited to elites in capitals. English, French, and Spanish shared crucial assets. One was a literature, which was the vehicle of linguistic prestige: the Cervanteses, Racines, and Miltons did much to make Spanish Spanish, French French, and English English. The second asset was some form of linguistic custodian. Spain and France went the route of the official language academy: the French Academy, founded in 1635, and the Royal Spanish Academy, founded in 1713. The guardians of English would be informal—lexicographers like Samuel Johnson and grammarians like Robert Lowth.

Perhaps most crucially, these states were powerful. Spain had conquered huge chunks of two continents in the sixteenth century. France emerged as the dominant continental power in the seventeenth, particularly after the Thirty Years' War (1618–1648), which devastated rivals to the east. And Britain's spectacular rise began in the eighteenth, as its colonists, merchants, and sailors built an empire on which the sun never set.

Spain, France, and Britain were not the only European countries with great languages and civilizations. But they were the only ones that combined them with heavy-duty, enduring political states. Russia was on the rise in the east but punched below its weight. Sweden declined after the Thirty Years' War. The Netherlands flourished briefly, gathering imperial possessions around the world, but lacked the economic and military power to keep them in the long term. Much the same could be said of Portugal.

From States Building Nations to Nations Seeking States

What brought Europe from the age of great but mixed states— essentially internal empires—to monolingual nation-states? Ernest Gellner, an eminent philosopher and social anthropologist, offered a theory of nationalism with one word at its core: industrialization. He wrote in 1983 that

> The proportion of people at the coal face of nature, directly applying human physical force to natural objects, is constantly diminishing. Most jobs, if not actually involving work "with people," involve the control of buttons or switches or levers which need to be *understood,* and are explicable, once again, in some standard idiom intelligible to all comers.

In agrarian society, only a few elite groups truly needed a standard language: military leaders, bureaucracies, and clergy. Their mastery of a high idiom (say, Latin or classical Arabic)—

learned among the religious, courtly, or military elites—put them at a comfortable, usually hereditary distance from the masses. But there was not yet an "education system" available to all. The masses themselves lived on the land, geographically separated from one another and speaking unwritten languages. Most people learned their trade—almost always farming—from their parents or village communities.

Industrialization changed all that. People had to be able to learn to pick up new skills faster, since the economy had not only to produce but to continually grow and become more sophisticated technologically. Learning one trade over many years would not do. People needed *generic* skills, to which only a small amount of extra training would allow them to move around the economy, taking new jobs and responding to innovation. This demand for generic skills created the need for the modern, standardized, centralized educational system to be extended to the masses. Gellner pointed out that such education is *useful*, not just good. This is why, though modern peoples have both a "right" to free speech and a "right" to education (through the United Nations' Universal Declaration of Human Rights, among other things), dictatorships usually respect one and not the other. Even tyrannies educate their people, because it is economically necessary to do so.

Gellner's theory that industrialization made nationalism necessary may be too neat. It ignores, among other things, how readily and happily common folk joined the nationalist wave. But there is no doubt that, once the nationalist spirit was loosed, industrialization and technology combined explosively with those emerging national identities. Britain, home of the Industrial Revolution, both Anglicized its islands and spread its culture to lands as far-flung as America and India with spectacular success. France's revolution released disciplined armies with universalist ideas upon Europe, spreading the notion that rationalism, nationalism, and progress could free and unify dormant "nations" stymied by tyranny. Spain, meanwhile, underwent a relative decline. (Still, Castilian Spanish continued to dominate not only Spain but most of South and Central America and much of North America, while Spain's regional languages languished, spoken but not fostered by the state, on the periphery. The growing Spanish insistence on Castilian only has caused conflicts that still boil today, as we will see.)

Meanwhile, two great European cultures still had no single state by the nineteenth century: the Germans and Italians. Germans were spread among dozens of states. The rickety Holy Roman Empire, created by the pope for Charlemagne in A.D. 800, was finally shoved into its grave by Napoleon in 1806. In the west, its successor states were multifarious free cities, duchies, and just two kingdoms of note, Bavaria and Prussia. In the east, the empire based in Vienna was hugely multilingual. Though dominated by Germans, it included Italians, Hungarians, Czechs, Slovaks, Poles, Hungarians, Romanians, various southern Slavs, Ukrainians, and Jews.

The lack of a single German state offended the "one people, one state" principle. Germans, in fact, spoke many local varieties of "German" that were only partly mutually intelligible. But they shared a literary language that depended heavily on the "High German" that had coalesced after Martin Luther's beloved 1534 translation of the Bible. In the true Protestant spirit, Luther had sought the people's language, trying to make his translation as close to the language he heard around him as he could. When his translation appeared, a contemporary opponent, Johann Cochlaeus (a Catholic), complained that

> even tailors and shoe-makers—nay, even women and ig-
> norant persons, who could read but little—studied it
> with the greatest avidity as the fountain of truth. Some
> committed it to memory and carried it about in their bo-
> soms. Within a few months such people deemed them-
> selves so learned that they were not ashamed to dispute
> about the faith and the Gospel, not only with Catholic

laymen, but even with priests and monks and Doctors of Divinity.

Though considerably older than the King James Bible of 1611, Luther's translation is easier for modern Germans to read than the King James is for the modern English-speaker. Luther's home region of eastern-central Germany, with its influence on his language, would contribute more than its fair share to what would eventually become the standard language we now call German. In contrast to the state-led creation of English, French, and Spanish, German's center of gravity would not be Germany's eventual capital, Berlin. The unified "high" language preceded the state.

The German that Luther helped form was crucial to a sense of Germanness that bound even Catholics and Protestants together with the sense of being a single people. This linguistic unity was crucial during centuries of political division among dozens of states, and left Germans ready for nationalism when it came—on the back of an invasion from the west.

After the French Revolution of 1789, Revolutionary and Napoleonic armies repeatedly marched into German lands. Even though the French invaders were defeated, they left behind the quintessential concept of their revolution: that of the modern nation-state, all people of a nation bound together in a single polity. This idea percolated for half a century, more decades of division and weakness, punctuated by a series of failed antimonarchical, nationalist revolutions in 1848.

In the end, Germans would not be unified by republican sentiments rising from below. Instead, the wily chancellor of Prussia, Otto von Bismarck, would provoke a series of wars (with Denmark, Austria, and France) that would unite most Germans from above. Under Prussian leadership, most of the German states (barring Austria) were united for the first time in a state called Germany: the "second empire" established in 1871. The king of Prussia was now the emperor of Germany. The new state quickly sought to catch up on building an overseas empire, seeking its proper "place in the sun" by racing France and Britain into Africa and elsewhere.

Italy underwent a similar crash nationalization. Italy, like Germany, was a patchwork of states in the wake of Napoleon's 1815 defeat. Despite that, like the Germans, Italians shared linguistic unity at least at an elite level. The writings of Dante, Boccaccio, and Petrarch, all Florentines, had led to a de facto literary standard. The linguistic scholarship of the Accademia della Crusca, which preceded even the French Academy by fifty years, helped too. Italy's "Prussians" were enlightened Piedmontese, northern Italians who gradually conquered the various states and annexed them to Italy. And Italy, unlike Germany, had no significant Catholic-Protestant divide.

But Italy was more geographically diverse, more rural, and poorer than the German lands, which had over the previous centuries produced many of Europe's finest thinkers and writers. Italy's sense of itself as a nation had further to go. Education had done less to spread the standard language to the people. *I Promessi Sposi* (*The Betrothed*), an early-nineteenth-century nationalist novel, was written in a Florentine Italian that was a deliberate attempt by its author, Alessandro Manzoni, to standardize Italy's language. By one estimate, just 2 or 3 percent of newly minted "Italians" spoke Italian at home when Italy was unified in the 1860s. Some Italian dialects were as different from one another as modern Italian is from modern Spanish. No wonder the pro-unification statesman Massimo d'Azeglio felt compelled to sigh, in the quotation that begins this chapter, that Italy was a state without a proper people.*

The creation of two big new countries on the European map gave other nations ideas. Success of the French nationalist citi-

---

* Even today, a movie in a regional dialect, such as 2008's *Gomorra* about the Naples mafia, must be subtitled in standard Italian in order to be understood nationwide.

zen army and the German state kicked off the stage of so-called "late nationalisms." The many non-German peoples of the Austrian Empire began to clamor: Hungarians, whose language, from the Finno-Ugric family, shares nothing with its neighbors; Czechs, who, despite historical Catholic-Protestant divides, considered themselves a nation united by language; Poles, whose great state had been gradually partitioned among Prussia, Russia, and Austria until the Poles were stateless; south Slavs, who developed a distinct identity between the hammer of Austria to the north and the anvil of Turkey to the south (despite their own tripartite Catholic-Orthodox-Muslim divisions); and so on. The territory of Western Europe had already mostly been filled by stable states. But Eastern Europe's borders began to change rapidly, as old empires frayed, and newly self-conscious nations began to seek states of their own. Most of those nations identified themselves mainly by their language.

This despite the fact that "language," in the case of the new nationalisms, was a touchy subject. Many languages of Eastern Europe had not been extensively written down. Unlike the Western Europeans, who had the benefit of strong states that had boosted standard languages for centuries, the Easterners had to create standard languages on the fly, with scattered raw materials. Linguistic nationalists collected folk tales, spawned language societies, and debated late into the night. Which regional pronunciation would be the standard? Which words were "foreign" and hence to be shunned? Should technical vocabulary be borrowed from English, French, or German or minted locally?

These efforts were sometimes farcical, as intentional language planning can be. Johannes Aavik (1880–1973), the father of modern Estonian, created nonsense words out of thin air for Estonian, of which forty survive in use today. Another purist, an overzealous Czech, coined a replacement for *křen,* "horseradish," because he thought it had been borrowed from German *Chren.* He didn't realize that *Chren* had earlier been borrowed from Czech. (His coinage, *mořska řetkev,* was, ironically, a part-for-part translation of the German *Meerrettich,* "sea radish." It didn't survive.) In both cases, the motive was to make the language distinct from that of the neighbors—to make a language worthy of a nation, so that the nation itself would be taken more seriously.

All of this linguistic nationalism is at least deserving of sympathy from our modern point of view. If nations have an understandable desire for a prestigious language, for small nations that urge was given a boost by centuries of being repressed. These many long-ignored nations of Europe were merely clamoring to join their bigger, more established neighbors at the table. But the orgy of nationalism that began with the French Revolution, gained strength with the creation of Germany and Italy, and sparked the awakenings in the east would ultimately lead to a century that would include the greatest bloodshed the world had ever seen.

It was a south Slavic nationalist, Gavrilo Princip, who assassinated Austria's archduke, Franz Ferdinand, in June 1914. Princip and his associates wanted a south-Slavic federation led by Serbia and free from control by Vienna. Germany, eager to flex its muscles, backed its ally Austria against Serbia. Russia came to fellow Slavic Serbia's side and France to its ally Russia's. Britain had allied itself to France too, and quickly, nearly all Europe was at war—the bloodiest war in centuries and the first truly mechanized war in history, killing millions of Europe's most promising young men. The United States, the Ottoman Empire, and others were also dragged into the fight.

Germany's defeat in that war planted the seeds of the next one. The former rising power lost big chunks of land to the east and west in the postwar Treaty of Versailles. Many Germans were now stranded outside Germany's newly shrunken borders. This humiliation, among the others that weakened the postwar Weimar Republic, eased the way for Hitler's rise in 1933. The two major steps toward that war—Hitler's *Anschluss* fusing Austria and Germany, and the annexation of the German-speaking Sudetenland from Czechslovakia—were the logical extension of the nation-state idea: that all Germans should live in one country. "National self-determination" had, after all, been one of Woodrow Wilson's celebrated liberal Fourteen Points at the end of the first war.

Irredenta elsewhere gave far too many other Europeans cause for complaint, ultimately pushing Europeans to war again just twenty-one years after the first Great War had ended. Slovaks and Croats, resenting their subordinate status, split away from Czechoslovakia and Yugoslavia (respectively) in the Second World War and joined the Fascist cause. So did Hungary: split from Austria-Hungary and shrunk by two-thirds after the First World War, it had lost millions of Hungarian-speakers to other countries. Many of the new Soviet Union's restive western minorities eagerly joined the Fascists as well. The "war to end all wars," the First World War, had done no such thing; it had merely primed the Europeans to try their hand at settling nationalist scores again. Two corporals wounded in the first, indecisive war—Hitler and Mussolini—became the instigators of the next.

It would be too glib to say that language purism and language identities caused the world wars. But the forces of modern nationalism unleashed them. And language was at the heart of those nationalisms more than any other single factor. In the high nationalist period that led to and included both world wars, religion was no good predictor of who would fight whom. Catholic and Protestant countries fought on both sides in both wars. (And some highly distinct peoples—the Hungarians, the Czechs, and the Germans themselves—were divided between the two confessions.) Instead, the new nations saw their conationals as those who spoke the most like they did. And those who felt that their nations were repressed, divided, or humiliated by others and not given a big enough piece of territory on Europe's crowded map wreaked bloody hell on one another for half a century, in service of the idea that the best possible state was one including all of one's conationals and no one else.

A Language for Israel, or a State for Hebrew?

It is one of the ironies of history that, as Europe was learning the painful lessons of nationalism, one of the peoples most oppressed by Europeans was taking the opposite lesson: that the ethno-nationalist state was the peak of human accomplishment, to be attained no matter the cost. There are few more painfully ironic examples of the triumph, and the pain, of nationalism than the creation of modern Israel in 1948, achieved with the help of the extraordinary resuscitation of Hebrew.

The Jews, dispersed throughout North Africa, the Middle East, and Europe after the destruction of Jerusalem and the second temple by the Romans, were one of the world's most storied nations without a state. Those in the Middle East—ironically, in the light of modern times—got along as second-class, but reasonably tolerated, subjects in largely Muslim states. But those in Europe suffered heavily. The oldest form of anti-Semitism was based upon the notion of Jews as the murderers of Christ. Jews were banned from professions, landholding, and simple rights granted ordinary Christian citizens.

But in the age of nationalism, the Jews became not mainly Christ-killers but an unloved ethnic minority. The Central European states had flourishing Jewish populations that had contributed hugely to European culture, through music, science, philosophy and other areas of learning, assimilating linguistically and nationally. Many Jews had abandoned Yiddish and tried to be good citizens of their countries. But they were still objects of suspicion and scorn. And in the eastern reaches of Jewish settlement, especially in Russia, a virulent anti-Semitism led to bloody pogroms against already impoverished, isolated, and unassimilated Jewish communities.

Near the end of the nineteenth century, Theodor Herzl, an Austrian, thought he had found the answer. In his pamphlet "Der Judenstaat," ("The Jewish State"), he proposed a solution for his stateless people: "Let the sovereignty be granted us over a portion of the globe large enough to satisfy the rightful requirements of a nation; the rest we shall manage for ourselves."

A minority taste at first, Zionism caught on gradually among a certain slice of Europe's Jews. The World Zionist Organization—which met for the first time in Basel in 1897—discussed where a Jewish state might be established, briefly considering even a home in British East Africa. But the focus of Zionist longing was the ancestral homeland itself: Palestine, then a backward and, as they saw it, sparsely populated province of the Ottoman Empire. Zionists began raising money through the Jewish National Fund and lobbying the Ottoman authorities to allow land purchases in Palestine. European Jews were encouraged to emigrate there to join a small community, the "old *yishuv*," of Jews who had never left.

At the same time, an astonishing cultural project began: the reconstruction of Hebrew as a living language. Hebrew had not disappeared. It was nobody's native language, but Jews in the diaspora still used it for serious writing. Several literary works had been composed in Hebrew: plays, essays, and a nineteenth-century novel. But no one spoke it spontaneously.

Some of those who wanted to revive Hebrew were *maskilim,* those who had assimilated into Europe's societies. For them, Hebrew meant scholarship and prestige, as compared to the isolation and provincialism of Yiddish. But another stream of interest in Hebrew ran in the opposite direction, feeding not integration but Jewish nationalism. One of those who caught the fever was a young Jew in the western Russian Empire, Eliezer Perlman, who gave himself an unprecedented task: to make an ancient language serve a modern nationalism.

Perlman fell in love with his people's sacred tongue not through religion—he was only briefly devout as a teenager. He instead was tickled by a Hebrew translation of a secular work, *Robinson Crusoe,* that the head of his yeshiva had shown him. Perlman wanted to see more Hebrew like that and became fixated upon reviving the language so it could live not only in the yeshiva but also in the kitchen, the market, and the street; it should be not only for studying and praying but for loving and fighting.

He was inspired by European nationalism. In his autobiography, he describes his growing fascination with the Bulgarians' struggle for liberation from the Ottoman Empire:

> Then late one night, after some hours of reading the papers and thinking about the Bulgarians and their future liberation, a flash of lightning seemed to pass before my eyes and my thoughts flew from the Shipka Pass in the Balkans to the fords of the Jordan in Eretz Israel. With astonishment I heard a voice within me calling out: *The restoration of Israel and its language on the soil of its ancestors!*

Perlman's passion for the language was so intense that it isn't clear which way his Zionism ran: he wanted a state for the sake of Hebrew itself, it seemed, nearly as much as he wanted a language to serve the Jewish state. Perlman would take the name Eliezer Ben Yehuda, converting his father's name (Yehuda) into his surname ("son of Yehuda") in the traditional Jewish way upon emigrating to Palestine in 1881, well before the formal Zionist movement began with the 1897 Basel conference.

Reviving Hebrew was far from uncontroversial, though. Herzl never mentioned Hebrew in "The Jewish State" and in fact seemed to think that German might be the language of the future Zionist state. "Who among us has sufficient acquaintance with Hebrew to ask for a railway ticket in that language?" he asked, practically enough. Yiddish, a German dialect that had spread from medieval Jewish settlements near the Rhine to Eastern Europe, was the language spoken by a majority of the world's Jews. Within the Zionist movement, it had its fervent partisans.

Moreover, many Orthodox Jews found Ben Yehuda's plans for Hebrew downright blasphemous. Hebrew was holy, not to be profaned by use for haggling in the marketplace. That was the job of Yiddish, Arabic, or German—anything but the language in which God had handed down the Torah.

But he would not be deterred. He isolated his first son, Itamar, from contact with any other language, refusing his frail first wife, Devora, a servant so that the child would hear only Hebrew. Itamar recalled Ben Yehuda flying into a rage upon coming home once and finding Devora (whose Hebrew was poor) singing a Russian lullaby to him. Itamar himself was once beaten up in downtown Jerusalem for speaking to his dog in Hebrew, the only language he knew. (Itamar's siblings would later master the language without being so harshly cut off.) Ben Yehuda's efforts to restore the language so angered the traditional authorities in Israel that when Devora died, they refused her burial in a Jewish cemetery: his family was seen as insufficiently Jewish. Ben Yehuda himself was excommunicated. But he carried on, marrying Devora's sister, becoming a teacher, and lobbying his fellow teachers to teach only in Hebrew in the schools they had begun establishing in Palestine.

The task was huge. Only 8,000 different words appear in the Hebrew Bible, compared to the 20,000 or more that the average adult needs and knows in most languages. There was obviously no word for Herzl's "railway ticket" or many of the other words needed for a modern state. Ben Yehuda labored to fill the gaps, writing a dictionary of modern terms coined from traditional Hebrew roots.

Meanwhile, Ben Yehuda's fellow Hebraist teachers contributed what they could, each becoming a one-man font of new words. They also worked to market the language, convincing incoming Zionists to abandon Yiddish—symbolizing weakness and disapora—for Hebrew. Obviously, the political motivation behind Zionism was an important reason Jews in Palestine worked to learn and use Hebrew. But the language was helped by the fact that many of those making the move from Europe didn't share a first language, and Hebrew became their lingua franca. The younger generation was particularly important. In the first decade of the twentieth century, the first children to learn not just Hebrew, but *in* Hebrew, began graduating from schools, marrying, and having children of their own. Those children became the vanguard, learning the ancient language from the cradle, and using it all the time. By 1922, just four decades after Ben Yehuda's arrival, Britain recognized Hebrew as the official language of Palestine's Jews.

That the creation of Israel was a nationalist project in the secular European mold, not a religious, messianic dream, can be seen in the stories of the early Zionists. Ben Yehuda classified himself, in his official registration in Palestine, as a "national Jew" but "without religion." The remaining bulk of the early Zionists was inspired by socialism, not the patriarchs and prophets. The Jews shared, by definition, a religion. But obviously this was not enough. Ben Yehuda's efforts, Herzl's eventual support, and the success of the project showed that a nation isn't a nation even if its people share a religion, history, and traditions. They needed a single common language.

Outside the ranks of the ultra-Orthodox, Yiddish would shrivel in Israel. A group of Zionists from the dominant Labor Party in the Jewish community in Palestine initially wanted to produce a Yiddish edition of their periodical but were attacked by the Hebrew-only faction and voted down, and Hebrew was made the party's sole language from 1907. The proportion of Yiddish-speakers in pre-1948 Palestine steadily declined, even with the influx of Yiddish-speakers coming from Europe after 1945. Hitler killed most of the world's Yiddish-speakers. The choice of Hebrew for Israel a century ago, and its stunning success since, is near to putting Yiddish itself into the grave.

Hebrew has expanded to all reaches of life. One need barely guess what the anti-Hebrew ultra-Orthodox think of Ben Yehuda's successful coinage of *dagdegan,* "clitoris" (from a root meaning "tickle"). And modern Hebrew has become far more than the creation of Ben Yehuda alone. Though he gets most of the credit, many of the words in his masterpiece dictionary are not in modern use. Instead, as it has grown, Hebrew has done what normal languages do: it has both settled and changed through daily use by millions. Beginning with no native speakers, it now has a distinctive accent, which some trace to the Russian of many early settlers. The European backgrounds of early Israelis moved Hebrew grammar away from Semitic forms toward more European ones. Hebrew has also borrowed words from abroad, with *telefon* replacing Ben Yehuda's *sach-rachok,* for instance. Israelis coin mongrel words, such as the English word and Russian suffix brought together to form *jobnik,* a soldier who has a duty resembling a normal civilian job. Hebrew even has—and this should not surprise readers of this book so far—declinist sticklers. "Ben Yehuda would be dismayed by the demotic Hebrew spoken today," said the Israeli author and journalist Hillel Halkin. Another Semiticist scholar, Edward Ullendorff, scoffs:

> Modern oddities like the grammatically impossible *mekir* instead of the *makkir* and similar monstrosities had not arisen in Ben Yehuda's Hebrew and I am glad it is left to those who nowadays watch over the health of contemporary Hebrew either to come to terms with such horrors or to endeavour to discard them.

Just a hundred years old, and already being ruined by the kids. A normal language indeed.

To say that the creation of Israel was not without controversy would be an understatement. No other people on earth suffered as mightily as the Jews in the first half of the twentieth century. But just as the Second World War was teaching much of the world the perils of nationalism, the Jews decided that they couldn't survive without it. Israel now had many of the trappings of a nationalist state, just like the nation-states it had imitated. It had a quasi-official religion—though Judaism isn't singled out in the constitution, any Jew worldwide may come to Israel with the promise of automatic citizenship. It had a sanctified semiofficial history—of dispersion, persecution, survival, and revival over incredible odds. (It would be decades before prominent Israeli historians critically reappraised Israel's creation and its catastrophic cost to Palestine's pre-1948 Arab majority.) And it had a thriving, robust single language for its Jewish population. The new state's third prime minister, Levi Eshkol (1963–1969), was one of the last prominent Israelis known for speaking what had been, a century earlier, the dominant language of Jewish life, Yiddish. Hebrew had triumphed.

Though other languages have been kept on life support as liturgical languages and small-scale revivals have succeeded in keeping (for example) Welsh and Irish alive, there is no parallel in history to the re-creation of Hebrew. Those who revel in linguistic diversity should take heart at the story. And those who argue—as I will in the next chapter—that official language planning by meddlesome experts is usually a bad idea must acknowledge this compelling success. Though Hebrew wasn't imposed, and hasn't been controlled, by strong-armed government pressure, its revival and flourishing certainly began with committed elites before spreading to the masses.

But one language and one religion for one people in one land have not brought Israel's Jews peace and security after decades of suffering; they have brought more insecurity and frustration. Even the admirers of Hebrew can see this as evidence for the perils, not the wisdom, of cultural planning wedded to muscular nationalism.

One Flag, One Homeland, One Language

At least Israel avoided one of the commonest, and stupidest, mistakes of linguistic nationalism. Hebrew is not the sole official language of Israel; Arabic shares that status, and the roughly 20 percent of the population that is of Palestinian Arabic origin learns in Arabic in schools, with Hebrew taught as well. Israel does push a symbolically Jewish-centered agenda by, for example, calling Jerusalem "Urshalim" even in Arabic script on signs. (The Arabic name is Al-Quds. I have seen Arabic-script "Urshalim" destroyed on Jerusalem signs. Sign defacing is a favorite outburst of linguistic discontent the world round and one inflicted by Israeli Jews on Arabic signs, too.)

But by and large, Israel has come to a pragmatic accommodation of its Arabic-speakers. Arabs campaign for seats in parliament in Arabic and debate in the Knesset in their language. A bill in 2008 proposed demoting Arabic to a "secondary language," putting it on par with English (widely used) and Russian (increasingly important since the influx of Soviet Jews after 1991). But the bill failed to pass, and Arabic remains in the top legal tier with Hebrew. Though most Israeli Jews do not make it far in learning Arabic, the basics are still theoretically required in high school.

Unfortunately, not all nationalists have had the pragmatism Israel has shown with Arabic. The true chauvinist must not only push his own language but suppress others. Modern history is, unfortunately, too full of examples. If Charles V boasted of speaking Spanish to God, Italian to women, French to men, and German to his horse, his successor, Francisco Franco, might have said, "I speak Spanish to God, Spanish to women, Spanish to men, and Spanish to my horse." Franco, who took power after a traumatic civil war in Spain (1936–1939), sought to erase Spain's long history of multilingualism.

Ironically, Franco himself came from Galicia, in northwestern Spain. Galician, or *galego,* is closely related to Portuguese. Speakers of the two can easily understand each other, but a Spanish-speaker will struggle with either. Franco spoke Galician, though he considered it Portuguese and never used it in public. He was like the Corsican Napoleon and the Georgian Stalin—a dictator from a minority background who persecuted minorities once he reached the top.

Galicia is the least nationalist of Spain's three major minority regions. In the east, the Catalans have long sought more autonomy or even independence from Spain. Catalonia was once a powerful political unit of its own, a principality tied to the kingdom of Aragon. The Catalan language was a vehicle for prestigious literature, and Aragon-Catalonia spread the language to the Balearic Islands, parts of Sardinia and mainland Italy, and even as far as Greece. After backing the wrong side in the eighteenth-century War of the Spanish Succession, Catalonia's language went into decline, banned from governmental use by the crown in Madrid. A nineteenth-century *renaixença* ("renaissance") saw dormant Catalan nationalism begin to rise again. It was aided—as nationalism often is—by economic considerations: Catalonia has traditionally been richer and more industrialized than Spain's Castilian heartland.

The third group to stick out from united Spain has been, from the Spanish nationalist's point of view, the most troublesome of all. The Basques speak a language unrelated to any other known on Earth. This is rare globally and unique in Europe. (Though Hungarian, Finnish, and Estonian are not related to their neighbors' languages, for example, they are related to one another.) Basque's distance from its neighbors can be seen in almost any common phrase: *dos cervezas* (two beers) in Spanish is *duas cervexas* in Galician, *dues cerveses* in Catalan, but *bi garagardo* in Basque. Basques proudly claim to be those who resisted the Islamic invasion of the eighth century most successfully, holding out in the mountains of northern Spain. In modern Spain, too, the Basques have reason to feel proud and unique: like Catalonia, the Basque autonomous region (which naturally doesn't include Basques across the border in France) is richer than the rest of Spain.

The only thing worse than uppity minorities are successful uppity minorities, from the centralizer's point of view. And Franco was a centralizer. Inspired and aided by nationalist Fascists in Italy and Germany, he sought strength through Spanish "unity." To this end, especially in early years, he cracked down on the minority languages. Official use of any language but Castilian Spanish was banned, as was the teaching of any other language in public schools. Films in minority languages were banned too, and parents couldn't register their children with regional names like Jordi (Catalan)—they had to be given Castilian equivalents (Jorge). Shop signs in the minority languages would incur heavy fines. Basques, Catalans, and Galicians were told to "speak Christian"—that is, Castilian. Bars and other establishments were made to feature signs reading "The language of the Empire is spoken here." A typical Francoist slogan was *Una bandera, una patria, una lengua:* "One flag, one homeland, one language." The similarity to *Ein Volk, ein Reich, ein Führer* is no coincidence.

Franco's militaristic unity policy kept the minority nationalists on the back foot, to be sure. Catalonia's leaders fled abroad, declaring government in exile from other corners of Europe, and many nationalist Basques headed to the United States. But those who stayed sought to fight back: ETA (Euskadi Ta Askatasuna, or "Basque Homeland and Freedom"), the Basque terrorist group committed to independence for the Basque country (including Basque parts of France), was founded in 1959, sixteen years before Franco's death. The Francoist regime gradually loosened its strictest controls on language, allowing books of poetry and plays, or limited radio broadcasts, on the assumption that they would reach mainly a few harmless cultural nationalists. But the minorities were unsatisfied, and ETA, in particular, stepped up a campaign of assassinations of police and officials representing the regime. Like Kemal Atatürk in Turkey, Franco not only failed to eliminate the hated minority languages, he gave their speakers an enduring grievance, the perfect symbolic issue to rally around. His death in 1975 was greeted with public jubilation in the Basque lands and Catalonia.

Spain's democracy was delicately restored after Franco. Galicia, Catalonia, and the Basque part of Spain won "asymmetrical" autonomy in the constitution, meaning that they were granted local privileges not given to other parts of the country such as Andalucía and Extremadura. The local languages were legalized and declared objects of national protection, supported for certain local uses including education. This accompanied a good bit of economic decentralization: the Basques, Catalans, and Galicians have more power to make their own economic policy than other parts of Spain do.

But independence movements continue to flourish. Galicia is largely happy with its semiautonomy within Spain. But the Catalans and the Basques continue to struggle, divided not between loyalty to Spain and independence but between far greater autonomy within Spain and independence. The Basques have sought to declare themselves a state "freely associated" with Spain, with diplomatic representation abroad. The Catalans, meanwhile, have used their minority position somewhat more cunningly: the small Catalan party in Madrid's parliament has often been a kingmaker, joining coalitions with the bigger, all-Spanish right- and left-wing parties to give them a majority. This status has been used to wring ever more cultural and economic concessions for Catalonia. Madrid, for its part, continues to insist on all the regions' integral status within a unified Spain. The country's territorial integrity was declared inviolable in the 1978 constitution, though this constitution did not pass majority votes in Catalonia and the Basque provinces, rendering those regions' national aspirations unconstitutional without their say-so.

On the linguistic level, a tense stability prevails. Catalan is seen everywhere in Barcelona—virtually every sign, even in this tourist paradise, is in that language, not the more widely spoken Spanish (which is sometimes but not always included underneath). But open your ears and close your eyes, and the impression is reversed: much more Spanish than Catalan can be heard in central districts. This is a direct legacy of Francoism: two generations were denied education in Catalan, which made it the language of homes and other private domains, not business in the streets. But Spanish prevails in Catalonia's heart also because wealthy Barcelona has attracted "internal immigrants" from other parts of Spain. They don't speak Catalan when they arrive. Their children, however, are immersed in Catalan at school, though Spanish is also taught. This has led to an ironic reversal of the old roles: Spanish-speakers claiming "intolerance" by the Catalans.

Joan Martí i Castell, the head of the Philological Department of the Institute of Catalan Studies in Barcelona, is a tanned, gray-templed gentleman who turns an appointed half hour into an hour to talk to me about the past, present, and future of Catalan. Though he is calm and kind, he is one of those Catalans who tenses up when he hears the Castilians talk about "tolerance." Noting that it is perfectly possible to live in Barcelona without speaking any Catalan, he says that it would be impossible to live there speaking *only* Catalan. True, you have a right to demand that a waiter speak to you in Catalan, but who wants to ruin dinner by insisting on a political point? And yes, you can insist that your passport renewal interview be conducted in Catalan, but who wants to annoy a civil servant in a position to make your life difficult? He goes on to argue why requiring schooling in Catalan is "fundamental":

> When a language isn't necessary—it isn't indispensible—it is destined to disappear. As long as it's only permitted, but it isn't indispensible for daily life, that's a language that is destined to disappear. Because anything that isn't indispensible is dispensible.

For him, Catalan in Catalonia must be like "Italian in Italy, French in France, English in the United Kingdom, German in Germany." The unspoken alternative is Welsh in Wales or Irish in Ireland: an accessory, not a necessity, consigned to an ever-smaller corner of life.

I ask whether Catalonia's independence is looking more or less likely as time goes on. Though I have always heard—from Castilians—that the Catalans get everything they want, Martí i Castell's face darkens. People in Catalonia are getting more and more frustrated. Besides "internal immigration," foreigners are coming from North Africa and naturally prefer to learn Spanish over Catalan. Latin Americans are also coming and continue to speak their native Spanish without learning the regional language. This has put Catalan nationalism back on the boil.

Franco's legacy was not a united Spain, *una patria* with *una lengua*. Rather, after three decades of democracy, ETA is still active, a majority of Basque-speakers still support independence, and even the wealthy and relatively comfortable Catalans are looking the same way. Spain still has found neither unity nor comfort in diversity, thirty-five years after the old dictator's death.

Apartheid's Overreach: South Africa and Afrikaans

Linguistic nationalism left enduring, perhaps unsolvable conflicts in Spain. Elsewhere, it may have even toppled at least one regime.

South Africa's Constitutional Court, in Pretoria, abounds in symbolism. In an unhappier, earlier era, it was a detention facility. It has the distinction of holding, at different times, two of the world's most famously righteous freedom fighters: Mahatma Gandhi was held there by British authorities in the early twentieth century, and Nelson Mandela would be locked up there half a century later.

Today, South Africa's Constitutional Court is a symbol of reconciliation and justice. Some of the old brickwork has been kept as a reminder of what the building once was. But the rest is new. The ceiling is designed to evoke an outdoor setting beneath trees, making semiliteral a traditional African concept: "justice under the tree" is dispensed by elders in traditional communal gatherings. Huge windows both offer transparency to the outsider and remind the judges and lawyers inside, during their legal disputations, of the real world they serve outside. And on the face of the building, in a font designed especially for the purpose, are the words "Constitutional Court" in eleven languages.

Officially, all eleven languages are equal. Oral arguments

and written submissions may be made in any of them and translated into any other; a glass booth for simultaneous interpretation overlooks the room, much as at the United Nations. But South Africa is no monodecilingual paradise. One language, spoken by less than a tenth of the country's population at home, is distinctly more equal than others.

Mandela was released from prison in 1990, after twenty-seven years. Four years later, he became president in South Africa's first democratic election. In 1996, a new Constitution, the product of years of negotiation between the apartheid regime and the African National Congress, promised a host of rights: not just the traditional ones of freedom of speech and assembly but socioeconomic rights such as housing and health care. Discrimination on the basis of race, sex, sexual preference, disability, religion, culture, age, pregnancy, and other categories is expressly forbidden in the constitution's Article 9, a far more expansive list of protections than in most democracies' constitutions.

Among those promises, the constitution required that the new South African state promote eleven newly declared official languages. Nine were African: Zulu, Xhosa, Ndebele, Tswana, Swazi, Sotho, Venda, Tsonga, and Pedi. The other two were European. The first, Afrikaans, is a distinct language, descended from the language of the Dutch who first landed in South Africa in 1652. The Dutch were the dominant white power in the region for centuries. Today, Afrikaans and Dutch are mutually intelligible, but Afrikaners take pride in their language's distinctiveness. At the Constitutional Court, judgments from lower courts often come in written in Afrikaans, and most judges speak it. But no case has ever been fully argued before the court in Afrikaans.

The last official language is English. The British came later to South Africa than the Dutch did but gradually supplanted them as the dominant European power there. In a series of clashes culminating in the turn-of-the-century Boer War (in which the young Winston Churchill served as a journalist), the

British defeated the Afrikaners. The Boers, or "farmers," as the Afrikaners were then frequently known, entered a half century of political submission to the British.

The Afrikaners' political self-awareness grew over that time. Most wanted little to do with the British Empire, of which they were now a part. They opposed South Africa's entry into the Second World War, quietly supporting the Axis. But three years after the war's end, in 1948, an assertive Afrikaner party, the National Party, won South Africa's elections for the first time. With this victory began the period of legally enforced "apartness" or, in Afrikaans, *apartheid*.

Before 1948, South Africa's white rule was not unlike that in other European colonies in Africa, such as Algeria or Kenya. Apartheid, though, was a different beast: the most legally elaborate, and stiflingly oppressive, system of minority rule in the world. Blacks couldn't move freely about the country, own land in the vast majority of it, work in skilled trades, join unions, have sex with or marry whites, or even, at apartheid's peak, learn mathematics in school. What was the point, mused apartheid's great architect, Hendrik Verwoerd, in teaching a subject they could never use? The stunted, so-called Bantu education became, by the 1970s, one of the greatest sources of black anger.

In 1976, however, the government overreached itself. Having raised Afrikaners' income levels and established an Afrikaans-speaking elite, the formerly derided Boers began to see the country as truly theirs again. English had been the predominant language of education (with African languages used at the lower levels). Now, the government declared, half of all education must be done in Afrikaans.

This was too much for the already fuming black majority, and the country exploded in protest. Protestors carried banners reading, in English, "To hell with Afrikaans!" and "If we must do Afrikaans, Vorster [the president] must do Zulu!" In Soweto, a huge black township outside Johannesburg, a thirteen-year-old boy was killed by an Afrikaner policeman in a confrontation. The protests became violent riots.

The hundreds dead, not to mention the thousands injured and imprisoned, marked the beginning of the end of apartheid. South Africa, after booming economically in the 1960s, became a global pariah. International sanctions, from those on investment and sporting events to a boycott of South African oranges, made the country an international leper. Even conservative Western governments sympathetic to the South African government's argument that Mandela's African National Congress was a communist front, had to keep their distance. Ultimately, the combination of increasingly violent domestic protests and international isolation forced the apartheid leadership to negotiate with Mandela. He left jail in 1990, and the ANC became a legal political party. At that point, the end of apartheid was only a matter of time.

How did Afrikaans help spark the fire that burned apartheid to the ground? Obviously it was the symbol of the hated apartheid government. English, remember, was also a language belonging to whites who had oppressed the black majority, yet its dominance was not a source of the anger. For black South Africans, Afrikaans was worse than foreign; it was useless. Its imposition in school served only as a symbol of the Afrikaners' attempt to dominate in every way, a humiliation with no redeeming features. Before 1976 most black students began primary school in their native languages, before moving gradually to English in upper grades. With English, they might speak to other Africans with whom they didn't share a language or with South Africa's large Indian population. They could read international resistance literature and get their own word out in English. Afrikaans was useful mainly in answering to the white boss.

Mandela is an extraordinary man for many reasons. One of them is that he studied the hated Afrikaans language in his decades of imprisonment, perhaps with a premonition that he would one day make peace with the Afrikaner government. His wearing of the national rugby uniform—which is associated with Afrikaners—at the 1995 world championship is a beloved memory of reconciliation. (South Africa won, too.) But Mandela also showed his feel for wounded Afrikaner pride in a quieter gesture, when he told an Afrikaner student audience, in their language, *"Wat is vorby is vorby."*—what is past is past.

Just 8 percent of South Africans speak English at home. Yet arriving at Johannesburg or Cape Town's airport, a visitor could be forgiven for thinking he was in California. Everything is written in English, with a rare few things also given in Afrikaans. Virtually nothing is written in an African language; only the title of South African Airlines' magazine, *Sawubona* ("Hello" in Zulu), gives any linguistic hint that this is Africa.

Modern South Africa might be impossible without English. Afrikaans would have been, of course, unable to bind the country. But that is equally true of all the African languages. It is English that knits the nation together. The vast majority of television broadcasts are in English. Government works overwhelmingly in English. English is the preferred language of education and research, not to mention culture and the media.

The facts on the street are more complex. The roughly 9 percent of the population that South Africans call "Coloured" consists of people of mixed European, African, and Asian ancestry, and a large majority of them speak Afrikaans at home. In urban areas, blacks from different language groups often use a creole—a stable, established blend of different languages—with one another. Of the African languages themselves, the biggest is Zulu, spoken by about a quarter of the population, but the elite, including Mandela, is disproportionately Xhosa-speaking. Neither could unify South Africa; Zulu nationalists and the ANC clashed violently in the early 1990s, as apartheid was unraveling. Zulu nationalism is still a force.

The constitution requires not only equality but promotion of all the official languages. Since the equality exists only in theory, the government is making small efforts to make good on the promotion part. The Department of Education is trying to develop teaching materials—reading samples, workbooks, and the like—for higher-level education in the official African languages. But African parents, perhaps surprisingly, have pushed back. Knowing the state of their country and the world, they want their kids to learn English as soon as possible. English is the ticket to higher education, perhaps to a stable civil service job or one of the jobs reserved for blacks in the big corporations under the mantle of "Black Economic Empowerment." Black it is, and empowering it may be, but to take advantage of it, they must learn a European language, English.

And what of Afrikaans? Jimmy Ntintili is one of Johannesburg's best-known tour guides, who boasts of having taken Bill and Hillary Clinton on his well-known tour of Soweto. He can chat comfortably in German and can also do most of his spiel in French and Italian. His high-pitched, slightly nasal English is, of course, impeccable. His parents are a Sotho and a Swazi. He claims to speak all of South Africa's languages. In a way, he is the perfect South African.

When he is asked what Africans think of Afrikaans today, to my surprise, he has nothing bad to say. "There's nothing wrong with the language. A lot of the Coloured people speak Afrikaans." But he continues, "It's some of the Afrikaner *behavior* that's the problem." He says that the Afrikaners he is friendly with sometimes introduce him by saying "this is my kaffir friend," using the Afrikaans word equivalent to "nigger." But toward the language itself, Jimmy has no grudge. Time has mellowed this native Sowetan's attitude toward the once-hated "Boertaal." Other things in South Africa, obviously, are going to need a bit more time.

English has utterly triumphed in South Africa, but not because English speakers forced it on hapless natives or convinced them that its civilized grammar and vocabulary were superior to African languages'. Instead, English's success there piggybacked on its success elsewhere, the success of Britain and then America. Afrikaans, meanwhile, has had its role humbled, in part because of the Afrikaners' attempt to force it on the population. Language was of course not the only or even the main grievance of black South Africans. But it was a symbol of language getting ahead of politics. Create a state that everyone hates and then yoke it to an official language, and both the language and the state may fail. Create a society people want to join, such as the international community of English speakers or a modern, tolerant South Africa, and it is never necessary to force a language on anyone.

Single Languages, Multiple Nationalisms: India and Yugoslavia

Language policy has contributed to communal war—whether ETA's bombings or the Soweto uprising. But sometimes communal wars come first, driving what was once a unified language apart. Such has been the case with India and Pakistan, and with Serbia and Croatia.

India is a wildly multilingual country with fourteen officially recognized languages and one especially designated "national language," Hindi. Pakistan has just one official language—English—and its own officially declared "national language," Urdu. Pakistan and India represent, in a way, the opposite of the linguistic nationalist stories we have seen so far. In the prototypical, European-style nationalist scenario, a group of people realizes that they speak alike (and share other aspects such as history, religion, culture, and so forth). They then decide to create a monolingual, monoethnic nation-state by drawing borders, moving people or suppressing languages, with one language per state the ultimate goal. British India was almost the opposite. The colony known to Britain simply as "India" included today's India, Pakistan, and Bangladesh. A sense of common history, geography, and personality gave the linguistically diverse colony a sense of unity. But one major divide, religion, would destroy it.

The first half of the twentieth century saw the birth of an Indian independence movement. Its chief political vehicle, India's equivalent of the African National Congress, was the Congress Party. (In fact, Mandela and the ANC learned from the Indian experience.) In freeing their country, India's independence leaders knew that they would also have to hold it together.

The Congress Party's leaders did not worry overmuch about language. They assumed that India's biggest language, which they called "Hindustani," would unite the free India they sought. These leaders included Mahatma Gandhi, a Gujarati-speaker who spoke Hindustani haltingly; Jawaharlal Nehru, who was descended from Kashmiris and spoke English best; and even the southern Tamil figure C.R. Rajagopalachari, who spoke no Hindustani at all. (Tamil is a Dravidian language, totally unrelated to the northern Indian languages, including Hindustani.)

"Hindustani," though, is these days a disputed concept. The languages now called Hindi and Urdu are its squabbling children. The two languages are, in fact, so similar at the colloquial, spoken level that most linguists consider them a single language, Hindi-Urdu. But what is a language and what is a dialect depends almost entirely on subjective judgment, not some clear test. Partisans of the two "languages" stress the differences, not the similarities.

Hindi is written in the Devanagari script, characterized by the vertical line that connects the letters from above. It takes its lofty literary or religious vocabulary from Sanskrit, the language of Hinduism's sacred texts. It is a marker of identity for millions of India's Hindus. Urdu, however, is the name given to Hindustani written in a modified Arabic script with a special flowing style called Nastaliq. Urdu takes its higher-level words, those needed for literature, scholarship, or religion, from Persian and Arabic. It is totemic for millions of Indian and Pakistani Muslims, just as Hindi is for many Hindus.

So are they really the same language or not? Robert King, a scholar at the University of Texas at Austin, relays an anecdote from a tour through Muslim Old Delhi by a Hindu-speaking historian:

Our guide was engaged in conversation with Muslims on the street, asking directions and engaging in casual

conversation. I detected no problems in his making himself understood and understanding himself what was
said to him in return.

But then the group meets and begins to talk with a Muslim
cleric about the history of the neighborhood:

> At this level of discourse communication was just about
> impossible. The conversational strain was impossible to
> overlook, in spite of the best will in the world on both
> sides . . . the architectural terminology was altogether
> different between Hindi and Urdu—specialized vocabu-
> lary usually is. The conversation was such that genuine
> communication was scarcely possible on any but the
> most mundane topics. . . . The situation was painful to
> endure, for both parties to the conversation had very
> much hoped to make this harmless and decent little in-
> stance of Hindu-Muslim-Western friendliness succeed.

Eighty years earlier, Gandhi (who, remember, was not fluent in
the language) was in denial about the divisions within "Hindustani":

> Hind[ustani] is that language which is spoken in the
> north by both Hindus and Muslims and which is written
> either in the Nagari or the Persian script. [It] is neither
> too Sanskritized nor too Persianized. . . . The distinction
> made between Hindus and Muslims is unreal. . . . The
> same unreality is found in the distinction between Hindi
> and Urdu. . . . There is no doubt or difficulty regarding
> script.

Nehru, meanwhile, thought a pragmatic technical fix was
available. After sending out a family wedding invitation in
Hindustani written in Roman letters, he wrote to Gandhi:

> I have no doubt whatsoever that Hindustani is going to
> be the common language of India. . . . Its progress has
> been hampered by foolish controversies about the script.
> An effort must be made to discourage the extreme ten-
> dencies and develop a middle literary language, on the
> lines of the spoken language in common use. With mass
> education this will inevitably take place.

For Gandhi and Nehru, Hindustani was iconic. They thought
that politics would lead and language would follow. Though
only about a third of Indians spoke Hindustani, it was the
biggest single language. After independence, Indians would
surely rally around it.

That made sense so long as the British were still the enemy.
But as independence began to come into view, the differences
between Indians, rather than between them on one hand and
the colonizer on the other, loomed larger and larger. The All-
India Muslim League, under Muhammad Ali Jinnah, began to
agitate for a separate state for India's Muslims, called Pakistan.
(The name was an acronym for the mooted country, the biggest
parts of which would be Punjab, Afghanistan, and Kashmir.)

Jinnah's wish was fulfilled. The British, who had clumsily
tried to prevent independence by dividing the Indians among
themselves, forced their own hands into creating two states
when they granted the colony independence in 1947. In the violent mayhem that ensued, some 15 million people scrambled
across the new border, Hindus fleeing Pakistan and Muslims
fleeing India. Hundreds of thousands—the exact number is un-
knowable—died in communal bloodshed that scars both communities still.

The creation of Pakistan and India could be seen as proof
that some forces—in this case, religion—can be more powerful
than language. No rule applies to all cases. But the case of Pakistan does not prove it beyond a doubt. Before partition, Muslim organizations, including the powerful Jamaat-e-Islami,

opposed or were ambivalent about the creation of Pakistan until the last minute. Prominent advocates for Pakistan were far from devout Muslims. Jinnah drank alcohol and wore Western dress. Sir Syed Ahmed Khan, a late-nineteenth-century proponent of Indian-Muslim consciousness and of Urdu, was so unorthodox that he was declared an infidel by the religious authorities.

Despite its status as Pakistan's national language, Urdu is spoken natively by just 8 percent of Pakistan's population today—mostly *mohajir*s, or emigrants from India and their descendants. The push for Pakistan's creation was at least partly an ethnonationalist one—with the Muslims an insecure *nation* within India, not a religious group. Among Urdu's biggest proponents were those whose status during the British Raj depended on mediating between the masses and the colonial power and on their linguistic skill—in Urdu. The *mohajir*s were a semiprivileged class who, by this explanation, created Pakistan to keep from losing their status in the Hindu-dominated India. This is one big reason Urdu is Pakistan's national language, despite being the native language of so few people there. Many more Pakistanis speak Punjabi and the other local languages as their mother tongue.

India has, for its part, struggled to unite around Hindi. The constitution declared it to be the "national" language, and independence leaders had high hopes for "Hindustani." However, almost as soon as India was created, regional leaders began to push for their own languages. Many demanded regional states with considerable autonomy, drawn on largely linguistic lines.

Nehru waffled. He had much more on his plate than language, including the threat of a new enemy abroad, Pakistan, and crushing rural poverty at home. But the hunger strike to death by Potti Sriramulu, a former Congress Party comrade in arms and advocate of a Telegu-speaking state in the south, forced his hand. The state of Andhra Pradesh was created for

Telegu-speakers, and, unsurprisingly, this led to other demands for language-based states that couldn't be ignored. Similar demands are a recurring feature of Indian politics to this day.

India now operates on a roughly three-language system: Hindi is encouraged and taught most everywhere, the major regional languages enjoy primacy in non-Hindi-speaking areas, and English is taught in secondary school. The constitution-writers anticipated a mere fifteen-year transition period for English after the constitution went into effect in 1950. Nehru waived its expiry, and English's major role in the country continues. It is a pragmatic policy that gives major regional languages, one big national language, and the world's most important international language each a place. But India is so multilingual that this isn't enough for everyone: it is the smaller, subregional languages (not dialects but often clearly freestanding languages) that are squeezed, creating lasting complaints from their speakers (and thus feeding the demands for new language-based states).

As for "Hindustani," its divergence into Hindi and Urdu has become a self-fulfilling prophecy. Nehru, a Hindu himself, complained that Hindi was being increasingly Sanskritized by Radio India. Meanwhile, increasing self-awareness among Muslims in South Asia, both in India and in Pakistan, has led to an Arabicization of their Urdu. Nehru had hoped for the opposite—a merger of the two over time into a "middle Hindustani," a language Hindus and Muslims alike could call their own. Like the united, secular India he sought and so many other fond wishes for South Asia, it never happened.

That so much of what we say about language is really about politics is seen in the history of a country that no longer exists: Yugoslavia. In the course of that country's disappearance from the map, something else vanished with it: a language called "Serbo-Croat" or "Serbo-Croatian" by most outsiders and various things by its speakers. The language did not die out as most languages "die," with the death of its last speaker. It died when the political unit that supported it met its death.

In the 1800s, the southern Slavs lived under domination by other empires: the Ottoman and the Habsburg. They were divided by religion—the Croats were Catholic and the Serbs Orthodox, while some of the local Slavs had been converted to Islam by the Ottomans. But they shared many aspects of their identity, most notably their Slavic language, of which there was no single variety but rather mostly mutually intelligible dialects. Until 1850, there was no written standard either. Serbs wrote in a semiartificial, lofty version of their language mixed with elements of Old Church Slavonic, the progenitor of the modern Slavic languages that had a long second life as a liturgical language. Croats wrote in various dialects. But in 1850, the Serbs and Croats decided, in their "Literary Agreement," to settle on one written version of their language. The agreement chose, as the basis of the dialect, forms used by most Serbs and the largest number of Croats. The Serbs would use the Cyrillic alphabet, like their coreligionist Orthodox Christians in Russia. The Catholic Croats would use the Latin alphabet.

The First World War resulted in the creation of the first Yugoslav state to support these aspirations: the Kingdom of Serbs, Croats, and Slovenes, renamed in 1929 the Kingdom of Yugoslavia. Its leader sought to emphasize the unity of the language. After all, most speakers of the various dialects could understand one another with few problems. What problems existed were not intercommunal: speakers of the biggest Croat and Serb dialects could understand one another easily, while there was far more variety among the Croats themselves. (They spoke three main dialects: Štokavian, Čakavian, and Kajkavian, named after *što, ča,* and *kaj,* different words for "what.")

But the merger never quite stuck. Most people, as has usually been the case with language reforms, simply continued to speak as they spoke, rather than consciously moving in the direction of the standard. As for that standard itself, many Serbs thought that too many concessions had been made to the

Croats. The Croats, for their part, saw the larger Serb nation as attempting to subsume them under the banner of a Serb-centered "Yugoslavism." So despite the efforts of a committed band of "Yugsoslavs" who sought to minimize the old identities, many continued to think of themselves as Serbs, Croats, Muslims, Slovenes, and so forth. Given the chance to bolt the federation during the Second World War, the Croats broke away under a pro-Fascist state. During this period, nationalist linguists revived many "historical" Croat words, purging those drawn from Latinate or other Western-looking roots and Serbianisms.

Yugoslavia was restored after the war. The Yugoslavs, uniquely among those European populations invaded by Germany, largely fought themselves out of Nazi domination by popular uprisings, "partisans" led by a charismatic mixed Slovene and Croat, Josip Broz Tito. After the war, every effort was made to bury or deny the wartime split-up of the country and enforce political and linguistic unity. But neither political nor linguistic harmony ever truly triumphed. A 1954 agreement sought to reaffirm that "Serbo-Croatian" and "Croato-Serbian" were one language, spoken in eastern and western varieties, with two alphabets. ("Western" was spoken by many Serbs as well as Croats, while "eastern" was limited mainly to Serbs. The two differ largely in one pronunciation, the sounds -*ije* versus -*e: vreme* versus *vrijeme* for "time," for example.)

Tito died in 1980, and though the country held together for a time, after the end of the Cold War in 1991, the bonds of Yugoslavia were only too ready to break. And in the nationalist muscle flexing that led to the Balkan wars, "Serbo-Croatian" was an early victim. Nationalist leaders such as Slobodan Milošević (Serbia), Franjo Tudjman (Croatia), and Radovan Karadžić (representing the Serbs in Bosnia-Herzogovina) whipped up their peoples' fears and resentments, emphasizing their differences and not their similarities. This found its way into language when, at political gatherings, nationalists began demanding a "translation" of the proceedings into Serbian,

Croatian, or Bosnian—despite the fact that everyone present had understood full well what had been said.

The war of words turned into a war of rifles and artillery. Slovenia escaped the union first, with only a brief civil war. The attempt by the Muslim "Bosniaks" to do the same, however, sparked Europe's worst bloodshed since 1945, dragging in both Serbs and Croats. (Both groups live within Bosnia-Herzegovina, as well as in Serbia and Croatia proper.)

The wars made the former Yugoslavs keener than ever to highlight their linguistic differences. Croatia, always wary of being treated as the little brother of Serbia, declared its national language to be "Croatian." The Bosnians declared their own new language to be "Bosnian." (It was indistinguishable from Serbo-Croat in most ways, save a few borrowed words or phrases from Arabic or Turkish.) The Serbs, for their part, continued to claim the heritage of pan-Yugoslavism.

The wars dragged through most of the decade, resulting in carnage televised around the world and the creation of seven new states: Slovenia, Croatia, Bosnia-Herzegovina, Serbia, Montenegro, Macedonia, and Kosovo (the last one not recognized by many countries, including those that sided with Serbia over its 1999 war with NATO). Besides Serbs, Croats, and Bosnians, other nationalities worked to emphasize the distinctiveness of their languages. In some cases this was more plausible than others. Slovenian had emerged in the nineteenth century as distinct, and Macedonian (which many Bulgarians still insist is a dialect of Bulgarian) had been officially recognized in Yugoslavia since 1944. But as the country began splitting, the former Yugoslavia also had the new Croatian, Serbian, and Bosnian, and one more would come. Montenegro would not be left out when it declared independence in 2006. Its official language is now one that almost no one (even in Yugoslavia) had spoken of much before: Montenegrin, another bit of the mutually intelligible, formerly "Serbo-Croat" continuum that was now declared to be its own language.

With what result? Robert Greenberg, an American expert

in the languages of the former Yugoslavia, visited several times for research in the 1990s. His experiences are worth quoting in some detail:

> [In 1990] I was back in Zagreb [Croatia] at the Institute for Language to disseminate my questionnaire on Croatian appellative forms. I had painstakingly produced two versions of the questionnaire—one in the Eastern (Belgrade) variant of Serbo-Croatian, and one in the Western (Zagreb) variant. I did my best to adjust my speech from Belgrade to Zagreb mode. However, in a slip of the tongue, I innocently mentioned something about my plans for July. Much to my embarrassment, my interlocutors chastised me for using the Serbian form *jul*, "July," rather than the Croatian form *srpanj*. To add insult to injury, one of the Institute's staff then took me aside and made me repeat after her all the proper Croatian forms for all twelve months. I knew that language was a sensitive issue, but did not realize the emotional and ideological baggage each word carried. Most Croats had simply praised my excellent "Croatian," even though I could have sworn that I had been speaking with a Belgrade accent.

Note that no one had objected until he made an unusual slip. They thought they had found a sympathizer, until an undeniable "mistake" gave him away.

After the Bosnian war, Greenberg returned to the former Yugoslavia:

> Having landed at Sarajevo [Bosnia] Airport in June 1998, I struck up a conversation with one of the airport's land crew. Her first comment was that she was impressed with my skills in the Bosnian language. Frankly, I had had no idea that I was even capable of speaking Bosnian . . .

The next morning I crossed the inter-entity boundary [between Bosnian-Croat and Serbian parts of Bosnia-Herzegovina] in order to catch the bus to Belgrade. In Bosnian Serb territory, I spoke the same language I had used the day before, only now I was treated as a Serb. When the Yugoslav border guards singled me out for extra questioning upon my entry into Serbia, the bus driver told them to let me through, because he considered me to be one of theirs.

Language *was* politics, as Greenberg experienced firsthand.

Since the dissolution of Yugoslavia, language nationalists have sought to push the languages apart. Croats, in particular, returned to the Fascist wartime practice of purging words deemed to be Serbian. A right-wing Croatian nationalist gave, with a straight face, the kind of chauvinistic justification the reader will find familiar by now: "The fundamental characteristic of native words in the authentic Croatian language is that they are for the most part semantically stable and unambiguous, i.e. they have a precisely defined meaning. . . . On the other hand, Serbian, like the majority of Balkan languages, is relativistic and undefined."

Many of the words purged by the Croatian nationalists, though, weren't even Serbian—they were the familiar Greco-Latin words present in languages across Europe. Croatian purists have sought to expunge *ambasada,* "embassy," and *avion,* "airplane." Books were issued telling Croatians how to replace *muzika* and *geografija* with *glazba* and *zemljopis.*

But the reengineering of "Croatian" has not entirely succeeded. A study of actual usage found language nationalism at a theoretical level—neo-Croatian coinages were seen as "more correct" than words of foreign origin—but not at the street level: a minority of people actually used many of the Croatian words, and some were barely known at all. Meanwhile, ironically, Latinate words such as *avion* provoked especially clear anti-foreign sentiment, while Serbian words, since they looked

Slavic, seemed familiar. Many Croats did not even realize their Serbian provenance and hence carried on using them, especially casually. The neo-Croatian words are more likely to turn up in newspapers and other edited prose than in people's daily speech and writing. Students are taught to use the neo-Croatianisms as much as possible. But the mask drops as soon as they get the chance. One student told the study's authors, "Among us young people there are some who try to be very careful how they speak in school because they know that the teachers will correct them, but outside [of school] they speak normally." "Normally" meant, of course, with the Serbian and other foreign words Croatians had always used.

So Serbs and Croats will probably be able to understand each other for some time yet. Not nearly enough time has passed for nationalist language fiddlers to render "Croatian," "Bosnian," "Serbian," and the new "Montenegrin" pure enough that the speakers can't rub along. It remains to be seen whether they will ever succeed. The result will depend not on real linguistic facts on the ground—remember that "Croatian" differs more internally than it does from "Serbian." It will depend on the old Yugoslav republics' political future, and that depends on the rest of Europe.

Polyglot Paradise? The European Union

The European Union has twenty-three official languages. Romanian and Bulgarian became official when Romania and Bulgaria joined the Union, in line with the traditional policy that each official national language is an EU language. But the European Union has another recent addition to its official roster: Irish. First-language speakers of the Gaelic language now number in the tens of thousands, but it has coequal official status with English in the republic. There are no monolingual Irish-speakers left. But the government of Ireland recently decided to insist on its right to make Irish an EU language. Now all official documents of the EU must be published in Irish, and Irish-speakers will have the right to speak it in the European Parliament. Simultaneous translation must, by law, be provided in all of the other twenty-two languages of the EU. There are, of course, vanishingly few living experts in both Irish and Maltese or Finnish; where needed, small languages are translated twice, once into English or French and then again into the other languages. The deadening effect on debate is predictable.

The EU experiment is an unwieldy one, binding together twenty-seven countries into a union far tighter than any other of the regional groupings in the world, such as ASEAN (Southeast Asia), Mercosur (southern South America), or the African Union. Laws passed by the European Parliament are binding on all members, judiciable through the powerful European Court of Justice. Europe has a common passport, anthem, holiday, currency, and many other trappings of a modern state. It has common policies on trade, agriculture, the environment, and other key areas and shares policy making with the member states on the economy, education, culture, transport, and more. The European Union is moving toward common foreign policy and possibly even common defense. In other words, it is somewhere between a garden-variety international club and a confederal state in the making.

Still, countries are clamoring to join. Turkey is particularly eager, enough so to change its old habits of linguistic nationalism. The prospect of EU membership has resulted in greater tolerance of Kurdish—spoken widely in the southeast but long repressed by the Turkish majority. Kurdish can now be broadcast, though only with translations (only music is excepted). Kurdish can be taught in private schools, though the first few schools set up to do so failed financially and it remains illegal to teach Kurdish in public schools. The progress is real, if fitful and partial, and the EU can take much of the credit.

The pull of membership has had results in the ex-Yugoslav would-be member countries too. Croatia has arrested high-level war-crime suspects and moved to near the top of the queue, trying to put the 1990s behind it since the death of Tudjman. Serbia, too, hopes to get in on the action. The other Yugoslavs watch, with envy, the benefits enjoyed by Slovenia, the small, Catholic, mountainous republic at the western end of Yugoslavia that escaped the worst of the wars and joined the EU in 2004. Slovenia uses the euro, and its citizens have the right to work and live freely in all other EU countries.

To get into the European Union, countries must show that they are functioning market economies and can put into effect some 80,000 pages of EU law. But they must also show that they are modern, stable democracies that respect human rights. Among those rights are language rights; trying to stamp out troublesome minority languages is an absolute nonstarter for would-be EU members. This has been one of the main levers for improving human rights in Eastern Europe and the Balkans: countries wanting to get in must be decent to their minorities. Implementation is not perfect; Slovakia is hard on its Hungarian-speakers and Latvia on its Russian-speakers. Among older members, France and Greece have often treated language minorities shabbily, and Belgium's linguistic squabbles between French and Flemish-speakers seem interminable. But all in all, the European Union is one of the most liberal and diverse places on earth, with proud and centuries-old nation-states respecting the principle of tolerance not only within the Union but within national borders.

Will the Balkan countries and Turkey make it into Europe's bureaucratic and boring, but also pluralistic and successful, postnationalist experiment? Or will the imperatives of nationalism—not least linguistic nationalism—continue to trap them in an atavistic zero-sum game, Turks versus Kurds, Croats versus Serbs, faith versus faith, and people versus people, fighting it out for the dream of one people, one state? The future of a large and volatile chunk of the world hangs in the balance.

6

Insubordinate Clauses

The Folly of Legislating
Language Rules

The principal function of the Academy will be to work with all care and all diligence possible to give certain rules to our language and to render it pure, eloquent, and capable of addressing the arts and sciences.

—STATUTE OF THE FRENCH ACADEMY

On May 4th, 2004, one of the world's oldest written languages underwent an abrupt official change. The government of Taiwan ordered that from then on, government documents in Chinese must be written from left to right. No longer could Chinese be written in its traditional ways, top to bottom or right to left. English characters and Arabic numerals running left to right, together on a page with Chinese characters running right to left, "looked confusing," said a government spokesman. Modernization required a single standard. That standard, naturally, was that of the world's dominant language, English—even though written English was centuries younger than written Chinese.

Most of the forms of top-down language policy—the kind that comes from governments or official and semiofficial elites—answer the question of what language, or what form of a language, will play a given role in society. What will be our official language, favored second language, liturgical language, language of education? But bureaucrats sometimes also sit down and make decisions on the actual *form* of a language—how it is printed, spelled, or spoken, which words are allowed and which forbidden, which alphabet must be used, and so forth. Linguists call it "corpus planning," the creation of rules affecting the body of a language itself.

Using state power to compel people to speak and write their native language in a certain way is a modern phenomenon. For the tens of thousands of years humans have been talking, they have mostly just done as they pleased. Communication was the only important thing that mattered to almost anyone. True, we have seen grammarians and language scolds as far back as ancient Rome. But they were mainly people who tried to lay down rules for the literary and formal spoken language only, and then only by example. The idea of passing a law telling people how to spell, which words were forbidden, or which grammar innovations were acceptable would have been hugely odd until modern times.

But the gradual development of nations and nationalism changed that. Building languages was necessary for building nations. In the last chapter, we saw leaders banning competing languages or dialects, in the name of gathering one nation into one state and giving one chosen language top-shelf status. In the modern world, they have gone a step beyond that. The long arm of the modern government has been tempted to fiddle with the language rule book itself: governments have banned words and phrases, coined new ones from thin air, changed the writing system, and otherwise used the power of the state to influence the natural growth of languages. The rougher governments of the world threaten harsh penalties when their linguistic laws are not observed: using banned "impure" words or a writing system that has fallen out of favor, for example. This kind of linguistic activism by politicians has rarely been successful. Yet still they try.

One of the most common rationales for top-down efforts to shape a language is modernization. Citizens are often told, as in the case of Taiwan's writing, that they must submit to an official change to their linguistic tradition because the demands of the modern world require it.

The world's societies have developed unevenly in the past five hundred years. Beginning in the middle of the last millennium, the European powers became the world's undeniable masters of technology and modern development. Later, their New-World offspring, and especially the United States, would join them in global dominance. From ocean-crossing vessels to railroads, from the telegraph to the telephone, from radio to television to the Internet, from the discovery of oxygen to the discovery of DNA, countries speaking European languages led the way in the world's modernization.

This was unsatisfactory for two other kinds of societies. Postcolonial states born in the twentieth century wanted to show the world that they were every bit as sovereign as the countries that had formerly defeated, dominated, or colonized them. This meant having modern languages that could cope with all of the world's technical and scientific challenges. The founders of Tanzania would seek, for example, to modernize Swahili—an East African lingua franca of African descent with a layer of Arabic vocabulary—to earn it a place among the world's must-know languages.

Another kind of society felt the need for language modernization keenly too: not newly independent, identity-building nations like Tanzania but some of the world's proudest countries, formerly powerful empires fallen on hard times. Countries such as China and Turkey could draw on hundreds of years of written history and a proud past of dominating huge patches of the world. To those former great powers, it was unacceptable to have their languages seem less than fully "modern," capable of holding their own among the other great languages of the contemporary world.

In most of these cases, modernization has been synonymous with "Westernization" and sometimes even "Anglicization" or "Americanization." The direction of a modernizing change is frequently in the direction of using the conventions, vocabulary, and sometimes even grammar of the main European languages, especially English. Traditionalists, of course, have resisted.

In other cases, language "reform" is really nationalist purification—the rejection of pronunciations, words, and even elements of grammar that come from another language. Such a reform is often sold as "modernization," too, even when the offending elements come from "advanced" languages. Instead of modernization, these purifying reforms are really addressing identity and insecurity: the fear that if a language becomes impure by borrowing, the nation itself will become corrupted.

These mixed, sometimes conflicting motives of modernizing, Westernizing, and "nationalizing" of a language are shown vividly in the language reforms in Turkey beginning in the 1920s. Ottoman Turkey was one of history's greatest empires, the equal of the Roman, Chinese, or British empires at its height. The Ottomans conquered Constantinople, a Greek-speaking center of Orthodox Christianity, in 1453. They renamed it Istanbul, turned the great Hagia Sophia church into a mosque, and proceeded from there to march farther into Europe, even reaching Vienna. The Ottoman state also expanded into the Middle East, extending nominal or real suzerainty over the Arab lands as far as Morocco and including the Levant, Syria, Iraq, and most of the populated parts of the Arabian Peninsula.

Like all empires of its size, the Ottoman Empire was heavily multilingual. Turkish, written in the Arabic alphabet, was the language of the Ottoman state. But Arabic, the sacred language of the Qur'an, was the indispensable language of religion. Despite their political dominance, the Ottoman Turks never sought to interfere with the crucial religious role of Arabic (and of course the empire included millions of Arabs). Persian, too, remained a major literary and diplomatic language, thanks to the presence next door of the culturally influential Iranian Empire. The empire's other language groups included many others from the Berbers of North Africa in the west to the Armenians of the east.

The Ottoman defeat in the First World War finished the long dismemberment of an empire that had weakened over the previous centuries. The Ottoman state and its sultanate were abolished, along with the Islamic caliphate—the symbol of the unity of the worldwide Muslim community. After Greece invaded the remains of the empire, however, the Turks fought back. The nationalist officers who sought to reverse Turkey's humiliation were ably led by Mustafa Kemal, who would later take the surname Atatürk ("father of the Turks").

In the aftermath of the war with Greece, 1.3 million Greeks were removed from Turkey, while 400,000 Turks were expelled from Greece, a forced migration, though agreed upon by the governments, that would today be called ethnic cleansing. Following the Ottomans' bloody campaign against the Armenians—which many consider the twentieth century's first genocide—the new Turkish state was more Turkish than the Ottoman one had ever been. No longer a multilingual empire, Turkey was now a modern, ethnonationalist republic, based on the land of the Anatolian Peninsula and on the Turkish people itself.

Ottoman Turkish had been a mixed product. Turkish belongs to a larger group of Turkic languages with origins in Central Asia. But by the end of the Ottoman period, the language also included a large tranche of loanwords from Arabic and Persian. Those two languages, with their cultural and religious prestige, even influenced the grammar of Turkish. Persian, however, is an Indo-European language (related distantly to

English), while Arabic is a Semitic one (related to Hebrew, Aramaic, Akkadian, and others). Reforms of the 1830s to 1850s had gone some way to removing foreign influence, but much of it remained, so much that even basic words such as "language," *lisan,* were Arabic.

This was a prime situation for a would-be language autocrat: a newly independent nation, formed mainly of one ethnic group, with a proud history, a recent humiliation, and powerful, equally assertive neighbors. A newly purified language would be the vehicle for a thrusting new nationalism. Atatürk would separate Turkey not only from its neighbors but from the Ottoman past: he wanted a republic based on nationalism, not religion. So to those ends, he undertook one of the most abrupt and far-reaching language reforms in recorded history.

At a stroke, Atatürk banned the use of the Arabic script for writing Turkish. This former alphabet reeked too much of Turkey's Muslim identity and of its connections to the rest of the backward Middle East. Instead, Turkish would now be written with the Roman alphabet of the Western European languages, of which Atatürk himself spoke French and German.

Language overhauls like Atatürk's are usually made on purported linguistic grounds. Proposed changes are sold to the people as more logical, more expressive, or truer to the native genius of the people. Sometimes this has the virtue of even being true, and in this case it was. The Arabic alphabet was poorly suited to Turkish: only the long vowels *a, i,* and *u* are written in Arabic, and none of the short vowels are written at all. Turkish, however, features eight vowel sounds, today written *a, e, i, ı, o, ö, u,* and *ü.* A few Turkish consonant sounds also required repurposing some Arabic letters. Meanwhile, certain Arabic letters were not needed at all in Turkish.

But other languages, like the Urdu of India and Pakistan, and the Pashto of Afghanistan, are also unrelated to Arabic but nonetheless written in Arabic script. Modifications allow non-Arabic sounds to be written in those languages and Turkish too. And Ottoman Turkish, imperfect as its writing in Arabic script was, had served the empire for hundreds of years. More-over, Turkish is genetically no closer to the European languages than it is to Arabic. So the move to the Latin alphabet wasn't obvious on linguistic grounds alone; an alphabet could have been invented, for example, tailored to the sounds of Turkish. Atatürk's real motive was purely political: by changing scripts, he wanted to bring Turkey out of the Middle East and into Europe.

To this end, he not only toured the Turkish countryside, teaching bewildered Turks their new alphabet on a chalkboard, he also decided that his language reforms needed the hard hand of state backing. It became illegal to write Turkish in the Arabic script on January 1, 1929. An alphabet was now a crime.

But the script was not the only object of Atatürk's reform. Arabic and Persian influences went deeper, not only into thousands of important words (especially in written Turkish) but also even into grammar. To carry out the wide-ranging reforms that Atatürk wanted required a new Turkish Language Association. Its remit was no less than to make a new language.

Turkish grammar was so heavily influenced by Arabic and Persian that half of a 1904 grammar book of the Turkish language, written in English, focused on teaching Persian and Arabic grammar. For example, native Turkish word order places adjectives before nouns, but Ottoman Turkish often adopted the Arabic order of noun before adjective and the Persian way of inserting "i" between a noun and adjective. The very name for the "Sublime Porte," the seat of the Ottoman government in Istanbul, was *bāb-i-ālī*: two Arabic words ("gate" and "high"), in Arabic order, joined using a Persian grammatical convention. (Imagine the White House being known as Das Maison Blanche.) Little wonder that a nationalist Turk could see his language as corrupted.

But Atatürk's solution was one of the most concerted assaults on a nation's linguistic heritage ever seen. The Language Association was tasked with coining new, purely Turkish words for Arabic and Persian ones. It took to its task with a vengeance. Words were either coined entirely from existing roots found in old Turkish writings or gathered in surveys of people's speech from around the country. This resulted in more than 100,000 new words. Newspaper editors were required to comb through articles and replace borrowings with the Turkicisms prescribed in an official new book. But that book was too generous. To replace the Arabic borrowing for "pen," for example, the editors had six choices, all equally obscure to most Turks. Chaos reigned.

Sometimes no Turkish word could be found. In those cases, the Arabic or Persian word was often kept—so long as it could be given a semiplausible Turkish etymology. This led to much amusing fakery. Atatürk himself was an exemplar; an amateur etymologist, he took on *asker*, soldier. It had been borrowed from the Latin *exercitus* via the Arabic *'askari*. But Atatürk convinced himself that the true origin was the Turkish *aşık*, "profit," and *er*, "man." A soldier, after all, profited his country.

The climax of this orgy of linguistic silliness was Atatürk's "sun theory": that Turkish was the world's first language and so all words that had been borrowed *into* Turkish had really originally been taken *from* Turkish. The theory was patently absurd, but it did solve a problem. The linguistic renovation had gotten out of control. In the face of so much difficulty and confusion, the forced Turkization of the language could now be slowed.

Geoffrey Lewis, an Oxford scholar of Turkish, called Atatürk's reform "a catastrophic success." A new Turkish did indeed exist, but it was so altered and invented that it was no one's native language. When the new Turkish was still young, Atatürk once even embarrassed himself by giving a speech in which he had replaced all foreign loanwords with his favored Turkish neologisms. An observer noted that he spoke "like a schoolboy who has just begun to read."

But the overhaul of Turkish was nonetheless eventually successful in Atatürk's stated aims. The reform did indeed rid the language of most of its foreign influences. The combination of the writing reform and his purge of the vocabulary and grammar left modern Turkish a substantially different language. Over time, thanks to the heavy but guiding hand of the state, Turkish editors of books and newspapers learned to use the new words and readers learned to read them. Turkish was reborn, but at a cost. Today, Turks cannot read most texts from the 1930s and before unless they are "translated" into modern Turkish.

Atatürk was a man so eager to break with the past that he ordered the banning of a hat—the traditional fez. This was just another manifestation of his urgent modernizing nationalism, willing into existence a new language that dragged Turks away from their heritage of the Ottoman Empire and the rest of the Islamic world. Though Atatürk's interest in language was keen, his real motivations were not linguistic. Language reformers like Turkey's first president talk about etymology and grammar, modernization and progress through a renewed language. But their real motivations are political. And in a dictatorship, like early Turkey, they can even succeed.

All this may seem distant and perhaps faintly amusing. But imagine that America had lost a war to France and, in the wake of its humiliation, tried to distance itself from the French language. Not only would obvious borrowings such as *tête-à-tête* have to go; a rich layer of vocabulary now considered perfectly good English—"royal," "guarantee," and so forth—would have to be replaced too. Vestiges of foreign grammar would have to be jettisoned as well. "Attorney general" and "surgeon general," which reflect French word order, would have to be reversed. (Of course "general attorney" wouldn't do either, as both words are Latinate; they would need replacing. "Head lawyer," perhaps.) The suffix *-ee*, which makes possible words such as "employee" and "refugee," would have to go too. Its closest native equivalent would be *-ed*. But of course "employ" comes from French too; an employee could now perhaps be a *hired*. Civilization itself would come to an end, since "civilization" had come from French. If all that seems too silly, just picture English-speakers not being able to read works as recent as those of Dickens or Henry James without a specialized education, or if their great-grandparents' old letters were in a foreign alphabet. That is what Atatürk did for his countrymen.

He didn't stop at encouraging patriotic Turks to use native words, he ordered them to, first banning the script and then forcing a new dictionary full of strange words on writers and editors. To ban an alphabet, and words themselves, is almost impossible to imagine in a democracy. Only a nation in the grip of both nationalism and anxiety would try it, and only a dictator could succeed.

Perhaps Atatürk dragged Turkey into the modern world. But he did so using means that no liberal-minded observer should approve. Turkey today remains plagued (though many Turks would say "preserved") by Kemalism, the aggressively secular and Western-looking philosophy that the republic's founder espoused. It remains illegal for women to wear the Islamic head scarf in parliament and in universities. The mildly Islamist prime minister, Recep Tayyip Erdoğan, was once jailed for reading a poem that seemed to authorities to be too Islamic. Turkey has experienced several constitutional crises, coups, and coup threats as traditional forces close to Islam do battle with the Kemalist guardians of modern Turkey, represented by the army. But while Islam is curbed, secular nationalism is sacred. It remains a crime to defame the republic, "Turkishness," or Atatürk himself, punishable by up to three years in prison. Ninety years on, the "success" of Atatürk's language reforms remains in place, but the Kemalist foundations of the republic are cracked and in need of some renovation.

If Turkey's language reform was an all-out assault on the past, the history of language planning in France is comparatively harmless. But while the Turkish case is little known in the West, the ineffectual meddling of the French is just too tempting for Anglophone journalists to ignore. For this reason, the French are known, not without some justification, as the most prickly protectors of their own language in the world.

In 1998, the BBC reported that the French president, Jacques Chirac, had received a letter that "demanded" the reversal of a creeping trend within his government. Politicians, of course, are accustomed to such letters. But this one dealt not with the economy, national defense, or education but with the weighty question of grammar—specifically, gender-specific pronouns. Women in the French cabinet had begun answering to *madame la ministre,* or Ms. Minister. According to the letter, written by the French Academy, the guardian of linguistic purity in France, they should be called *madame le ministre.* No matter that they were women and *la* is the feminine article in French. *Ministre,* whether male or female, was grammatically masculine, argued the Academy. Not only that, but allowing the *la* would only exacerbate the notion that men and women ministers were different. *La ministre* was an affront to equality. Man or woman, said the Academy, everyone had the right to be *le ministre.* But the government did not change its practice.

In 2007 the BBC was at it again, reporting that "a new French resistance" was under way. A center-right member of parliament was arguing publicly that the invasion of English words was very dangerous, because "the French language is the spirit of France and of every Frenchman." A union leader bemoaned the fact that 7 percent of French companies were using English as their official language. The article cited *les e-mails, le web,* and *l'Internet* as proof that the English were invading back across the Channel. The British press loves a good tale at the expense of the French—perhaps in revenge for the Norman Conquest of 1066 and all that.

But this genre of story also works so well because the French passion for the language is so well known. French waiters and shopkeepers are thought to be rude to customers who don't speak French. French writers publicly decry their eroding heritage, and French politicians sometimes refuse to speak English, even when they can, to the outside world. And then there is the famous Academy, which journalists so enjoy chronicling as it tries to stave off English words and natural language change.

All this overlooks the fact that the modern, standard French language itself is hardly the pure maiden its defenders would have it be. No doubt recent years have seen the import of *Web* and *Internet,* and earlier decades saw *le week-end* and *le foot* (soccer). But French borrowing goes back into history well beyond the supremacy of wily capitalist Anglo-Saxons and their devilishly successful ways.

One scholar has counted 2,613 borrowings from English in a modern dictionary of French words of foreign origin. But she also counted 1,012 from "Gallo-Roman dialects," Romance languages related to French such as Provençal. She also found 694 words from Old German and 408 from modern German. The older borrowings include such venerably French *mots* as *bleu, blond,* and *blanc,* to name just color words, and *soupe, haïr* (to hate), and *honte* (shame). Whatever modern defenders of purity may think, France has been borrowing for a long time. *L'Internet,* in its way, is part of a grand French tradition.

This is all too easily forgotten by the modern era's French elites, who, like declinists elsewhere, have for many years been convinced that their language is under threat. Unlike many others, they have been unusually active about addressing the "threat," and the Academy embodies their determination to protect the language.

Cardinal Richelieu, the first minister to King Louis XIII, established the Academy in 1635 to promote the refinement of French letters. In 1694, it published its first dictionary of the French language. Its members have included Pierre Corneille, Jean Racine, Voltaire, and Victor Hugo. Limited to a total number of forty, they serve for life and are humbly styled "The Immortals." They occupy not "chairs" at the academy but

"armchairs" (*fauteuils*).* The Academy is thus sometimes referred to synecdochically as *les 40 fauteuils*. And well they
might want comfortable chairs: in 2008 the average age of
Academy members was seventy-nine years old.

Election to the Academy is an elaborate ritual. New members are chosen by the sitting members. Upon being selected to
fill an empty *fauteuil*—which can take more than a year—the
new member makes a speech eulogizing the member he has replaced. The new *académicien* must then listen to a speech by a
sitting member. After eight days, the newcomer must once
again make a speech, this time giving thanks for being chosen.
Academy members wear traditional green garb, hats, and cere-
monial swords. Perhaps unsurprisingly, a few iconoclastic or
loner writers have refused to join the elaborate ritual; Marcel
Aymé, a novelist, said upon being invited that he was a solitary
type who wouldn't know what to do in such company. Others,
including Descartes, Molière, Balzac, Flaubert, and Proust, for
one reason or other were never invited, were rejected, or died before they could take their seats; such eminent non-academicians
are collectively known as the "41st *fauteuil*." Besides them,
there are two other groups that have rarely joined the Academy: only five women in its history (the first in 1980) and only
two full-time language scholars in the last century.

A 1996 letter to the conservative newspaper *Le Figaro* by
one of its members, a literary historian and essayist named
Marc Fumaroli, captures how the average *académicien* sees his
language in relation to the world's others:

> Well-taught French is more than just French: it is the
> human spirit placed in possession of a symbolic system
> which opens the door to all the others . . . the Latin of
> modern times is in itself a human education.

* Early in its history, only the director had an armchair, but one ailing cardinal demanded something more comfortable than his ordinary chair, and
Louis XIV ordered armchairs for all forty.

The Academy may seem merely stodgy to the outsider, but its habits cross the French political and intellectual spectrum. A detour in the Academy's history is illustrative. After the French Revolution of 1789, the new republican government suspended the Academy in 1793, as it did all the royal academies. To the instincts of the revolutionaries, the Academy smacked of the Ancien Régime. (Later, Napoleon would restore it.) French political culture has long included an authoritarian strain that respects powerful men such as Napoleon, Philippe Pétain, and Charles de Gaulle and is conservative in believing in the virtues of tradition, the Catholic Church, and elites. The revolutionaries wanted to do away with all that.

But the revolutionaries introduced another cultural strain that, for the purposes of language, is little different from the elitist tradition it replaced. In opposition to the authoritarian streak, the revolution brought what the French call "republican" values. These include egalitarianism, secularism, rationalism, meritocracy, and science. Its radical form was Jacobinism in the revolutionary period and is reflected in the ongoing French sympathy for communism and socialism today. The products of French "republican" thinking range from the successful (the metric system, invented by the French revolutionaries) to the embarrassing (the new months and ten-day week of the "revolutionary calendar" and the guillotine).

What French republicanism and traditional elitism have in common is that they are top-down, statist, *dirigiste*. The revolutionary republicans were no less tempted to meddle with language than the elitists of the Academy. In 1794 theater directors were ordered to excise from the plays they produced the noble titles *duc, baron, marquis,* and *comte,* and even *Monsieur* and *Madame.* (*Citoyen* and *citoyenne* were preferred in place of the last two.) The order was repealed after a week. But a public notice in 1799 nonetheless told inhabitants of the capital, "The Citizens of Paris must reshape and correct anything which is contrary to the laws, to decency and to the rules of French."

Language control was as important to the revolutionaries

as it ever was to the old regime before it. According to the two traditional streams of French politics, society must be run either by a great man or by a group of self-selected rationalists who know what is best for you. There is little room in French political culture for the political strand that is called "liberal" in Europe and "libertarian" in America: leave people alone, let them work, live, and love, whether they succeed and fail, and use the power of the state as little as possible.

The two French strands—traditional nationalism and republican rationalism—occasionally join forces. The attempt to eradicate *la ministre* can be defended on grounds of French tradition ("We have always done it this way") or on the basis of universalism and equality (*"Le ministre* can be a man or a woman"). Though France is internally politically divided between left and right, language policy is an area of broad agreement: from right to left, there is a national concord on the need to promote and defend French. The Academy's members include a former center-right president, Valéry Giscard d'Estaing, and a well-known socialist (and formerly Communist) journalist, Max Gallo. The right and the nationalists support French language planning in the name of national prestige, while the left argues that French is a key to universal values like liberty, equality, and fraternity. But in the end, they support the same thing: government language planning.

The Italians had their Accademia della Crusca before France's, but the French Academy's model has by far the most celebrated and imitated. Spain was an early adopter; in 1713, King Philip V founded the Real Academia Española. Sweden founded an academy in 1786 and Prussia one in 1779. (Germans, such as the philosopher Johann Gottfried von Herder, have always had a soft spot for the notion that language represents the organic genius of a people.) And the trend has spread beyond Europe: Israel and Indonesia have language academies; Brazil's Academia Brasileira de Letras, founded in 1897, so slavishly copied the French model that it has forty permanent members, called *Imortais*.

But how successful has the French Academy been? Its dictionary is not the most prestigious one in France, though it is widely respected. Its first grammar, having taken three centuries to appear, was considered a "scandalously poor piece of work." Judging by its own standards, its success should be considered mixed at best. A few simple pieces of evidence demonstrate. At the time of this writing, the phrase *madame la ministre* appeared 321,000 times on Internet pages indexed by Google. *Madame le ministre* appeared just 87,400 times, or one-fourth as frequently.

Besides rare cases like *madame le ministre,* has the Academy managed to freeze "proper" French in place? Many foreign students who first try to use their book-language skills on the streets will answer in the emphatic negative. The *ne* that is supposed to go along with *pas* in negative constructions is routinely dropped, especially in speech: *Je ne sais pas,* "I don't know," is usually *Je sais pas.* The *est-ce que* construction in questions (*Est-ce qu'il est parti?,* "Has he left?") is less and less frequent, and the more elegant *Est-il parti?* is rarer still. (Most people just say *Il est parti?*) Even a prestigious academy like the French one can't simply change natural language behavior. The best it can do is freeze a formal written variety of the language that diverges more and more from the living, moving spoken language and everyday writing.

What about preventing infiltration by English? The Academy's website frankly admits that the commission is charged with "forging new words and recommending French words in place of English." In 2008, the institution announced its opposition to some five hundred English words, including *blog, supermodel,* and *Wi-Fi.* The Academy is assisted in its work by terminology committees in each ministry, which coin technical vocabulary, under the Délégation Générale à la Langue Française (DGLF). But the march of English has not been so easily stopped by the Academy's elite or the ministries' technocrats.

Technology is, of course, the area in which English words

have had the strongest tendency to appear in other languages. *Courriel,* the official word for "e-mail" (borrowed, in fact, from Quebec but no less official in France for that), appears on 16 million French Web pages. But another borrowing is far more prominent: *mail* (words are often chopped or altered when they're borrowed) appears on about 122 million French pages, an eight-to-one advantage. But *mail* in the sense of "e-mail" doesn't appear in the section of the Academy's dictionary that would contain it. (The dictionary is updated not all at once but in successive alphabetical volumes. Of the series of volumes making up the most recent full publication, *"Logo-machie"* to *"Maîtrise"* was published in 2000.) There is an entry for *mail*—a kind of sporting mallet used for an old ball game, the game itself, and the field where it is played. No one plays *mail* anymore, while virtually everyone sends e-mail. But only the archaic, not the living, word was included in the Academy's dictionary, which had not been published in full since 1932–1935. Maybe it will be included it in the next edition, half a century or so hence.

When I visit the French Academy for an interview, I am a little nervous. My French is perfectly workable, but it is hardly Proustian, and I know there's a chance I will make small mistakes. If the French are famously insistent that foreigners use their language, how much higher a standard will the French language's own guardian expect from me? Fortunately, my contact is Jean-Mathieu Pasqualini, the Academy's surprisingly jovial chief of staff, a small, spry man who sounds on the telephone as if he's about nineteen years old.

A former professor of philosophy, Pasqualini takes me in and defends the Academy's positions while registering on his face that I don't always buy them. Boasting that the Holy See uses French for its diplomatic correspondence, he says, "The reason given is the precision, the surety, the clarity of the French language" but goes on to offer, "I don't know if attributing these qualities to the language makes sense on a linguistic level." When he notes that the Academy's dictionary is "normative," not descriptive, he almost seems sorry to have to break the bad news to me. He thinks that *courriel* is a delightful word but admits that it is barely hanging on to life.

The French love their language. They even hold televised dictation contests, which bear witness to their fascination with getting their beloved tongue right. And they largely admire their *Immortels*. But the aversion to English, and the haughty, authoritarian tradition may be more of an elite phenomenon than a nationalist groundswell. Many of the French share Pasqualini's cheerful realism. In 1994 the Ministry of Culture commissioned a poll, intended to show that the French were worried about "Franglais." Instead it showed a mixed result: 60 percent said they were "strongly attached to French," but only 44 percent said that the use of English words was "bad" and 42 percent said it was "good." Asked to characterize the use of English words in French, 41 percent said it was "modern" and 30 percent chose "useful." Just 14 percent chose "annoying" and 6 percent, "stupid."

So the Academy and the terminology committees may be out of touch. The DGLF cannot keep *le mail* from dominating *le courriel*. The Academy's dictionary tries to keep up with the times and accepts some English words (the dictionary currently being produced, in sections, includes *dope* and *joint*), but cannot accept *le mail*. The Immortals' forceful pronouncement on *madame le ministre* is robustly ignored by most speakers. Seven of the Academy's elderly membership died over eighteen months between 2007 and 2008, prompting national concern about how connected to the vital world of a living language its members were. The French may admire the Academy and say that they want to be told how to speak and write. But that doesn't mean that they listen.

If the dented self-image of a Turkey or a France makes us see their language policies in a sympathetic light, we might have even more fellow feeling with newly independent countries. In the twentieth century, the number of the world's independent states exploded. Most escaped colonial domination from a greater power. Many had only recently begun to write in their languages. When such nations achieve statehood, we can understand their efforts to shore up their languages, particularly against foreign elements.

The story repeats itself again and again. In Balkan Europe, the new states that broke away from the Ottoman Empire, like Bulgaria and Serbia, sought to purge Turkish words from their vocabulary. The Poles shunned Russian influences. Those dominated by the Austrian empire, like Czechoslovakia and Hungary, sought to cleanse German from the body linguistic.

Even one of the world's most peaceful, prosperous, and homogeneous democracies has not been free from the purism born of language insecurity. Norway was formerly ruled by Denmark, and even though Denmark was not exactly known for its heavy colonial yoke, the nineteenth century saw Ivar Aasen, a Norwegian linguist, create Nynorsk ("new Norwegian"), a freshly minted standard based on various Norwegian dialects and Old Norse. Aasen's real target was, of course, Danish. Nynorsk was successful, after a fashion. It has survived and is used by about 10 percent of Norwegians. But the rest use Bokmål, the older, Danish-influenced form. This leads to the absurdity that the modern and ethnically homogeneous state of just 4.6 million Norwegians has two written versions of its language. Divisions over which is the "real" Norwegian divide the country to such an extent that the youth wing of a political party burned a Nynorsk dictionary in one of its television commercials in 2005, causing a mini-scandal.

English has had some attention from purists, too. Great writers such as Winston Churchill and George Orwell have praised and encouraged the use of Anglo-Saxon words instead of their Latin or French equivalents. In the essay "Politics and the English Language" examined in chapter 4, Orwell memorably recast a famous verse from the King James translation of Ecclesiastes:

> I returned and saw under the sun, that the race is not to the swift, nor the battle to the strong, neither yet bread to the wise, nor yet riches to men of understanding, nor yet favour to men of skill; but time and chance happeneth to them all.

In Orwell's disdainful view, had that verse been written in the twentieth century, with Latin- and Greek-derived bureaucratic vocabulary in fashion, it would have come out

> Objective considerations of contemporary phenomena compel the conclusion that success or failure in competitive activities exhibits no tendency to be commensurate with innate capacity, but that a considerable element of the unpredictable must invariably be taken into account.

Churchill was another fan of earthy, Saxon words. In one of his most famous Blitz-era speeches to his countrymen, he growled

> We shall go on to the end, we shall fight in France, we shall fight on the seas and oceans, we shall fight with growing confidence and growing strength in the air, we shall defend our Island, whatever the cost may be, we shall fight on the beaches, we shall fight on the landing grounds, we shall fight in the fields and in the streets, we shall fight in the hills; we shall never surrender.

Just five of those seventy-five words are Greek- or Romance-derived: ocean, cost, defend, confidence, and surrender. (Even "France" takes its name from the Germanic-speaking Franks.) Churchill liked this rhythm; he said that "short words are best, and the old words when short are best of all." The "old, short" words in English tend, of course, to be of Anglo-Saxon stock.

But the most active and elaborate English purist is little known and even less followed—which speaks volumes of the Anglophone world's attitude toward purism. William Barnes

(1801–1886) was a schoolmaster, minister, and poet from Dorset, in southern England. He was a keen student of languages—an admiring biographer says he knew fourteen fluently (though for someone who rarely left Dorset and Wiltshire, this seems far-fetched).

Barnes typified a populist purism that is in a way the opposite of the elitist prescriptivism of the French Academy. His most famous poetry was written not in standard English but in his Dorset dialect:

> O zummer clote! when the brook's a-gliden
>> So slow an' smooth down his zedgy bed
> Upon thy broad leaves so seäfe a-riden
>> The water's top wi' thy yollow head,
>>> By alder's heads, O,
>>> An' bulrush beds, O,
> Thou then dost float, goolden zummer clote!

Barnes sought not to drag the barely worthy masses up to his lofty language, as did the French Academy. Rather, he wanted to purge Latin- and Greek-derived words from English, replacing them with coinages of Anglo-Saxon stock so the masses could more easily understand and learn literary language. "Photograph," he though, should be *sun-print*. "Botany" was to become *wort-lore* and "enthusiasm," *faith-heat*. When not inventing words, he used, and encouraged others to use, old country words that had been replaced with borrowings: *inwit* for "conscience," *earthtillage* for "agriculture," and *bodeword* for "commandment." He used his invented language, too: he wrote an 1878 grammar called *An Outline of English Speech-Craft* and in 1880 *An Outline of Rede-Craft (Logic)* in which he employed his inventions liberally.

To those who might call him a rustic boob for writing in his Dorset way, he said, "I cannot help it. It is my mother tongue, and it is to my mind the only true speech of the life that I draw." This argument is typical; countryside purists like

Barnes portray the language of the peasant as the "only true speech," not layered with foreignisms and fancy words like the language of the cities or the universities.

But even Barnes never sought to push politicians to impose his project. He was a Little Englander (before that term was common), anti-imperialist and apolitical, a member of no party. Deeply religious, he longed for a return to what he saw as an England uncorrupted by materialism and swaggering nationalism.

His work as an idiosyncratic rustic compares starkly with the elite language planners of other countries. The Anglophone world has long preferred a mix of nostalgia, shame, and patriotism to the setting up of a national language academy to rule on proper usage and allowable words. Something in the English mind resisted this even as other European countries set up their language guardians.

When the United States was born, it seemed briefly as though the new nation would engage in some of the kind of top-down language planning we associate today with France. After all, insecurity about a nation's status in the world often prompts this kind of attempt, and America was just finding its feet.

Noah Webster (1758–1843), who gave his name to America's most famous dictionary, decided that the new United States needed a new idiom to shore up internal solidarity and to distance America from other powers and its colonial past. He was honest about his motives, writing that even the seemingly prosaic matter of spelling "is an object of vast political consequence."

But Webster's results were modest. He introduced some of the best-known differences between American and British English, prescribing "color" for "colour," "traveling" for "travelling," "theater" for "theatre," "check" for "cheque," and the like. But English speakers today can flit from British to American texts hardly finding those words, or hardly noticing when they do. To the extent that American English differs from the

British variety, this has little to do with such top-down reforms as Webster's. Much more important was the natural additions to the language, from "bronco" and "lasso," borrowed from Spanish, to Native American words such as "tomahawk" and "wigwam."

Webster's new nation flirted with the idea of an academy. The first proposal came even before independence, in 1774. The first bill to create such an academy was introduced, unsuccessfully, to Congress in 1806. Finally, in 1820, the American Academy of Language and Belles Lettres was created, and John Quincy Adams, soon to be the president of the United States, was president of the body. It seemed ("belles lettres" and all) that America might follow the French path.

Mostly ignored and unloved, the American Academy broke up after just two years. It left no mark to speak of on the American language or on English generally. It was never replaced, and America's short-lived experiment with language planning is so obscure to modern memory that while the Klingon language has a 3,000-word entry on Wikipedia, as of this writing, the American Academy of Language and Belles Lettres has no entry at all.

It is tempting to argue that the French regulate their language only because they are insecure, while Britain, unconquered since 1066, and America, a global superpower, are not. But this is too simple, ignoring the chronology. America rejected government language planning well before it was a superpower. The White House was burned down by the British during the War of 1812, the same era during which the American Academy went belly-up for lack of attention. Meanwhile, the French Academy was founded when, under the "Sun King," Louis XIV, France's status as Europe's greatest power was undisputed.

This leaves us seeking additional cultural explanations. France has both an authoritarian-elitist streak, reflected by its Academy, and a rationalist-"republican"-technocratic tendency, represented by the official terminology committees set up in each government ministry. There is nothing, it seems, that the French can't improve by decree or regulation. But then again, France has had five republics, four monarchies, and a military dictatorship since its revolution in 1789. Britain has only gradually changed its constitutional form bit by bit since the Magna Carta of 1215, while America has made do with one Constitution, rarely modified, since 1789. If language policy reflects politics, as this book argues that it does, the different attitudes of the Anglophone and Francophone worlds provide a perfect example. The French relentlessly try to regulate and tinker, with mixed results. The Americans and British accept a flawed product, rarely if ever trying to change it with government action, under an attitude that if it isn't broken, no law should try to fix it.

Though many top-down language policies are overtly nationalistic, many are fairly technical, presented on grounds of practicality. Often they even make sense. The Taiwanese example that begins this chapter may be one of them. It is hard to imagine many stable language situations that would tolerate writing left to right, right to left, and up to down, often on the same page. The Taiwanese government took a fairly sensible position: that in official documents at least, left to right would be the only way to go. The public will probably eventually go along, setting a new, accepted standard.

But even when writing reforms make sense, politics is rarely far from the scene. Usually, some groups win and other groups lose. Those in the dictionary business feed off of public demand for a codified, perfected language. Traditionalists, older people, and those simply opposed to government interference prefer to see language left alone. There is no purely technocratic approach to language.

If there were, we might expect to see it in a place like Germany: a modern, well-developed nation-state that has exchanged its history of nationalism for a reputation for efficiency and rational modern politics. If a country like Germany can't impose sensible reforms on its writing system without chaos and howls of protest, we should generally be skeptical about virtually any government-run language reform. And, indeed, Germany can't impose sensible reforms on its writing system without chaos and howls of protest, as the country's response to its recent spelling reforms shows.

German, like most European languages, has a relatively straightforward letter-to-sound correspondence. The letter *z* is always pronounced the same way, and *ei* always rhymes with the English "eye," never "see," and so on. But most writing systems have their quirks, and German is no different. German famously runs words together into long compounds, but when the first part of a compound word ends in a doubled consonant and the second part starts with that same consonant, the possibility results of the same letter appearing three times in a row: add *Kongress* ("congress") and *Sitzung* ("session") and you get *Kongresssitzung*. Or maybe *Kongressitzung*—traditionally, triple consonants were reduced to two. Or is it *Kongreßsitzung*? Another quirk of German is the letter *ß*, called an "ess-zet" or sometimes a "sharp *s*," sitting in for two *s*s.

Confusion about how to handle triple letters, when to use the sharp *s*, and a number of other wrinkles led to a movement to reform German spelling. The ß was to be abolished except after long vowels and diphthongs; that meant it would disappear from many common words like *daß* ("that") and *muß* ("must"), which would become *dass* and *muss*. The reasoning is that in German, ending a syllable with a double consonant usually means that the previous vowel is short (*hoff* rhymes with English "off"), while a single consonant means that the vowel is long (*Hof* rhymes with English "oaf"). The sharp-*s* change was meant to bring *s* into line with the other consonants.

Elsewhere, the triple consonants would be restored, but in most cases, the compounds in question would be hyphenated (*Kongress-Sitzung*). Other changes were made, including to two-part verbs such as *kennenlernen,* "to get to know," which became *kennen lernen,* and modifications to capitalization. But the sharp *s* accounted for most of the changes the average reader or writer would see or use.

The rules seem complicated to the foreigner, but mostly they made basic sense—as well they should, having been debated from the formation of a working group in 1980 to the announcement of the proposed changes in 1994. Germany, Austria, Switzerland, Belgium, Liechtenstein, and Italy (which has a German-speaking minority in Trentino–Alto Adige) agreed to the rules in 1996, planning to phase them in from 1998 over a period of years.

The intense pushback surprised the reformers. Several German states refused to implement the reforms in their schools. A newly formed group, Teachers Against the Spelling Reform, gathered to resist the changes, with intellectual support from a host of intellectuals including the novelist Günter Grass. (He did not, however, start writing his name *Graß.*) The state of Schleswig-Holstein held a referendum, which rejected the reform. A legal challenge reached the Constitutional Court, Germany's supreme court. The court supported the reformers, agreeing that the state culture ministers could put the new spelling into place without further parliamentary approval.

In 2000, the *Frankfurter Allgemeine Zeitung,* the most prestigious daily newspaper in Germany, announced that it wouldn't abide by the reform. In 2004, the Springer publishing group, along with *Der Spiegel* (Germany's biggest newsmagazine), the *Süddeutsche Zeitung* (another major daily), and *Die Zeit* (a famed weekly newspaper) rejected it too. (To get a sense of their media heft taken together, imagine all the Dow Jones publications, plus *The New York Times, The Washington Post, Time,* and *The New Yorker.*) Parts of the reform were proposed for rollback, and a modified version of the reform later entered force—though only in fourteen of Germany's sixteen states. Some three-quarters of Germans opposed the reform, according to one poll; the rest supported either the full reform or some "reform of the reform." To this day, Germans put up with a partial reform and a chaotic situation; Germany's neighbors have taken various stances, while the different German states have their own attitudes. The most prestigious publisher of language reference books, Duden, observes a partial version. And most Germans now think the whole thing was a bad idea from the start.

This result of Germany's botched reform should be a cautionary tale to anyone who thinks that devising a "logical" set of rules—even for something as straightforward as spelling—and then imposing them through government fiat is a good idea. It can lead to disaster even in a modern, fairly homogeneous, and well-run state. Language is usually best left to its own devices.

Even though Germany's spelling reform was modest and made a good deal of sense, it has produced little but confusion and anger. Why? Maybe language reform simply doesn't work in a democracy. Whether people say they want to be told what to do by a body like the French Academy, or, as in Germany, they say they don't, in practice, it's simply hard to enforce language diktats. All things being equal, people will do what they have always done—write and speak the way they learned in school and go by their instincts when they don't know the rules.

But we have also seen a language reform that was successful—"catastrophically" so—in Turkey. The difference lies in the political context, as well as the political system. Atatürk was revered. A hero during the First World War, he also turned back a subsequent invasion of Turkey by Greece. Plus, Atatürk governed a state that was, in effect, a one-party dictatorship. The popular autocrat was in a perfect position to drag his language into the future.

There is one major reform that might make more sense than almost any other reform to any language anywhere else in the world. But it will probably not happen anytime in the remotely near future, and only a dictatorship would be able to pull it off. This is the often proposed, but never implemented, shift to the Roman alphabet for writing Chinese and Japanese.

Everyone knows that Chinese and Japanese are written with a set of complicated characters that look nothing like Roman letters. Most know that there are quite a few of these characters. But there are many exoticizing myths about the writing of Chinese and Japanese that need to be dismissed before looking at Romanization.

One belief is that Chinese characters are "pictograms," direct pictorial symbols of what they stand for. This idea is fostered by menus in cheap Chinese restaurants in America, which invite diners to kill time by reading about how Chinese characters developed from concrete pictures to stylized modern versions.

"Oracle bone"–style character for *ri,* "sun," ca. 14th–12th century B.C.E.

"Seal script" character for *ri,* Qin Dynasty era, ca. 9th–3rd century B.C.E.

日

Modern character, *ri.*

This story is so easy and pleasing that most people won't get around to thinking, before the hot-and-sour soup arrives, "Wait: I can see where it came from, but that last character doesn't look anything like the sun, really. And how do they depict other things? Does the character for 'car' look like a car? And what does the character for 'intuition' or 'to reconsider' look like?"

Chinese characters are not pictograms for the simple reason that most things can't be illustrated pictorially. A purely pictographic writing system would never be extensive or flexible enough for a natural human language.

A more tempting version of the legend of Chinese characters is that they are "ideograms," with characters representing *concepts,* not concrete things, through visual symbolism. A simple ideogram might be the character for "one":

一

Or "middle," "inside":

中

This notion gets more enticing when we hear intuitively appealing stories, as for example that the character for "good" combines "woman" and "child":

女　　　　子　　　好
"woman"　　"child"　　"good"

The relationship between a mother and child can certainly be very good indeed. But would you guess, if you didn't know, that the abstract representation of a mother plus a child meant "good"? Or would you maybe guess it meant "motherhood," "parenting," "filial," or something like that? What of the many other "good" things that could depict "good"?

If Chinese were really a system of symbolic representation, we should see those who don't know it able to pick up on the symbolism to some degree. The research, however, shows no such thing. One experiment asked nonspeakers of Chinese to guess which of a pair of Chinese characters with opposed meanings corresponded with their translations. Shown forty-two pairs such as 好 and 壊 they were asked to guess which meant "good" and which meant "bad," and so on with beautiful–ugly, heavy–light, weak–strong, alive–dead, and a few dozen others. The average percentage of correct guesses was 54 percent— barely better than chance.

In another experiment with new subjects, the forty-two antonym pairs were lined up in the subjects' native language (Hebrew) on one page and in different order in Chinese on the other. The subjects were then asked to find the pairs "good–bad," "heavy–light," and so forth from among the Chinese pairs. The average subject got just one of the forty-two guesses right. So much for universal symbolism.

But do those who speak Chinese and know the elements gain some kind of wisdom from how they are combined? Maybe the most common ideographic myth among Westerners is that the Chinese for "crisis" combines "danger" and "opportunity." The appealing notion has been repeated by John F. Kennedy (on the Cold War), Al Gore (on climate change), Condoleezza Rice (on the Middle East), and countless investment advisers urging clients to buy during a dive in the markets. Perhaps the Chinese knew something, in that ineffable Chinese way.

But Victor Mair, a scholar of Chinese at the University of Pennsylvania, has shown it to be untrue. *Weiji,* "crisis," is actually two characters, not one, as in the common rendering of the myth. The first does indeed mean "danger," but the second, *ji,* means "incipient moment, crucial point," and the like. So *weiji* means "the crucial point of danger," or crisis. But *ji* can be combined with many other characters to mean a host of things and must be combined with a totally separate character, *hui,* to mean "opportunity." *Weiji* and *jihui* share less than the English words "community" and "communism" do. To argue that *weiji* implies upside opportunity makes as much sense as arguing that people who live in communities are communists.

What Chinese characters most closely resemble are what linguists call "morphemes," or the smallest unit of meaning. In English, "sun" is a morpheme (the smallest unit meaning what it means), but so are "un-" and "-y," so that "unsunny" has three meaningful parts conveying "not," "sun," and "[adjective suffix]." Most Chinese characters are morphemes too. Since they are also all single syllables in Chinese, some linguists call them "morphosyllabographs." The Chinese call them *hanzi* and the Japanese, *kanji,* but it is easiest just to call them "characters."

How do they work? The truth is interesting but stubbornly unromantic. Once pictographic, Chinese characters developed over time through what is sometimes called the "rebus principle." This is the process whereby a picture of an eye stands for the word "I," the capital letter *C* stands for "see" and a picture of a bumblebee might represent "be." Chinese characters similarly went from being pictographs to symbols that stood not for the original referent but for something that sounded like it.

As the Chinese characters evolved, many homophones (words pronounced identically, like "bear" the animal and "bear" the verb) had to be distinguished. The solution was to combine a "phonetic," which showed how the character was pronounced, with another piece called a "radical," which gave an idea as to the general domain of meaning. The character 口 means "mouth." But it is part of a common radical, 言, that represents words coming out of a mouth. That radical in turn is used in many characters like 語, "language."

The same piece of a character can be both a phonetic and a radical: 木 stands alone for "tree" (*mù* in Mandarin). It's the radical in the character 柏, *bò, "cypress"*—a kind of tree. But it's the phonetic in 沐, *mù,* "to bathe," a semantically unrelated word but one pronounced just like *mù,* "tree."

Even with a radical (conveying a bit of meaning) and a phonetic, characters can't simply be decoded by anyone who knows the (huge) inventory of pieces that make up the characters. There are about 200 radicals and perhaps 800 to 1,000 phonetics, and it isn't always obvious which is which in a given character. At best, there are a few rules, which often break down. Chinese learners must use the phonetics and radicals as mere helpers. These can aid in memorization, and they are use-

ful in recalling hazily learned characters. But they will be un-
helpful in recognizing or, especially, producing novel characters. Sometimes the radical is on the left and the phonetic on
the right, sometimes vice versa. Sometimes the radical is on
top, other times on the bottom. To make things harder still, not
all characters have a radical or a phonetic. Some have just one,
and some have neither.

Without the radical-and-phonetic "system" (such as it is),
learning to read and write Chinese would probably be impossible. Very large dictionaries include about 60,000 or more characters. No one learns that many, of course. Estimates of the
number in use average about 7,000. Learning all of them isn't
required for literacy, but at least 4,000 to 5,000 are required
for any kind of advanced reading and writing. Knowing just a
thousand characters would limit reading and writing ability to
simple domains.

This makes it hard to estimate what is needed for "literacy" in Chinese. Italian uses just a couple dozen letters in predictable ways, allowing the Italian peasant who has learned
them to read any word in his vocabulary, even if his vocabulary
is small. A Chinese with a large vocabulary may not be considered truly "literate" if he can read only a fraction of the words
he knows. And since the characters are hard to recall from
memory, writing is even harder than reading.

If the thousands of characters of Chinese are daunting, the
Japanese system is more difficult still. The government specifies
1,945 characters to be taught in schools, though a few thousand more than that are in common use. But though it uses
fewer characters than Chinese, Japanese ladles on the complexity.

The Chinese characters were borrowed by the Japanese
from perhaps the fifth century A.D. The Japanese, who had no
writing system to that point, began to adapt the Chinese writ-

ing system to Japanese, despite the fact that Japanese and Chinese are utterly unrelated and have totally different grammar, vocabulary, and sounds. This adoption happened in several parallel streams, leading to the incredibly intricate modern Japanese system. In some cases, Chinese characters were adopted for native Japanese words. In addition, Chinese words made their way into spoken Japanese, bringing the corresponding characters with them.

For this reason, modern Japanese uses the Chinese characters with a wide variety of different "readings." In Chinese, most characters have one pronunciation (though many have two, and some have more). Chinese characters in Japanese, however, have pronunciations (called *on*) derived from borrowed Chinese words, as well as native Japanese ones (*kun*). Learning a character means learning its meaning as well as its *kun* and *on* readings, which are usually not remotely alike.

One typical character, 影, has the *on* reading *ei,* and the *kun* reading **kage.**

Tōei suru

means "to project an image," and

kage *boshi ga utsuru*

means "a person's shadow is cast." Someone learning the system, upon seeing the character, will need to know the meaning and readings of neighboring characters to know if he should pronounce it *kage* or *ei.*

A simple character has only two readings in Japanese; at the extreme, twenty readings are possible. The character 生, with the base meaning "birth" or "life," has the readings *sei, sho, umu, ikiru, ikasu, hayasu, haeru, shoujiru, shoujizu, nama, ki,* and others. On its own, it can mean to give birth, to be born, to be alive, to grow, and the adjectives "raw" and

210   **You Are What You Speak**

"fresh"; it is also part of compound words including *sensei,* "teacher," and *gakusei,* "student." Meanwhile, forty-nine different characters can be pronounced "shi."

To add to this, the Chinese characters coexist in Japanese with two syllabaries, *hiragana* and *katakana,* simplified from Chinese characters centuries ago. *Hiragana* and *katakana* have no meanings, only pronunciations; unlike alphabetic writing, though, each symbol represents a syllable (*shi* or *ma* or *yo*) rather than a single sound (there is no way to write just the sound *y*). There are only forty-six characters in each syllabary. In Japanese writing, the Chinese characters are the main parts of words: key nouns, verb stems, and so forth. The *hiragana* denote word endings, tense, possession, and other crucial bits of grammar. (At a glance, it is the presence of the simpler, gently curved *hiragana* that distinguishes Japanese from Chinese.) The other syllabary, *katakana,* is used only to write foreign words and names, to write certain brand names, for onomatopoeia, and for emphasis.

If Chinese and Japanese sound daunting for natives to learn—not to mention for foreigners—they are. Students in both China and Japan spend thousands of hours studying their character sets to be able to read and write. This is, needless to say, time that could be spent on other subjects. Some Western linguists even think that so much rote learning teaches Chinese and Japanese students to value form and process over creativity, though this is controversial.

Do Chinese and Japanese convey advantages, though? Some nationalist linguists in both countries claim that they do. Higher-level words in English are usually built from Latin or Greek roots. "Mesolithic" is from *mesos* (Greek "middle") and *lithos* ("stone"). This is a fancy word pertaining to the Middle Stone Age that English-speakers must learn from a dictionary when they first encounter it. Similar learned words in Chinese and Japanese can be built from two characters that the reader already knows—or so the theory goes.

But William Hannas, an expert in Asian languages for the U.S. government (he speaks Japanese, Mandarin, Shanghainese, Taiwanese, Korean, Vietnamese, and Tibetan—"all well!" his former Ph.D. adviser, Victor Mair, says with amazement), has dismantled the theory. One Japanese study "proved" that the writing system helps Japanese readers learn advanced words, but Hannas, a former academic, showed how it relied on cherry-picking a few erudite English words that had simpler equivalents in Japanese. Meanwhile, some Japanese and Chinese native words can't be figured out by knowing the individual characters—but Chinese or Japanese readers will try to analyze them anyway, making mistakes.

Other defenses of the system are vaguer: that the effort spent learning them trains the mind generally, for example. This notion enjoyed a vogue period in Japan when that country was booming economically but has lost its shine with Japan's economic stagnation. The fact is that the enormously difficult Chinese and Japanese writing systems have not withstood careful scrutiny of their supposed advantages. And the disadvantages are more than obvious.

There are alternatives. Both Japanese and Chinese have standard systems for Romanizing their languages. Japanese has no sounds that can't easily be written in Roman letters using only the existing alphabet, plus the macron for long vowels (like *ā,* which can also be written *aa*). The system, called *rōmaji* after the Latin alphabet's home city, is seen all over Japan, and Japanese children learn it early, as an aid to learning the Chinese characters.

Chinese has a Romanization system too: *pinyin,* established by the Communist government in the 1950s. It is more complicated than Japanese. Mandarin Chinese has four tones, which are as crucial to Chinese meaning as the vowels and consonants of an English word. For example, *ma* with a rising tone and *ma* with a falling tone mean "hemp" and "scold," respectively. In pinyin, the four variants must be written as *mā*, *má*, *mǎ*, and *mà*. (Pinyin replaced earlier systems, which is how Mao Tse-tung became Mao Zedong.)

Computers have made typing Chinese characters easier—but they have ironically also made Romanization more tempting than ever. Obviously, keyboards don't have thousands of keys, so Chinese and Japanese users employ various workarounds. The most common is simply using the Roman letters on the standard keyboard. To type "I am Chinese" in the standard Microsoft Windows Chinese support system, you type *wo* in Roman letters, then pick the right *wo* character from the offering, and so on through each of the characters *wo shi zhong guo ren*. Modern computers are clever enough to guess at the most commonly sought characters, so users can also type *woshizhongguoren* in one go, and Windows will offer the correct characters. This won't work for more unusual sentences and characters, however. Japanese works much the same way.

But if Chinese and Japanese both use Roman letters to get to Chinese characters, why use the Chinese characters at all? The pressures to make reading easier go back a long way and often come from nationalists with impeccable credentials. But Romanization has failed again and again. And it has failed thanks to political concerns of identity and cultural heritage, not the purely linguistic concerns that are sometimes trotted out.

Japan's first notable advocate of Romanization, Nanbu Yoshikazu, proposed accepting the alphabet as far back as 1871—just decades after the American Commodore Matthew Perry steamed into Tokyo's harbor and forced Japan open to the world. The Japanese leadership realized that the country was well behind the West in scientific, technological, and military advancement. The push for Romanization thus came when many other Western technologies were being eagerly adopted, during Japan's spectacular drive to modernity.

Romanization's fans competed with advocates of another radical simplification: those who, first organized in 1866, favored adopting the *kana* syllabaries for Japanese writing. They are simple to learn and have the political advantage of being locally derived. But the *kana*-only movement fell out over arguments about how Japanese-derived versus Chinese-derived words should be written.

Movements in favor of *kana* or Romanization ground to a halt in the 1930s, as radical nationalism took hold of a Japan that was fighting wars on several fronts. (Japan even stopped teaching English as a foreign language in schools.) In the postwar period, however, Japan was defeated and occupied by the Americans and was rapidly remade in the image of a Western democracy. An acclaimed novelist, Shiga Naoya, even proposed that Japan adopt French.

So the advocates of Romanization and *kana* had another chance. The Americans were divided on what to do about the writing system. Some supported a switch to *kana* or Roman letters, on the grounds that it would symbolize a break with the past, render wartime propaganda harder to read, improve education, and make censorship easier. But the Americans ultimately decided against imposing a reform, and once again the opportunity slipped. Japanese proponents fell out among themselves—advocates of one *rōmaji* standard (called Hepburn) even denounced other *rōmaji* supporters as wartime collaborators. While the *rōmaji* camps squabbled, a new national language body appeased critics of the writing system by abridging the *kanji* set to 1,850 characters (later expanded to 1,945).

Japan still has proponents of *kana* and Romanization, and it seems as though the increasing computerization of everything will gradually turn up the pressure. But the "inevitability" of Romanization or adoption of *kana* only has been confidently predicted since just after the war. No one can say that it won't happen or that it will, but the forces of linguistic conservatism are powerful and determined.

Where does the resistance come from? Modern Japan isn't

particularly xenophobic regarding foreign words. The language has a big, and old, layer of high-level vocabulary from Chinese. And in the modern era, Japanese have happily borrowed words from *aisu kariimu* and *kohii* (ice cream and coffee) to *boifurendo* and *garufurendo* (boyfriend and girlfriend). Such "Japlish" is the source of many jokes on both sides of the Pacific, but it is a simple, mostly uncontroversial fact of modern Japanese.

Despite this openness to new words, the characters persist. Why? Besides nationalist motives, psychological factors favor inertia. All the bureaucrats and lawmakers in a position to reform the writing system have already learned it—indeed, their presence among the elite required it. People are strongly attached to things they've given a great deal of time and painful effort to learn. This kind of thinking is well known to everyone from soldiers looking back on the screaming and yelling of basic training to a senior fraternity brother hazing his pledges: "I went through this, and believe me, it was no party. But it made me who I am today, and it bonded me to this community. It didn't kill me, and it won't kill you either." With this argument in place, secondary ones for Chinese characters, such as "It trains the mind for higher thinking" and "It is good for instilling discipline," settle in unchallenged. If the infinitely more modest German spelling reform is any guide, any change in Japan would have to be demanded from below; to introduce it from above would be to spark ferocious opposition. Japanese adoption of the Roman alphabet is a long way off, if it is ever to come at all.

In contrast to Japan, China, a one-party dictatorship, could introduce *pinyin* in place of Chinese characters any day it liked. Yet China is unlikely to Romanize soon for its own reasons, some of which do overlap with Japan's. The Chinese believe to some extent that the characters *are* the language and that understanding them means understanding Chinese. Western linguists wouldn't agree—they tend to see writing systems as artificial structures built on top of the real language, which is the organic product of people's brains and mouths. But changing Chinese minds on this is unlikely.

A more important reason China will not adopt *pinyin* is that it logistically can't, not without exploding a notion to which the Chinese are inalterably attached: that there is one Chinese language, of which different varieties, such as Mandarin, Shanghainese, and Cantonese, are "dialects." This is simply untrue. The major different classes called "Chinese" are, without any serious debate among linguists, mutually unintelligible different languages, at least as different as the major Romance languages of Europe are from one another. Saying that Mandarin and Hakka are dialects of Chinese is like saying that French and Italian are dialects of Latin.

Max Weinreich, a Yiddish linguist, noted that in the popular imagination, *"En shprakh is en dialekt mit en army en flot"*: "A language is a dialect with an army and navy." How different two varieties should be to be called "languages" rather than "dialects" is not fixed, because the main criterion—whether two speakers can understand each other—isn't an either-or phenomenon but a continuum. Speakers of Danish can understand Swedish, and Swedes can (with somewhat less success) understand Danish. To some linguists, that is a case for calling these varieties one language ("Scandinavian") with several dialects. But for most people, the real criterion is political: since both countries have armies and navies, we consider Swedish and Danish different languages.

Any objective look would render the opposite judgment of China. It has a tremendous army and a growing navy. But, simply put, a Mandarin-speaker from Beijing and a Cantonese speaker from Hong Kong, if they have not learned the other language, cannot understand each other. Cantonese has six tones to Mandarin's four; it can end syllables with the consonants *p, t, m,* and *k,* while Mandarin has just two syllable-ending consonants, *n* and *ng.* The actor Chow Yun-fat, a Cantonese-speaker, had to learn Mandarin for the movie *Crouching Tiger, Hidden Dragon,* and he was ribbed by some Mandarin-speaking viewers for his accent in Mandarin. (The movie is also available dubbed into Cantonese.) The same levels of difference, broadly, exist among the other major Chinese languages, including Wu, Hakka, Min, Gan, and Xiang.

The differences among the different "Chineses" are so well known that Mandarin-speakers have a rhyming saying:

Tian bu pa, di bu pa, zhi pa Guangdong ren shuo Putonghua. ("I fear neither Heaven nor Earth, I only fear Cantonese speakers trying to speak Mandarin.")

The Cantonese have their own version:

Tin mh geng, deih mh geng, ji geng bak fong yahn gong gwong dung wah mh jehng. ("I fear neither Heaven nor Earth, I only fear Mandarin speakers speaking Cantonese so inaccurately.")

Note how different they look.

But the Chinese nonetheless insist on speaking of one Chinese language with different dialects. Why? It's not a government plot to deny China's linguistic divisions and keep the country together. Han Chinese (the majority of Chinese, but not speakers of smaller languages such as Mongol, Tibetan, or Uighur) do share a strong identity, bolstered by China's millennia-long history of political independence. Mostly they really do believe that they speak the same language.

Besides the strong sense of national identity, one reason so many Chinese are in denial is that the writing system hides the differences. Written Chinese, based on Mandarin, is a standard that speakers of all the Chinese languages are taught in school, even though they pronounce the individual characters completely differently in their own languages. The fact that a Mandarin- and a Cantonese-speaker read the same characters tricks them into thinking they speak the same language, when really they are both just reading Mandarin.

Romanization would change all that. No longer would written Chinese unify the country, because *pinyin* is a Mandarin-only system. (The Cantonese equivalent is *pingyam,* used in the "Heaven and Earth" saying above.) Writing Mandarin in *pinyin* would expose to all non-Mandarin-speakers the fact that they are looking at a foreign language. This is a headache that China's authorities, already fearful of non-Han separatist movements in Tibet and the Muslim, Uighur-speaking region of Xinjiang, can do without. Stoking nationalism among the Han majority is increasingly tempting for the Chinese leadership, to head off challenges to its authority in the face of corruption, inequality, environmental degradation, and the like.

Surprisingly, Romanization nearly succeeded in China. One 1934 experiment with an early Romanization system "proved beyond a doubt that ignorant farmers and laborers need only a hundred hours" to learn alphabetic Chinese, according to proponents. But the nationalist Kuomintang government lost interest.

After the Communists' 1949 victory in the Civil War, the political will for reform came in a new form. Mao Zedong, now the unquestioned leader of China, had said earlier that alphabetization was inevitable. After taking power he seemed to change his mind, saying in 1951 that "The writing system must be reformed, and it should take the phonetic direction common to the languages of the world; it should be *national in form;* the alphabet and scheme should be designed according to the existing Chinese characters." (Emphasis added.) A more concrete statement could not be possible: Chinese must be phoneticized, though the system should be Chinese-based.

It looked as though some radical simplification was inevitable, and a national commission was set up to study the question. After mulling over Chinese-derived options and one using the Cyrillic alphabet, the commission recommended *pinyin.* (It considered, perhaps, that a made-in-China system, even Roman-based, would be "national in form.") But Mao's interest had moved on. His premier, the powerful Zhou Enlai, elaborated the new policy: that Chinese characters would be simplified, not abandoned, and *pinyin* would be used only for teaching purposes. Meanwhile, a standard language based on Mandarin was to be promoted. One famed poet and scholar, Chen Mengjia, dared to oppose the abandonment of traditional Chinese characters during the brief "Hundred Flowers" movement of intellectual openness in 1957. After the "Hundred Flowers" experiment ended, he was labeled a "rightist" and exiled to three years of farm labor in Henan. He killed himself during the Cultural Revolution.

The real reform was now the simplification of the characters. Many of the *hanzi* were stripped of brushstrokes, making them easier to write and learn. The simplified character set is now standard in the People's Republic, though Hong Kong still uses the traditional characters, as does Taiwan and as do most overseas Chinese. The reform was ultimately conservative, and full Romanization was dead.

China still may introduce *pinyin,* but only if an important precondition is met. The government strongly promotes *putonghua,* the official "common tongue" based on the Mandarin of Beijing. Signs in Shanghai read "Speak Mandarin—be a modern person." Toilets in Beijing's Capital Normal University have signs above them reading "Your excellent Mandarin provides convenience to everyone around you." ("Provides convenience" puns on a Chinese euphemism for going to the toilet.) And the government has even objected to the dubbing of the American children's cartoon *Tom and Jerry* into Shanghainese for children: in 2004 the state broadcasting authority ordered an end to the show, though it later relented.

As China's economy booms, the spread of Mandarin may accelerate: more people will move around the country and need a common language to communicate. Education is in Mandarin, and the spread of computing, broadcasting, and other technologies may put stronger wind into Mandarin's sails. Those same forces may also militate in favor of Romanization. The more people use computers—using Roman letters to call up a menu of characters they can choose from—the more they forget how to write them from scratch and think in *pinyin* all the while.

It would be ironic if China switched to *pinyin* before Japan adopted *rōmaji* or *kana*. The characters, after all, come from China, not Japan. It's not inconceivable that China may make the switch for practical, economic, and technological reasons someday, and it has a dictatorship to force it through. Meanwhile, Japan hangs on to Chinese characters for the sake of its national identity, a position encouraged by nationalist politicians. Neither China nor Japan looks as if it will make any changes soon. Politics, as ever, trumps clear thinking about language.

Several themes emerge from the different stories of language planning. Usually the planners make some form of argument based on the state of the language itself, whether its integrity, expressiveness, or modernity is at stake. The linguist George Thomas has collected the metaphors that language nationalists use, and each involves something reminiscent of physical wholeness or purity, often biological: language is an ore that needs refining, a grain that needs milling, a genealogical organism that needs pure breeding, a tree that needs pruning, a body that needs surgery, and so forth. Foreign elements—Arabic in Turkish, Anglicisms in French, Latin and Greek words in William Barnes's view of English—these are somehow poisonous, contaminating, corroding. And change is usually equated with decay or rot, rarely considered neutrally as mere change.

But the real motivation behind most language planning is usually political. Language reforms have winners and losers, and so appeasing the "losers" (including those who have already mastered an old system and will have to learn a new one) makes it tempting to appeal to linguistic factors, to convince everyone that the planners know best about how the language should work.

If forcing through change by fiat is usually a bad idea,

sometimes it makes some sense. Newly independent countries establishing their identities may have the most sympathetic arguments for planning their language: coining and codifying native elements, choosing an appropriate writing system, trying to keep foreign elements out. But even when we are sensitive to those political motives, they should be made clear. Language planning is almost always about identity creation, the gathering of an in-group and the exclusion of an out-group, the process called "nation building." Nation building happens through the creation of artificial symbols such as a flag, a national anthem, or national myths. There is nothing wrong with these and nothing necessarily wrong with nation building through language, either. But language planning will be not only more honest but also more successful when its nation-building motives are front and center, rather than dressed up in bogus arguments about language itself.

7

The Microsoft and Apple of Languages

America, France, and Languages in Competition

They come in droves, and are becoming the majority, except in one or two counties. Few of their children in the country learn English. They import books from Mexico, and of the six local TV stations, two are entirely Spanish, two half Spanish half English, and just two are all English. They have one Spanish newspaper, and one half Spanish. Advertisements intended for everybody are now printed in Spanish and English, the signs in our streets are in both languages, and in some places only Spanish. They write their legal documents in their own language, which (though I think they shouldn't be) are allowed in our courts, where there's so much Spanish nowadays that they constantly need more interpreters. I suppose in a few years we'll need them in the Assembly too, to tell one half of our legislature what the other half says.

Hearing someone speak an unknown foreign language is enjoyable for some, bewildering and even frightening for many others. Hearing a foreign language *in their own country* is, for millions of Americans, downright infuriating. It vexed so many Americans that the U.S. Senate, in 2006, passed an amendment to a bill declaring English the "national language" of the United States, a status it had happily done without since 1776. The amendment would also have declared that no one would have rights to government services in any languages except English, except such rights as already guaranteed by law. Then-Senator Barack Obama voted against the amendment, which died anyway in the House of Representatives.

We have seen how so many of the conflicts of the world arose from the idea of nationalism and that nationalism, for many, included something like "all of the speakers of my language should have a state to themselves—without speakers of any other language." But the United States was largely immune to this thinking. After all, all white Americans were descended from immigrants themselves, and for centuries many have proudly carried their heritage with them in happy hyphenation. From Germans and Scandinavians and Irish in the middle of the nineteenth century to Italians, Poles, and Jews at the turn of the twentieth, America has continually been enriched by immigration, new ingredients to the melting pot.

Only recently, with a long-term, heavy-flow history of immigration, has this started to change. Hispanics in particular are seeking special legal rights to use their language in public life and cluster in closed communities that slow their transition to English. America is in danger of becoming a bilingual society. As the eminent political scientist Samuel Huntington put it in his 2004 book *Who Are We?*, the bilingualism of cities such as Miami offers a clue to what the United States may look like in the future if nothing is done. Other language groups— Asians on the West Coast, in particular—cluster in large enough numbers that they too may someday seek special language rights, threatening to destroy America's English-speaking unity and turn it into a modern Babel. Today's immigrants simply have too little in common with the mainly European-descended whites who came a hundred years or more ago, and they are unwilling to assimilate. A softheaded, mostly left-leaning belief in "multiculturalism" abets those who would adulterate the identity of the United States. Throw in those who would sanction "Ebonics," and English-speaking America may be headed for crisis.

All of the above beliefs are widespread—and wrong. They get the history, at both ends, nearly exactly backward. America has a long track record of nativism, including fear and distrust of immigrants speaking languages other than English. States and the federal government have made nervous attempts to ban the use of foreign languages in the public square for a hundred years. Most of those efforts have been spottily enforced embarrassments. Nonetheless, even without official shoves or punishments, the immigrants whose languages so worried our forebears, wherever they came from, have become fully Americanized, most of them monolingual—in English. Don't believe me? Try finding a German-speaker who doesn't speak English in Texas, once home to a wave of German-speaking immigrants to towns such as Fredericksburg, New Braunfels, and Weimar. Pick your traditional ethnic enclave—Italians in Brooklyn, Scandinavians in Minnesota—and you would be hard-pressed to find someone raised from childhood in those communities who today doesn't speak English.

Is today's immigration from the Spanish-speaking world different, though? We hear *Oprima dos para español* on the phone; was there ever any *Drücken Sie zwei für Deutsch* during the period of heavy German immigration? Of course not, because there were no automated phone menus. But lost to our shortsighted vision of history is the fact that German-speakers were so heavily concentrated at the turn of the twentieth century that they shed their German more slowly than today's Hispanic immigrants are losing Spanish, according to the most careful studies. We have seen fears for English, and skittishness toward a foreign-speaking community in our midst, many times before.

The irony, of course, is that Americans' fears for English is misplaced because English is, to put it simply, the most wildly successful language in the history of the world. Though Mandarin has the most speakers, nearly all of them are in China. English boasts half a billion native speakers and is the official language of at least one country on all six inhabited continents. It is the language of the world's only superpower. It is the world's auxiliary language, learned by Swedes and Italians so that they can speak to each other. It travels as part of the world's most successful pop culture, whether films, music, or television. And all this, of course, is given a massive boost by the Internet, which as it brings people from around the world together puts an even bigger premium on a common medium of communication: English. Saying that English is "under threat" is something like saying that gravity and the use of the fork are under threat. It was once said that "rooting for the Yankees is like rooting for U.S. Steel." But English isn't even just as dominant as U.S. Steel in its near-monopolistic heyday. Today, Microsoft would be a better comparison: millions of us can't get through a day without using a Microsoft product, especially its ubiquitous Windows operating system. But even an analogy with Microsoft can't do full justice to the worldwide power of English. One can imagine Microsoft disappearing in fifty years. English is all but certain to be even more dominant then than it is today. There simply has never been a linguistic success story like it in world history.

The above is so obvious to the rest of the world that it takes an American to miss it. The last chapter looked at language purism practiced by official government bodies: bureaucrats and academicians who toil away coining technical and cultural terms so that their languages will resist importing English words. But countries do another kind of planning, too: bolstering the status of their language as a whole vis-à-vis others. They might forbid government work from being done in English, forbid English advertising or business communication, even specify a maximum amount of television or radio content in English (and a minimum in the local language). Officials who can speak English might refuse to do so even in international settings. They might refuse to allow English to be designated the main or only official working language of a multilingual body. The overarching position is that other major languages must be given an equal seat at the table in international arenas and must be legally protected from English at home.

No people in the world is as famous for doing this as the French. France aggressively promotes the use of its language in international forums: the European Union, the Council of Europe, the United Nations, and the like. France assures that any prospective secretary-general of the United Nations speak passable French, threatening a veto of any candidate who doesn't.

If English is the world's Microsoft, then French could be its Apple. Like Apple's sleek silver computers, French is the self-consciously cool alternative choice of many creatives and thinkers who hate the idea of relying on the subpar product that represents the behemoth. If it is a minority preference, the choice to use French is one that many make with pride, and with disdain for those who can't or won't. Think about the architect who works from your local coffee shop and wouldn't dream of working on a PC (even though he's perfectly capable of doing so, with the same end result). That's how much of the world feels about French.*

The French and the Americans often see themselves as polar opposites, but they are not always so different. Both are insecure, and for related reasons. Both are nervous in the face of globalization. Both are nervous about their failures to fully assimilate big immigrant populations. These challenges have shaken both countries' very sense of identity.

The United States and France are also more alike than they

---

* Like all analogies, this one shouldn't be taken too far. I am thinking of operating systems for full-scale computers, in which Windows has, at the time of this writing, over a 90 percent market share. But with the success of its iPhones and iPads, Apple's market capitalization actually surpassed Microsoft's in early 2010.

think for deeper reasons: traditions of liberty and universal values that rocked the world when they emerged from two revolutions that took place just thirteen years apart. Both America and France have given themselves the mission to remake the world with their values. (In the colonial period, the French called it, charmingly without artifice, *la mission civilizatrice*.) The spread of a language is seen as a proxy for success in this endeavor.

And finally, both great countries need to relax. The English language is not threatened; nor is French. The "idea of America" is not threatened, either, however much Samuel Huntington thought it might be. And Charles de Gaulle's *certaine idée de la France* continues to be a big part of the French identity. Whatever powers may rise in Asia and elsewhere, America and France still have much to offer the world—and in English and French.

Samuel Huntington wrote in *Who Are We?* that "The role of English in schools and other contexts had come up before in the United States, but the profusion and intensity of controversies at the national as well as state and local levels [in the 1980s and 1990s] were unprecedented." Anti-immigration Republicans can often be heard saying the same thing. In January 2009 a Nashville city councilman who sponsored an English-only bill, Eric Crafton, told *The New York Times* that some California legislators needed interpreters because they couldn't speak English. He didn't want California's future for his city, which had seen a boom in immigration. To make his point, Crafton introduced his motion in Japanese, which he had learned in the navy. He wanted to show that he wasn't against foreign languages in every way but merely pro-English. He worried that it was possible to live—even be elected to office—without learning English in America.

But in fact, as the *Times* later corrected, Crafton was wrong. There are no California legislators who can't speak English. Crafton got the factoid from a television program, he said later in retraction. And Huntington was wrong, too. The fevered defense of English in the face of allegedly overwhelming waves of immigrants is no new phenomenon. The epigraph beginning this chapter is not a contemporary complaint about Spanish-speaking immigration to the United States. With "German" changed to "Spanish," "printing houses" changed to "TV stations," and the wording modernized slightly, it comes from a letter by Benjamin Franklin in 1753. The original reads

> They come in droves, and carry all before them, except in one or two counties. Few of their children in the country learn English. They import many books from Germany, and of the six printing houses in the province, two are entirely German, two half German half English, and but two entirely English, they have one German News-Paper, and one half German. Advertisements intended for to be general are now printed in Dutch and English, the signs in Our Streets have inscriptions in both languages, and in some places only German, they began of late all their bonds and other legal writings in their own language, which (tho' I think it ought not to be) are allowed good in Our Courts, where the German business so increases, that there's continual need of interpreters; and I suppose in a few Years They will also be necessary in The Assembly, to tell one half of Our Legislature what the other half says.

Franklin goes on to make sweeping generalizations about German immigrants: that America got only the most ignorant of the Germans, that they had a tendency to cussedness and rebellion, and so forth. This echoes Samuel Huntington's worry about what he patronizingly called the *mañana* ("tomorrow") culture of Latin America: trust of family and friends over society and public institutions, lack of economic ambition or planning for the future, and so forth. Franklin's Germans and

Huntington's Hispanics stand in negative contrast to what Huntington called America's "Anglo-Protestant core."

Not all early Americans worried about foreign-language speakers coming to American shores as Franklin did. The French Revolution sent French émigrés in large numbers. The Germans continued coming after the American Revolution. They established their own schools and churches in self-contained colonies, using their own languages almost exclusively. The early American leaders, with exceptions like Franklin, did not worry too much about this. They thought about language like they thought about much of the rest of politics: people should be left alone unless there was a good reason to interfere in their lives. The royal language academies of France and Spain were well known but seen as monarchical examples to be avoided. Meanwhile, Benjamin Rush, a Founding-Father-era congressman, wrote that a German college, specifically designed to assimilate incomers and their families with language and other patriotic lessons, would be the best way to integrate Germans: "It will open the eyes of the Germans to a sense of the importance, and utility of the English language and become perhaps the only possible means, consistent with their liberty, of spreading a knowledge of the English language among them."

The attitude toward assimilating immigrants persisted in its split personality. On one side, roughly speaking, was the notion that people would assimilate when they were good and ready and couldn't be forced to do so. On the other was the idea that life for non-English-speakers had to be made uncomfortable to make them learn English. It was the former, accommodationist principle that led to a 1795 bill in Congress—which failed by one vote—that all laws be printed and disseminated in German as well as English. (This is, by the way, the source of a persistent myth that German was nearly made America's official language.)

The early American fear about German was not due only to the existence of big German communities in America. Further contributing to the new country's sense of insecurity was the fact that German had just enjoyed centuries of prominence in science, literature, and philosophy in Europe, while America was finding its voice as a culture as well as a republic. The same worry led Noah Webster to distance American English from that of Britain with his spelling reforms.

While most immigrant groups dropped their languages in a typical pattern of two to three generations, the Germans held on the longest. They lived in large and contiguous communities refreshed by immigration, particularly in Pennsylvania and the Midwest. Some schools in Cincinnati (where three-quarters of immigrants were German) spent half the day teaching in German—a program that persisted from 1840 to the First World War. Denver opened a German-only school in 1870. Other schools taught at least some of the time in German, especially in cities such as Indianapolis, Baltimore, Cleveland, Milwaukee, and Saint Louis.

The Germans were the biggest and most persistent group of foreign-language speakers. But other foreign bogeymen, with new origins, faiths, and languages, would appear over the nineteenth century. In the middle of that century, the American Party (most frequently known as the "Know-Nothings") won several big election victories in places like Massachusetts and Illinois. The Know-Nothings worried primarily about Catholic immigration, especially that from Ireland. They feared a popish plot to flood the Protestant-majority country with loyal disciples; like many paranoid movements in American history, its adherents kept it a partly secret society. (They were told to say merely "I know nothing" when asked about it.)

Immigrants have tended to cause the biggest backlashes, unsurprisingly, when they cluster. Hence even white, Protestant Scandinavians were the target of anti-immigrant sentiments in places such as the upper Midwest, where laws aimed at "promoting" English were targeted at Swedish and Finnish. But as today, numbers strengthened the immigrants' hands: large German-speaking communities successfully pressured local politicians to allocate funding for German-language education. In 1900 fully 4 percent of students in the United States were being taught at least partly in German—a far higher proportion than all bilingual programs for all languages combined today.

It was the end of the nineteenth and beginning of the twentieth century that saw waves of immigration—and backlash—that most resemble today's. It was the biggest period of immigration in America's history; in 1920, 13.6 percent of the population was foreign-born, as against 11.7 percent in 2003.

Moreover, the backgrounds of the newcomers didn't make their arrival easier. Many were Catholic, coming from Ireland, Poland, or Italy. Pogroms in Eastern Europe led to an influx of Yiddish-speaking Jews, linguistic outsiders with the double disadvantage of not being Christian. Overall, 27 million people came to the United States in the fifty years from 1880 to 1930.

But the flow would be shut off quickly. The First World War led to a boost in red-white-and-blue nativism across the board. German signs were destroyed on the streets and German newspapers required to publish English translations, putting many of them out of business. Some states and towns forbade German conversations over the telephone, and one Ohio town introduced fines for speaking German on the street.

The nativist wave was symbolic as well as practical. Washington McCormick, a congressman from Montana, proposed in 1923 making "American" the official language of the United States. He was motivated, perhaps surprisingly, not by the most recent waves of immigration but by a still-existing Anglophobia, sensing that too many Americans continued to live in Britain's cultural and political shadow. McCormick's national bill failed, but it sparked a wave of similar bills in state legislatures. Only one succeeded, in Illinois, though "English" was quietly reintroduced in 1969.

The state of Nebraska went furthest, however. In the same First World War–era fervor, it scrapped an earlier requirement that official proceedings of county boards be published in Ger-

man-, Swedish-, and Czech-language newspapers. More sweep-
ingly, in 1919 it banned the teaching of any subject whatsoever
in any language other than English—and that included the
teaching of foreign languages themselves before the eighth
grade. The law applied not only to public schools but even to
private and religious ones. Even in private settings, no one
could be taught any language other than English. Exceptions
were made for religious teaching (and then only on Sundays or
other recognized Sabbath days) and parents teaching their children at home. Coincidentally or not, it is at that age, around
the onset of puberty, that children tend to lose their cognitive
abilities to learn foreign languages to near-native skill. Nebraska was taking no chances.

The state's version of "English only" would make modern
English-only activists cringe. The measures were clearly xenophobic, aimed, in particular, at Germans and German-Ameri-
cans. The arguments were often primitively Whorfian. One
lawmaker said, "I, for one, believe that there is no language
spoken by man that breathes the spirit of American liberty like
the language that has come down to us from our Anglo-Saxon
forefathers." Proponents agreed that something about English
was particularly suited to the ideals of the republic.

The law was overturned by the U.S. Supreme Court in
1923. The "Sunday only, and only for religious teaching" pro-
vision was key: Nebraska was forbidding religious instruction,
foreign language or no, six days a week. The defendant had
committed the crime of teaching Bible stories to a ten-year-old
from a book in German in the parochial school of a Lutheran
church. The Supreme Court of Nebraska had returned to
Whorfian thinking when it upheld the law, arguing that to
teach a child even a separate subject (religion) in a foreign language

> was to rear them with that language as their mother
> tongue. It was to educate them so that they must always

think in that language, and, as a consequence, naturally inculcate in them the ideas and sentiments foreign to the best interests of this country.

The federal Supreme Court disagreed. It did not specifically reply to Nebraska's coarse psychologizing that learning a foreign language "naturally inculcate[s] in [children] the ideas and sentiments foreign to the best interests of this country." It also agreed that public schools could, certainly, be required to teach English. But to *prohibit* a *private* school from teaching anything in any foreign language was unconstitutional. Even if the promotion of a common language was a legitimate interest, "a desirable end cannot be promoted by prohibited means," Justice James Clark McReynolds reasoned.

The foreigner-phobic feeling in the land was not banished, however. In the early twentieth century, the spotlight of suspicion swung around once again to the most "undesirable" immigrants: often Catholic, Jewish, or nonwhite, from southern and Eastern Europe or from Asia. New laws from Congress included the unsubtly named National Origins Act, which slammed the door to immigration completely for Japanese immigrants and limited the numbers coming from the European countries. The Chinese Exclusion Act had done the same for that nationality in 1882. (One almost misses the days when lawmakers were so frank in naming bills. One wonders what the USA PATRIOT Act would have been called back then.)

At the San Gennaro festival, a cheesy but fun annual street fair of Italian-American pride in New York's shrinking Little Italy, I once saw a T-shirt for sale reading "Welcome to America: Now Speak English." Yes, in *Little Italy*.

In fact, the United States has a remarkable ability to grind down foreigners' languages, turning them into monoglot Anglophones, no matter where they came from. I live in another heavily Italian neighborhood, Carroll Gardens, in Brooklyn.

Statues of Christ, the Virgin Mary, and Saint Anthony of Padua abound; Italy's red, white, and green tricolor dots shop windows. Al Capone was married down the street. There are enough Italians that, a few blocks from my apartment, there is a social club for immigrants from a single Italian town, Pozzallo (in Sicily). The block was ceremonially renamed "Citizens of Pozzallo Way."

And yes, you can hear Italian on the streets and in the parks—but almost exclusively among people over seventy. They all speak English, too, of course, but Italian is both more comfortable and a mark of solidarity with one another. One occasionally hears a middle-generation adult speaking Italian with her parents, but that is rare. And though the kids wear the blue jersey of the Italian soccer team (or, more likely, *Sopranos* T-shirts), I have never once heard someone under forty speak Italian in the neighborhood.

In 1918, Theodore Roosevelt, by then out of the White House for ten years, feared publicly that America was becoming a "polyglot boarding house," in a famous speech that modern opponents of immigration have eagerly e-mailed each other in recent years. But linguists have a different nickname for America: "the graveyard of languages." Despite past waves of immigration—large and sustained surges that created big and homogeneous foreign communities—inevitably social forces render immigrants' children English-speakers and their grandchildren monoglot English-speakers.

The process is virtually identical across groups and has been the same for two centuries of American history. The first generation to come arrives speaking only the language of the home country. These new immigrants may learn English imperfectly; those who come as adults will nearly all have an accent. (Henry Kissinger, for example, arrived as a teenager and had not shed his accent seven decades later; his brother, a few years younger, had no German accent.) It is the presence of this first generation in large numbers that gives native-born Americans the idea that immigrants can't or won't learn English.

But the key isn't the arriving generation; it's the over-whelming forces that turn the first generation born in America into Anglophones. It is, to put it simply, nearly impossible to raise a child in the United States without the child learning English; it would require isolation from the outside world bordering on child abuse. Children born in America, and even those arriving at a young age, inevitably pick up English.

Of course, members of this bridge generation will typically speak the old country's language, too, learning it in the kitchen from their parents. But it is the bridge generation's own behavior as parents that eventually, and inevitably, dooms the "heritage" language. Parents are not stupid, nor do they typically perform cruel tricks on their children. Parents of children in the United States know that wherever they live, however many bilingual signs surround them, however many phone menus offer *"Oprima dos para español,"* and however many fellow speakers of their language surround them, their children will need English to survive and thrive in America.

Thus I have never met a child born and raised in the United States who doesn't speak English, but I know many who have never learned their grandparents' language and often not even their parents'. Cliff, a journalist friend of mine, was charmingly given the English name closest to his Chinese one, Shan ("mountain"). But he doesn't speak the Mandarin of his mother and father. They came from China but sought to speak English to him as often as possible. Minh Thu, another friend, was born in Vietnam and arrived in the United States as a young girl. Unlike Cliff, she speaks fluent Vietnamese—but only because her parents made a constant effort to speak it to her while she was growing up in North Carolina. Her cousins, who came at a similar age, speak virtually no Vietnamese, their parents having worried so much that it would convey a disadvantage that they spoke broken English to their children.

But as economists like to say, the plural of "anecdote" is not "data." "English-only" proponents worry that, whatever the historical precedents, the situation has changed. Today's waves of immigration are from more concentrated linguistic sources, and there is no greater fear than that of Spanish.

Spanish-speakers come not only from populous and poor nearby Mexico. They also make the long trek across Mexico from poorer countries in Central America; they come from Cuba to Miami and from the Dominican Republic to New York. They even come from an American territory, Puerto Rico, where heavy "Americanization" efforts after it was captured from Spain in 1898 failed to turn the island to English. Immigration has increased steadily since the 1920s-era quotas were relaxed in 1965, and with illegal immigration bolstering the legal kind, Hispanics are now the largest minority in the United States.

In 2009, Barack Obama nominated Sonia Sotomayor, born in the Bronx, to be the first Hispanic justice on the Supreme Court, in a tacit recognition of Hispanics' growing political clout. When it came to light that she had once praised the virtues of being a "wise Latina" in a speech, conservatives were apoplectic, many flatly calling her a racist. Mark Krikorian, a professional worrier about illegal immigration, found even the prosody of her name galling, writing in the blog of the conservative *National Review* magazine:

> Deferring to people's own pronunciation of their names should obviously be our first inclination, but there ought to be limits. Putting the emphasis on the final syllable of Sotomayor is unnatural in English . . . and insisting on an unnatural pronunciation is something we shouldn't be giving in to.

All this reflects a fear that Hispanics will keep their Spanish, while clamoring for rights such as Spanish ballots, Spanish-language education, and interpreters in public offices, pushing America gradually toward bilingualism—in other words, that there is something new and different about this wave of immigration.

Once again, though, there are data to be had. The key isn't looking around. It is certainly easy to find people in America who don't speak English or signs and services catering to them. As a New York City resident, I see more of them than most Americans, and I am frequently surprised at the number of signs in Chinese or Spanish with no English translation, even public-service announcements from the city government. This kind of thing serves the millions of foreigners in America who can barely get past "Hello."

But this is nothing that couldn't have been seen in 1900s Cleveland or 1750s Philadelphia. The way to find out if things are truly changing is to look *back*—at what the American-born children of immigrants have done over time as they grow up in America. It is that generation, the bridge generation, that tells us what will happen in the future.

Alejandro Portes and Lingxin Hao decided to take a close look at this generation in San Diego and Miami–Fort Lauderdale. Both cities have some of the highest concentrations of immigrants in the country, the former from Mexico and Asia, the latter primarily Cuban, Haitian, West Indian, and South American. Their subjects were 5,266 eighth- and ninth-graders who answered detailed, anonymous surveys: on which languages they knew, which ones they used at home, and which their close friends spoke. The researchers also compared these numbers against social variables such as the average socioeconomic status of the school, the concentration of immigrants in the surrounding community, and the like.

The study found in detail what so many other studies have shown that linguists nearly take it for granted. Virtually all of the bridge generation speaks English "well" or "very well": 93.6 percent of the total students surveyed, who either had been born in the United States or had lived there for more than five years. Just about one in twenty children of immigrants had failed to learn English "well" by eighth or ninth grade, and even they had learned it passably.

The numbers are robust across language groups, too: 94.7

percent of Latin Americans spoke English well or very well; the same was true of 90.3 percent of Asians. There were interesting differences within the groups, however. Not surprisingly, second-generation children of Mexicans—by far the largest group of immigrants in America today and often found in contiguous communities that make it easier to live without English—were the least likely to speak English well. But even 86.1 percent of them did. Among Asians, Laotians were the least likely to speak English well—but three-quarters of them still could do so. This was the worst-performing of all national groups studied by Portes and Hao.

In fact, the two set out not to study English learning. So many studies had already shown that second-generation immigrants learn English just as they always have that another such study would have been old news. Portes and Hao were also looking to find which groups held on to their native languages longest, to see whether it was still true that America is the "graveyard of languages" and whether the second generation preferred their parents' languages or English.

On the preference question, once again, the nativist fears that immigrants want to create a multilingual society are misplaced. Of all the groups surveyed, only one group of the second-generation children slightly preferred their heritage language: just 44.8 percent of Mexican-descended subjects preferred English to Spanish. But overall, 71 percent of Latin American–descended children preferred English, as did 73.6 percent of those of Asian heritage.

What about retention of the heritage language? If the bridge generation is learning English, is it bilingual? In short, no. Just 27 percent of the children studied spoke both their parents' language and English well. This is because only 44 percent of the whole sample spoke their parents' language at least "well," and just 16.1 percent spoke it "very well." The language drop-off was fastest among Asians. Of Latin Americans, 60.6 percent spoke Spanish at least "well," perhaps supported by the profusion of Spanish-language media, not to mention the big immigrant communities they live in. But one in five of the Latin American sample spoke Spanish "very well"—hardly a hard core ready to turn America bilingual. The Cuban group was most likely of all groups to be bilingual; 61.3 percent speak Spanish well, but they overwhelmingly prefer English (83 percent). Higher socioeconomic status was also correlated with bilingualism. In other words, richer and better-educated parents were more likely to have the time and motivation to make sure their children learn the heritage language.

With 71 percent of the bridge generation preferring English and just 16.1 percent speaking their heritage language very well, Spanish (like Vietnamese, Cambodian, and the others) seems headed the way of Finnish, German, and Swedish: to a near-inevitable demise as first languages spoken by large groups of Americans. The mistake Huntington made was looking at immigrants and not their American children.

The behavior of the bridge generation is confirmed by another study. Rubén Rumbaut, Douglas Massey, and Frank Bean looked at 5,702 people across four immigrant-derived generations in southern California. Generation "1" arrived in adulthood, generation "1.5" arrived in childhood, generation "2" comprised American-born children of two immigrant parents, generation "2.5" comprised U.S.-born children of one immigrant parent, members of generation "3" had three or four immigrant grandparents, and those in generation "3.5" had just one or two grandparents from abroad. The results are best seen graphically. The first graph shows the proportion of each generation that speaks the language "very well," and the second shows the proportion that prefers to speak the immigrant language at home. Both are good predictors of language death. Parents who speak the immigrant language only "well" and not "very well" are far less likely to speak that language routinely to their children—especially given the high economic premium on English. And those who don't prefer the immigrant language even at home are especially unlikely to pass it on to their kids.

**Proportion of immigrant group members who
speak mother tongue very well by generation**

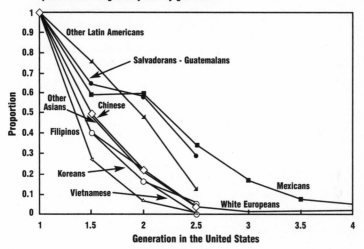

**Proportion of immigrant group members who
speak mother tongue at home by generation**

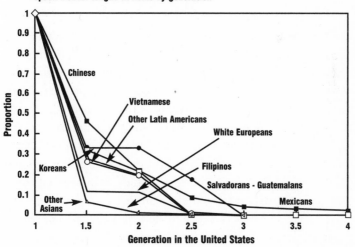

Rumbaut, Massey, and Bean note that Huntington's thesis seems only partly correct. Their sample all comes from the five counties of southern California, which taken as a community would form a medium-sized Spanish-speaking country. They note that the community is supported by huge and sophisticated Spanish-language radio stations and television networks. It is also close to Mexico. For this reason, Mexicans and their children stand out on the first graph as keeping their ability to speak their language for longer than Asians or non-Latino whites. But ultimately it is the shape, not the location, of the curve that counts. The authors reckon that those still speaking and preferring Spanish will fall below 5 percent among even Mexicans in the third generation.

It is not only clear that immigrant children are still being transformed into monoglot Americans; it comes at a big cost. Not the abstract "diversity" and culture, beloved of the multicultural left, however important they may be. There are real losses that even proud, English-only, America-first types should regret when languages die out among immigrants' children in America.

One is that the loss of immigrant languages may literally make us dumber. Repeated studies have shown fluent bilingualism to be accompanied by higher intelligence and intellectual performance. Bilinguals show not just better verbal skills but better overall grades in school and college, higher test scores, and even superior math skills. And studies looking for the direction of causation—are bilinguals smarter or do smarter people become bilingual?—seem to have shown that it is the first: those who become fluently bilingual, especially at an early age, gain a cognitive bonus. One recent study even showed fluent bilingualism warding off old-age dementia.

It isn't clear whether proud and nationalistic Americans would be happy to throw these gains away in their pursuit of an English-only America. But the types who would prefer English only, who are patriotic and often conservative, may be persuadable by another cost of monolingualism: America is losing a vast and valuable resource, a potential pool of bilinguals who could serve America's interests. The fields where America is desperately short of language skills is long and well known. America's intelligence agencies lacked the Arabic-speakers to translate and analyze many intercepted e-mails and phone calls before September 11, 2001; it is similarly short-handed with Arabic, Pashto, and Dari speakers in Iraq and Afghanistan. U.S. diplomats must be expensively and lengthily trained in foreign languages—the Defense Language Institute expects that it takes eighty-eight weeks of *full-time* study to master one of the difficult languages, such as Chinese and Arabic, that English-only types are so intent in stomping out of immigrant children's heads as quickly as possible. In business, Chinese and Japanese negotiators often understand their American partners and rivals' language and culture (as do virtually all Europeans); Americans must rely on translators and local agents and hope they are competent and honest.

Speaking in favor of foreign languages, of course, should not be taken as downplaying the crucial unifying role of English. Many on the left—including no small number of academic linguists—associate the American attachment to English mainly with a negative, excluding, and unhealthy nationalism. Those on the far, multicultural left associate it especially with the abuse and murder of Native Americans, racism against Latinos, the intentional mixing of African slaves from different language groups to keep them from uniting, and so forth.

But English has a hugely important function. Though the framers thought better than to include it in the Constitution, English *is* the national language, so obviously so that it really is in no need of protection. Though it varies slightly from region to region, a more or less unified American English binds a diverse and continent-sized country together. It has been a path to assimilation for many groups that earlier, "Anglo-Protestant" Americans thought unassimilable. Americans are rightly proud of this history and of the language that made it possible.

Ethnic minorities in America—and Latinos themselves know they are no exception—need English. In fact, they need it more than richer, far more secure white Anglos do. It is good and proper to encourage English learning, as Arnold

Schwarzenegger, the governor of California, courted controversy in 2007 by doing. The Austrian immigrant made good
told his Latino audience to "turn off the [Spanish-language]
television" and learn English as he had.

To tell them to abandon their home languages because they
are a threat to American unity, though, is ignorant of the facts
and long overdue for consignment to the dustbin of bad ideas
from an earlier age. One hesitates to criticize brilliant men such
as Ben Franklin, Teddy Roosevelt, and Samuel Huntington, but
history has shown the first two to be wrong about English, and
the numbers make it look likely that Huntington will be wrong
too. From each man's era to the next, English has grown more
powerful in the United States and the world. It's doing just fine.

The United States, of course, isn't alone in worrying about the
influx of foreign languages. My plane touches down at Charles
de Gaulle airport in Paris. The airport is named after the general and president whose *certaine idée de la France* still ani-
mates many among the French. De Gaulle developed a nuclear
bomb for France, yanked his country out of NATO's military
command, and booted the alliance's headquarters out of Paris.
He believed in a strong Europe, with France its undisputed
leader, an independent pole of power between the Soviet- and
American-led blocs. The main center-right party in France,
which has changed offical names repeatedly, is still universally
known as the "Gaullist" party, and its leaders—notably
Jacques Chirac in recent years—share the America-wary DNA
of the general himself.

So what greets the visitor arriving at Charles de Gaulle airport today? Among other things, signs reading "The department store capital of fashion," "Only the brave," "I ♥ Italian
shoes," and "Duty free like nowhere else." The computer company Oracle boasts in an advertisement that it serves "20 of the
top utilities." The American credit-card company MasterCard
riffs on a famous ad campaign with a poster reading "Keeping

up with fashion? Priceless." All of these are written not in the language of de Gaulle but in that of George Washington. Even the French ads are infused with English: Peugeot, a French car company, advertises a vehicle—somewhere between a car and an SUV—it calls the Crossover, "avec technologie *grip control.*"

French intellectuals are known for bewailing this kind of thing, as we saw in the last chapter. But resistance to foreign influences, with the corresponding instinct to build up French, is nothing new to France; building the French state alongside the French identity has meant fighting off competitors to French for centuries.

Today, France stands for many as the emblematic "nation-state": the complete merger between a people, a state, and a language. (Whenever I ask my students to "Name a nation-state, quickly," the first reply is nearly always "France.") But though it may seem axiomatic today, this powerful identification of French and France, the making of France as the nation-state par excellence is actually a remarkable historical achievement—and the result of a long, conscious process. Not only outsiders but many Frenchmen themselves forget that France was not always so Francophone. Shortly after the French Revolution, in 1790, the Abbé Grégoire's census (mentioned in chapter 5) found that just 3 million French citizens were native speakers of French. Another 3 million spoke French with some competence as a second language. Another 25 million spoke another first language and had little or no standard French to speak of. France was less than one-fifth French.

It took a conscious and assertive policy of extending French, pushing it from its heartland around Paris out to the north, south, east, and west, to make France speak French. Along the way, other languages have suffered—and their speakers have sometimes pushed back.

Take just one of France's traditionally non-French regions. Brittany was settled by Celtic peoples coming down from the British Isles near the end of the Roman period. It remained a sovereign duchy from 938 to 1532, when it was conquered and incorporated into France. Brest, the regional capital, lies in the westernmost bit of Brittany and so is nearly the westernmost point in mainland France. Breton is a Celtic language, thus part of the Indo-European family. But it is a close cousin of Welsh and Cornish (the latter now extinct), and, though utterly unlike French to the ear and eye, it survived Brittany's incorporation into France. In the two centuries after the French Revolution, though, Breton was suppressed in the state's drive to extend French (and only French) to all of France's territory. Beginning in the 1970s, after centuries of repression, and accompanied by a slow but steady rise in the popularity of Breton music and culture, Breton enthusiasts began fighting for their language.

Not that it is apparent to me as I visit Brest to look into the state of things. In this, the largest city in Brittany, the train station has a large kiosk with books and magazines—not a single one in Breton. A humor book, *Ils sont fous, ces Bretons!!* ("They're crazy, these Bretons!!"), pokes loving fun at the culture, the people, and the language—but is written in French. A glossy magazine, *Bretons,* is dedicated to modern Breton life and features a cover story on Jack Kerouac, who was of Breton heritage. But it, too, is entirely in French.

Striking out trying to find any Breton-ness on my own, I ask at the tourist office whether I might find some Breton culture or people knowledgeable about the language. I'm told that I might find them in Carhaix, a town an hour and a half away, which has an Office de la Langue Bretonne. Hoping to find some help a little closer, I ask the staff of young women whether anyone in the tourist office speaks Breton. Cécile, who has been helping me, frowns with her mouth as she laughs with her eyes, as if thinking carefully how to answer this ridiculous question without embarrassing me. After holding this expression for a few seconds, she recommends a small museum in

Plouguerneau, forty minutes or so to the north, where, she thinks, the director might know Breton.

Instead of giving up on Brest, I strike back out on the street to see if I can find any Breton there. But the language is nearly invisible. Some of the official street signs are in both French and Breton—a major symbolic victory for the Breton movement, France being France. But another large newsstand I visit also has no material, among hundreds of magazines and newspapers, in Breton. When I think I've finally found a Breton spot—a convivial and crowded bar and restaurant called Tir na N'og—I get excited until I get a little closer and see the sign that means death for all seekers of cultural authenticity: "Irish Pub & Restaurant."

Moving on, I find the largest bookstore in town; among about twelve cases of books on Brittany and its culture and history, just two carry books either teaching the Breton language or written in the language itself. I peruse one, *Le Breton pour les Nuls,* a French edition of the familiar, yellow-covered, and American-born _____ *for Dummies* series, for about twenty minutes. As I read, I periodically look up to see if anyone approaches the Breton-language books in the busy store. No one does.

The last piece of the picture falls into place when I walk past a crowded school playground. Dozens of children are playing and shouting as children do, and all of them in French. With Breton, as with any language, children learning a language from their parents, not instruction at school, keeps that language alive. Just as none of their parents were buying books in Breton, none of these children were playing in it. If the current trends continue, it may be that in a century's time no child will.

At last I discover a small Breton cultural office (one that even the tourist office staff had not seemed to know about). Bernez Kerdraon, the director, sits down to tell me more. Brest isn't the best place to look for Breton, he says—though it is geographically as deep into Brittany as it's possible to get, it harbors a big naval base, the headquarters of France's Atlantic fleet. Perhaps Rennes, the other biggest city in Brittany, would have been a better choice? I ask. No, not really there, either, Kerdraon says. You have to go to the countryside and talk to older people. This, I remember silently, is a terminal prognosis for a language.

Kerdraon was raised by Breton-speaking farmers himself— but they spoke French to him. They were born into the era when signs reading "No spitting on the floor or speaking Breton" were common in public places. Dunce caps or a sign of shame around the neck were given to students caught speaking Breton in school. The children had to wear them until they could pass them on to another student they caught in the act. Children learned to police themselves and one another, saving the authorities the work. And Bretons learned to associate their native language with humiliation.

But beginning in the 1970s, Breton music and culture enjoyed a vogue in France, Bretons saw their Celtic cousins in Northern Ireland battling British domination, and political groupings, many left-wing, began to form. Kerdraon and many others began to feel shame at their cultural prostration and began agitating for their language. More militant members destroyed signs only in French, visible symbols of the state that was seeking to erase their language. Gradually, French national policy moved away from active suppression.

Today, the highest guidance on French language policy is a simple statement inserted into the constitution in 1992: "The language of the republic is French." But the simplicity of that sentence is misleading: it avoids the words "only" and "official," each of which would trigger extra consequences. It is no longer seen as the done thing to attempt to destroy indigenous languages, and the attitude of the government in Paris has become what some call "hostile tolerance" of the regional languages.

In Brittany, a system of bilingual schools called Diwan

("the seed" in Breton) was set up in 1977. These are the hope of the Breton movement: they provide bilingual education designed to get students to master both Breton and French. (Even the staunchest Breton activist accepts the economic and political need for French mastery.) But in 2009, Kerdraon estimates, 12,000 students studied in these schools—of a regional population of 3 million. With the Diwan movement thirty-four years old, a cadre of committed and bilingual adults raised and steeped in Breton activism could lead the way to a truly bilingual future. But it is far from clear that a big enough cohort of such dedicated Breton boosters exists. Meanwhile, modest cultural centers like Kerdraon's offer mainly a kind of optional heritage tourism for those with spare time and money. These centers do teach Breton to adults, but this is no way to save a language. Only native acquisition by children can do it.

Kerdraon describes the situation, hopefully, as "the bottom of the wave." Fifty-five hours of Breton-language material appear each week on the privately funded Radio Kerne. One of the two regional papers prints a single page in Breton every Thursday. Asked if he is optimistic, he says it is hard to be in the circumstances. And when asked if the French government is improving in its attitudes, he shrugs and gives me a look that says simply "You know how it is."

If Breton is threatened—consigned to old folks in the country and a core of partisans—the other regional languages of France are on different parts of the slippery slope toward language decline and death. Basque and Catalan are spoken in the south, and though they are declining in France, they benefit enormously from the presence of larger, organized, semiautonomous regions in Spain that vigorously promote both languages. Speakers can watch television or hear radio broadcasts and quickly pop across the almost nonexistent borders of modern Western Europe to visit regional capitals such as

Barcelona and San Sebastián. The same is true of the Flemish speakers in France's northeast, who share a language with half of Belgium and all of the Netherlands.

The situation in Alsace, though, is unique. Not only do language groups straddle the border, but that border itself has moved back and forth in recent centuries. Alsace and neighboring Lorraine were part of France until 1871, until they were taken by Germany in the Franco-Prussian War. France grabbed them back in the next round of the Franco-German grudge match, the First World War. France initially offered special laws to the region, many of whose inhabitants speak standard German, Alsatian dialectal German, or Alsatian dialectal French. But these linguistic privileges were gradually rolled back to integrate the region further into France. The presence of Germany next door means that more and more Alsatians, whatever their home language, will learn both standard German and standard French at school; the Alsatian dialects of both are the likely losers.

Finally, there are the Romance dialects: Picard, Gallo, Nissart, Occitan, Provençal, and the like. These are all closely related to French, and their speakers often themselves regard them as little more than substandard "patois." They are different enough from French to be reasonably classified as separate languages, however, and they do have their ardent backers. But they are either small—as with the northern varieties—or divided, as in the south. "Provençal" and "Occitan" are dialects of each other, or Provençal is a dialect of Occitan, or they are the same thing, depending on whom you ask. But the supporters of "Provençal," in the southeast and near the Alps, are associated with the political right, and the fans of "Occitan," in the central south and southwest, are tied to the left. They don't get along and so have been unable to form a strong united front for the single strongest and uniquely French Romance tongue after French itself.

In other words, French language policy, not unlike Atatürk's reform of Turkish, has been something of a "catastrophic success." French is undeniably the national language, in a position of such supremacy and so staunchly backed by the government that there is no indigenous threat to it whatsoever. Just to make sure, France, in a small club of other grouchily nationalist European states, continues to refuse to sign the Council of Europe's European Charter for Regional or Minority Languages, saying that it would contravene French law (and that anyway the regional languages are being cared for). The cost of this success of French, however, may well be the death—or confinement to a museum, at best—of several full-blown languages.

But as all those signs at Charles de Gaulle airport show, just as France was completing its linguistic conquest at home, it was invaded from abroad by English. What are the French doing about it?

In 1994, Maurice Druon, the permanent secretary of the French Academy, published *Letter to the French About Their Language and Their Soul*. In it he captured the attitude that is often taken by foreigners as typically French: "Lack of respect for language reveals a lack of respect for everything" and "France cannot retain its rank as a great country, and carry out policies on the world level, unless she continues to have a military deterrent and a mastery of a universal language." The odd conflation—what are "military deterrent" and "universal language" doing side by side?—seemed to showcase a particularly sharp-edged linguistic nationalism.

That same year, France took the most notorious step to protect the language in modern French history: the National Assembly passed the Toubon Law, named for the culture minister of the Gaullist-conservative government of the day. The Toubon Law made French "obligatory" in five domains: education, employment, advertising and commerce, media, and scientific meetings and publications. It begins grandiloquently, "French is an essential element of France, the language of teaching, work, commerce and public service, and is the special link for the Francophone community." The law—and its application—are responsible for much of France's reputation as panicky and heavy-handed when it comes to language.

The law's provisions seem harsh on their face. For this reason, many French politicians and pundits, especially on the left, mocked it upon its appearance—some called it the Loi Allgood, "all good" being a rough part-for-part translation of Toubon (or *tout bon*). The critics were partly right and partly wrong. The law has gone some way in protecting French but in other domains has been ineffective at best and embarrassing at worst.

Toubon originally envisioned that the law would extend so far as to cover even private speech and writing and broadcasting on private radio and television. It would have required individual companies to use official words, coined by special "terminology commissions" in government ministries, instead of popular English borrowings. The Constitutional Court quickly decided that this would be an unconstitutional infringement on freedom of speech, violating the French Revolution's Declaration of the Rights of Man and of the Citizen.

But the Toubon Law still did provide for punishing individuals and entities who flaunted the requirement for French in public domains such as advertising. Semi-official groups, such as the Association for the Defense of the French Language and The Future of the French Language, were sanctioned to act as complainants in legal cases. The consumer-protection and fraud office was appointed official watchdog.

Several high-profile cases have made the Toubon Law seem both effective and harsh. Georgia Tech, the engineering college based in Atlanta, runs a satellite campus in Lorraine. The program's website was at one time entirely in English. For this, the Association for the Defense of the French Language and The Future of the French Language brought legal charges: as a piece of public advertising in France, the website was required to be in French. The case was thrown out on a technicality, but Georgia Tech was required to translate crucial parts of the website into French and refer visitors to the main, American-based website for other information.

Most of the cases brought under the Toubon Law have been piddling. France Télécom was taken to task for offering services called Tatoo (not "tattoo") and Wanadoo, but the case was thrown out for lack of French translations of these nonsense words. Guilty findings are relatively rare, and fines are small—one reason, no doubt, that so many English words can be seen around France. On the walk between the Saint Michel Métro station along the Seine to the French Academy, where I had an interview for this book, I took pictures of every English word I saw on the street. In just those few hundred meters, I saw a dozen examples of English: "brunch," "city tour," "Canadian pub," and more. This is admittedly a touristy part of town, but it shows that Toubon has hardly eradicated English in France.

French law did take a big bite out of one big offender, however, when in 2005 a court found GE Medical Systems, which had an office in France, guilty of providing technical documentation for internal employee use only in English. A 2006 appeals court upheld the original ruling and a fine of €580,000—almost $700,000.

On examination, though, French policy as applied in cases like this is not entirely unreasonable. GE had been asked repeatedly by its French union to provide translations for the documents. GE (a huge multinational that could easily pay for translations) claimed that the documents were intended primarily for foreign workers in France. The union replied, reasonably enough, that this effectively marginalized French workers who did not speak English in their own country.

Elsewhere, the Toubon Law nicely disguises its anti-English intent: one subsection declares that anything translated from French for the benefit of foreigners must be translated into at least two foreign languages. Though clearly aimed at English, this is neatly dressed up as a nod to diversity and multilingualism, and so English sits alongside Spanish on many signs.

Some French-language policy is positive, not negative. A "Pascal Fund" provides generous monies for international conventions and scientific gatherings to provide translation and interpretation services—a practical gesture, given that requiring such proceedings be entirely in French would immediately drive all international scientific meetings from France.

French law in this regard is thus a mixed bag, not all as bad as the Toubon Law. It has not resulted in quite the catastrophes predicted by many when the law was being debated and when it came into effect. My magazine, *The Economist,* in 1995 quoted an analyst who (incorrectly) predicted that it could make complex financial deals 60 percent more expensive, making pools of capital available to the French economy dry up. Others saw it as nakedly protectionist, motivated not by cultural but by economic insecurity—onerous French laws would make it harder for high-tech products (requiring extensive technical documents) to be exported to France without French translation. This would make it harder for multinationals such as GE to set up and operate in France.

Some opponents of the Toubon Law thought it was aimed not at rich multinationals but at nonwhite immigrants to France and their children. The idea, thought critics of Toubon, was to make life miserable for immigrants so that they would leave. The law was in fact passed around the same time as the tightening of immigration laws (the Pasqua Laws, under the same conservative government). But the Toubon Law has not been a "solution" to immigration, because language is not the chief problem for France's immigrants. Many come from former colonies where French is prevalent and already speak French. The issue is not language but the stigma of immigrants' darker skin and their relative poverty. Many Arabs in France don't even speak Arabic properly. One prestigious private school in Paris accepts only bilingual students. It can find many French-English and French-Italian bilinguals but can't find enough Arabic-French bilinguals to fill classes designed for them.

As for globalization, Toubon has done little to alter the playing field for France one way or the other. France's resistance to globalization is in fact vastly overreported: the country is host to big, high-tech, successful multinational companies in carmaking, pharmaceuticals, and armaments, even if they are less well known than those in luxury, fashion, and food products. The vast majority of Americans would be stunned to disbelief to find that the French worker is more productive, on a GDP-per-hour basis, than the American worker is.*

The problem of both globalization and immigration is the French reluctance to certain *kinds* of change, not an aversion to all things new or non-French. The economic system protects those already in comfortable jobs. Since the law makes it hard to fire workers, it makes it unattractive to hire them, the single biggest cause of France's stubbornly high unemployment rate. And of course those most likely to be unemployed are immigrant-descended youth, mainly of Arab and African descent. France's economy is not sickly any more than its culture is. But France's unique ethos, the "republican" values that insist that anyone playing by the rules can make it, ignores a hard truth. Societal racism has made it effectively impossible for, say, a young graduate named Khaled to get the same shot at a job interview as an equally qualified but luckier young man named Pierre. But many among the French, who don't even collect census statistics on ethnicity or race—prefer to stop their ears and insist on the equality of opportunity in France. When things get rough, the French—hardly alone in this sin—squeeze their eyes shut, insist that there is nothing wrong with the French model, and seek a scapegoat. To some extent, that scapegoat has been the "cultural invasion" of English.

---

* A caveat to this remarkable fact is that French workers work shorter weeks and fewer weeks per year, and a smaller proportion of them are in the workforce at a given time. America's labor market has relatively larger numbers of less productive workers working, and the long hours worked reduce the productivity of the average hour.

France is an anxious power—and both of those words must be remembered when thinking about the country, because it is a power. It holds only one of five veto-wielding seats on the UN Security Council, is one of the world's few nuclear states, is an undisputed leader of the European Union, and has one of the world's largest, most sophisticated economies. Rumors of the decline of France, like those of Mark Twain's death, have been vastly exaggerated.

The same goes for the language. France is the world's ninth-most-spoken language. Even if, as linguists fear, half the world's six thousand languages disappear in the next century, the vitality of French is utterly unthreatened. (Even if they keep on disappearing at a rate of half the world's languages each century, France has a good thousand years or so left in it.) At the EU, in Brussels, English is gaining ground, but much business is still done in French, and even Britain would hesitate to send a diplomat there who did not speak French. At the United Nations in New York, there are six official languages: English, French, Russian, Spanish, Arabic, and Chinese. English, of course, dominates, but one can frequently hear an official or a reporter start speaking French midmeeting—something that never happens in Chinese or Arabic. French is a well-established alternative there, as so many other places, and it is a minor rite of passage for UN diplomats to find their first opportunity to flaunt their French confidently.

That French represents cool in quarters all over the world is shown by the odd case of the organization known as the Organisation Internationale de la Francophonie. Founded in 1970, the club was meant to tie together France's former colonies, as well as other French-speaking countries such as Belgium and Switzerland. The organization does little, meeting only once every two years. But the fact of its existence—and its unofficial leadership by France, the anti-America in the eyes of many countries around the world—has made its membership expand in surprising directions. Francophonie doesn't require members to have large French-speaking populations, merely affiliation to French culture. So the fifty-six members include territories where French is nearly universal (Canada/Quebec); where French is one of several main languages (Switzerland); where French is official (Senegal); and where French is common among the educated (Lebanon, Morocco). But it also includes countries with virtually no discernible link to French language or culture. Whatever "Francophonie" is, apparently it includes Albania, Bulgaria, Greece, Macedonia, Ghana, and Egypt. Many of these countries have joined in the past twenty years, another sign that Brand France and the French language are alive and well.

French is an official language of thirty-nine countries, second in the world only to English with seventy-three, but well ahead of the next competitors, Arabic (twenty-five) and Spanish (twenty-one). Countries like Nigeria—never colonized by France—have considered making French an official language for geopolitical reasons. And as mentioned earlier, France is the world's second second language, a lingua franca for people around the world who don't share a first language and can't or won't speak English. Unlike Arabic or Spanish, it isn't concentrated but truly global, spoken by native speakers on six continents. French is the official language of (French ex-colonies) French Guyana in South America, New Caledonia in the South Pacific, a slew of countries across Africa, and a massive province that could one day be a country, Quebec, not to mention its European heartland, where it is official in France, Belgium, Luxembourg, Switzerland, and Monaco.

In other words, the notion that France is threatened should be treated more with a light laugh than with alarm. Perhaps the best reaction was that of Anthony Steen, a Conservative member of the British Parliament, after the introduction of the Toubon Law. Steen introduced a bill authorizing traffic wardens to fine people on British streets £10 on the spot for speaking French. Steen described the situation ominously:

Mr Toubon's Bill tears up completely the entente cordiale which was signed by Edward VII on 8 April 1904 at the end of 100 years of hostilities between the French and the English. . . . Every country in the European Community is proud of its status as a nation state, but the French have tipped the scales towards chauvinism.

His real attitude soon became clear:

We should forget words like baguette or croissant—they are out. We would not be able to visit a café or brasserie. There would be no aperitifs or hors d'oeuvres—in fact there would be no restaurants. We should forget the table d'hôte; there is no question of the à la carte instead. There would be no left- or right-hand side of the menu and no nouvelle cuisine. Bon viveurs would be banned. One would not be able to shower one's fiancée with bouquets, meet at a secret rendezvous, or buy her haute couture clothes. There would be great difficulties in having a ménage-à-trois. Crime passionel would be out of the question and negligée would make a liaison dangereuse a little risqué.

After another member cried out "guillotine him!" Steen's fines-for-French measure was duly put to a vote and rejected, 149–45.

By whatever measure—countries where they are official, number of first-language speakers, number of second-language speakers, volume of written publications, or the slipperier quantity we might call simply prestige—English is the most successful language on Earth, and French is the only other with a global reach in the same league, despite the fact that other languages have more native speakers. Mandarin Chinese is spoken by more people as a first language than any other tongue on Earth. Hindi's first-language speakers outnumber English's. Will we not all one day be speaking Chinese? Should we not all maybe dust off that Hindi book, too?

Not so fast. To be sure, those Upper East Side parents in Manhattan who have looked high and low for Mandarin-speaking nannies for their children haven't gotten a bad idea into their heads. As we saw above, bilingualism is good for our brains regardless. And speaking the difficult (for English-speakers) language of a crucial rising power is a very good idea indeed.

But the idea that since China is rising, Chinese might even come to rival English is based on false premises. The amount of Chinese is growing on the Internet, for example, because China's billion-plus population is gradually going online. But this trend cannot, obviously, go on forever. The really relevant question is how many *non*-Chinese communicate in Chinese on the Internet. The number is doubtless tiny; Chinese's dreadfully difficult orthographic system, described in the last chapter, requires years and years of study for native speakers and is harder still for nonnatives. English's predominance, not only on the Internet but in all forms of international written media, is unchallenged.

It is in this sense alone that French is challenged: not in France, not French people's right and ability to speak and write in their language, but French's role as a global standard. For better or worse, English's advantages are locked in by the fact that so many people have already learned it. To replace it would take a tremendous shift. France is healthy; English is dominant. It is most other languages that have cause for concern.

But Americans somehow worry that their language is threatened in its superpower bastion, the United States. And the French had to pass one of the world's most restrictive language laws to protect French in France. What is going on?

The rise of immigration and globalization have hit both countries at awkward times. France's diplomatic importance, role at the United Nations, and unquestioned leadership in the European Union mean relatively less in the face of the spectacular economic (if not yet political) rise of Asia. And though America's dominance looks set to last a while, the challenge from China and the post–September 11 prominence of Islamic terrorism have made the giant unusually uneasy.

Once again we see that arguments about language are usually arguments about politics, disguised and channeled through one of our most distinctive markers of identity. America longs for an overwhelmingly "Anglo-Protestant" model that never existed in the form in which most people imagine it. The French dominance of continental Europe and much of the world is a recent memory and a source of nostalgia. Both countries are challenged from without by globalization and from within by immigration and the struggle to create a new meaning for "American" and "French." Their challenges are not the same—France is the prototypical "nation-state," while America has long been peopled by recent immigrants and their children. But France and America are nonetheless more similar than they appear on the surface. That many proud Frenchmen and Americans would bristle at the comparison only makes it, to my mind, truer.

Clouds, Not Boxes

And Other Better Ways
of Thinking
About Language

*Human mental identities are not like shoes, of which we
can only wear one pair at a time. We are all multi-dimen-
sional beings. Whether a Mr. Patel in London will think
of himself primarily as an Indian, a British citizen, a
Hindu, a Gujarati-speaker, an ex-colonist from Kenya, a
member of a specific caste or kin-group, or in some other
capacity depends on whether he faces an immigration of-
ficer, a Pakistani, a Sikh or Moslem, a Bengali-speaker,
and so on. There is no single platonic essence of Patel. He
is all these and more at the same time.*

—ERIC HOBSBAWM

Steven Pinker, in his book *The Stuff of Thought,* has a fascinating chapter about metaphors. "The Metaphor Metaphor" is about cognition itself: some people think that to think
is to think in metaphors or that metaphorical thinking is a
metaphor for thought. It is a powerful idea. He begins with the
famous first paragraph of the Declaration of Independence and
finds it rife with metaphors: to "dissolve . . . the bands which
have connected them with another" is a metaphor: *alliances
are bonds.* "The course of human events" contains the
metaphor that *a sequence of events is motion along a pathway.*
"Independent" meant originally "not hanging from" (think of

a "pendant," which hangs). This relies on the metaphor *reliance is being supported*. And so on.

Pinker's trick was to identify metaphors that most readers did not even see as such. Language, through natural evolution, recruits metaphors from the concrete world to represent abstract ideas. When the first political bonds began to form, there was no previously existing need for the word "independence," so someone had to coin it from the idea of physically hanging from something else. Over time, metaphors become worn out and dull until they are no longer seen as metaphors. Did you ever realize that "behind" came from a bodily metaphor meaning "near your hindquarters"? So much of language develops this way that the linguist Guy Deutscher refers to language itself as "a reef of dead metaphors" (itself a vivid metaphor).

Metaphors can be powerful enough to affect our thinking, which is why they can be the subject of fierce efforts to control them. Pinker has debated bitterly with another linguist, George Lakoff, about the role of metaphors in politics. Lakoff, as we saw in chapter 4, thinks Republicans "out-frame" Democrats, by, for example, rebranding "estate taxes" as "death taxes." When you think of an "estate," you think of a wealthy patriarch: his lands, stocks, bonds, and antique furniture. To haul off a few grandfather clocks and bottles of thousand-dollar Bordeaux and sell them for the commonweal before his spoiled kids get the rest seems little more than common decency. But death is the tragic fate that awaits us all, after we watch many of our loved ones die. The phrase "death tax" conjures up the gray-faced IRS man showing up at your dead grandmother's bedside, hounding you to write a check through your tears. These two utterly different visions are framings of the exact same (fairly abstract) public policy. He who wins the framing war, Lakoff thinks, wins the political war.

Pinker, for his part, thinks this goes far too far. Lakoff tries his hand at a few novel, Democrat-friendly coinages, such as calling taxes "membership fees." Pinker sees this framing as unlikely to succeed. But he doesn't disagree that metaphors are hugely powerful. If you think your love is "a red, red rose," as Robert Burns did, you are likely to behave differently from Pat Benatar, who sang "Love is a battlefield."

In thinking about languages themselves, most people succumb to a simple vision that might be called languages-as-boxes. Just as boxes have a rigid geometrical shape, people want a language to have one rigid, supposedly perfectly "logical" variety: the correct one handed down in prescriptive dictionaries and grammars. Moreover, people also want or expect those boxes to correspond exactly with national boundaries. Only *one* variety of *one* language called German should be the language of *exactly one* country called Germany, which should include *all and only* German-speakers; and so on for Italians, French, and so forth. One crucial step to realizing the boxes metaphor in the real world is to create "nation-states," largely achieved in Europe but elusive in most of the rest of the world. The other step is to standardize the language so that everyone within their borders speaks the same dialect; variation is to be scorned, as against unity and patriotism, against the nation itself. This metaphor is taught, overtly or tacitly, to children in schools when they are told to stop speaking their Alsatian/ Cajun/Scots/Ebonics and start speaking the "real" language, the only one worthy of the name and the one that defines the society the children live in.

In the language-as-boxes metaphor, people would walk cleanly across a border from one country to another, from one box to another, and the language would change as abruptly and neatly as the uniforms on the border guards. *"Wo ist der Bahnhof?"* ("Where is the train station?") in Germany would neatly become *"Où est la gare?"* in France, just as the German black-red-gold flag gives way to the French tricolor.

But language doesn't work that way. As we saw in the last chapter, if you crossed from Germany into France through Alsace, you would hear distinctive local varieties of German and French on the street, even if standard French and German ruled the airwaves and the newsstands. This kind of border isn't an anomaly but is found all around the world, whether in the Dutch-like "low German" spoken in northwestern Germany near the Dutch border; the Spanish-Portuguese hybrid Portuñol spoken on the border between Uruguay and Brazil; the Galician spoken in northwestern Spain, which is almost identical to the Portuguese just to the south; and so on at blurred boundaries around the world. The box metaphor is a dud.

A better metaphor, though it isn't perfect, is clouds. Clouds move in space and shift in shape over time. So it is with languages as well, which move around the map over time, changing in form, sometimes breaking apart, sometimes joining together. We may want to see rigid boxes, but the reality is clouds.

Think of the famous American political notion of red states and blue states. The map of U.S. elections typically shows two bright hues, fifty big chunks that are either one or the other, giving rise to the political fiction that every family in Texas lovingly polishes a picture of George W. Bush hung just under the shotgun over the mantelpiece and every family in California sleeps with a picture of Barack Obama under the pillows of their same-sex conjugal beds.

American politics as boxes.

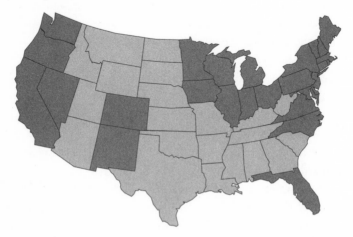

The reality is not only truer but more interesting. A better map is both more granular—looking at county levels rather than states—and more fine-tuned, looking at the intensity of preference for one party or another, rather than coloring a 51 percent "red" territory just as red as an 80 percent "red" territory.

American politics as clouds. *Source:* Mark Newman, University of Michigan, www.personal.umich.edu/~mejn/election/2008

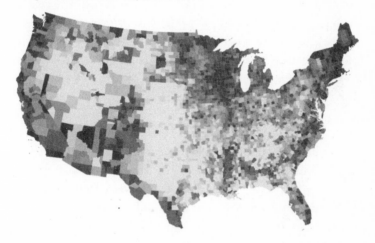

At this level, we see Dallas, Houston, Austin, San Antonio, and the heavily Latino borderlands in Texas voting for Barack Obama. We see a red streak that runs through the heart of California's Central Valley. We see many other features too: the Democratic-friendly African-American belt of counties running through the Deep South; the way counties on the Mississippi River voted Obama while those in the Appalachians voted for John McCain, and so forth. This is the real world; not red states and blue states but mostly purple towns and communities and ultimately real human beings.

A map of the world by language, if such a thing were possible, would be equally complex and utterly fascinating. It would also destroy our notion of monolingual nations. The average country (by simple mathematical mean) is home to forty-four languages, far more than most people would guess. Of course, these are unequally distributed—New Guinea has more than a thousand, and Iceland has just one (though even without native linguistic minorities, nearly all Icelanders are multilingual). But nonetheless, even in continental Europe, the home of the nation-state, the linguistically pure state is nonexistent.

So the first step toward peace and happiness in thinking about language is an acceptance of the actual reality, however much people would like it to be otherwise. The world is a mess, linguistically. Monolingual states are almost nowhere to be found. The world of language isn't a collection of neat boxes but a mass of overlapping clouds. How, then, can we keep our sanity amid this messy reality?

We can do so by finding a better metaphor for thinking about "good" and "bad," "right" and "wrong" in language, to understand why prescriptivists and descriptivists can both have a point, how both can love language, and why there needn't be an all-out winner in the grammar wars. Prescriptivists see language as law. There are statute books (the grammar and dictionary), and in a perfect world there should be punishments for breaking the rules. Thou shalt not kill, thou shalt not shoplift, and thou shalt not split an infinitive. Many sticklers "fondly" recall a nun's ruler on the back of the hand after making some trivial grammar mistake—as if this were any decent way to learn to use this most delightful human faculty.

If you think about it for just a moment, law as a metaphor for language is grossly inapt. Laws are made to prevent people from hurting one another in a chaotic and competitive world. Language—slander and "fire in a crowded theater" aside—is not a means of hurting other people. It is human expression itself. It is the spontaneous composition of thought and emotion through speech and the slightly more considered composition of the same things through writing. Language is not law; it is in fact a lot like music. Speech is jazz—first you learn the basic rules, and then you become good enough to improvise all the time. Writing is somewhat more like classical composition, where established forms and traditions will hold greater sway. But nobody sought to punish Franz Liszt for using Hungarian folk songs in his compositions, nor to put Jimi Hendrix in jail for playing "The Star-Spangled Banner" on his guitar (though Jimi did spark indignation). We need to put away the idea that someone speaking a way we don't like is some kind of offense against the public order.

But in the prescriptivism-versus-descriptivism battle another metaphor may be handy, too: remember Lynne Truss in chapter 2 saying that punctuation was like traffic signals—use the wrong ones, and you get a pileup or everyone ends up lost. In a way, the prescriptive-versus-descriptive combat is a fake one, because descriptive linguists certainly accept the existence of rules. Especially in writing, conventions dictate certain forms of organization, grammar, spelling, mechanics, and so on. They also happen to be fantastically useful, giving rise to the written culture that is the bedrock of modern civilization. I have yet to find a descriptive academic linguist who wants to do away with rules.

Of course, descriptive linguists decry some of the most baseless rules—not splitting the infinitive and so on. But this is because they have been ignored by the majority of English-speakers in the main throughout the history of good English writing. In this case, let us borrow another metaphor: descriptivism is like common law, which works on precedent and accumulates slowly over time. Prescriptivism is an authoritarian version of code law, which says precedent be damned: if the rule book says this is the law, that's that.

If we accept that language is more like music or traffic rules—a set of conventions, which can be violated harmlessly in most cases (music, most like speech) or which are best observed most of the time (traffic rules, most like writing)—we realize that we have been tearing our hair out over nothing in the language wars. Accept that speech and writing are different;

that some situations call for highly formal and rigid styles and some call for innovation and rules-be-damned daring; accept that every country houses people who speak different dialects or even languages; that even speakers of the same dialect speak differently; that it has been this way throughout human history and always will be; and some of the anger and urgency will come out of our language debates. Relax, everyone. Language is too enjoyable to get so angry about it.

Returning to the question of nationalism, though, is it so bad that people seek to belong to a nation and look for language to serve as a mark of belonging? After all, if nationalism has caused so many wars, and if language has been a touchstone of nationalism, shouldn't we get rid of the idea of standard languages so that this bloody thing called nationalism can stop plaguing the planet?

This is one question where I have more sympathy with traditionalists and less with linguists, who tend toward the antinationalist Left. Writers such as Eric Hobsbawm, the Marxist historian famous for coining the "invention of tradition," and Ernest Gellner (an anti-communist, incidentally), whose industrialist theories of nationalism we saw earlier, may have come up with utilitarian explanations of nationalism. (In Hobsbawm's case, conscious manipulation by the ruling classes; in Gellner's case, the demands of industrial society.) They may even have found some kernel of truth. But they, like other social scientists and many linguists as well, are too quick to dismiss nationalism (and the language-building that is part of it) as a cynical tool of manipulative leaders. The fact that masses do embrace nationalism so enthusiastically should tell us something, and not just that people are easily misled.

People like to belong to groups. It is very likely part of our genetic makeup to identify with, and seek to support and protect, others like ourselves. People who look like us, for example, are likely to share our genes, and thus it makes a certain kind of sense to stand with them, making it more likely that the shared genes will be passed on. Nationalism works because it harnesses a feeling that has existed throughout human history—group identity and solidarity—only it drew that "group" as a larger circle, making it the nation rather than the family, village, or clan.

And there is nothing inherently wrong with that. As Europe moved from the dark ages to modernity, a unit bigger than the village or region made sense, even if only for economic reasons. The state system was born, and with it flags, anthems, passports, borders, customs, the Olympics, the Eurovision song contest, and 192 member states of the United Nations. Semiartificial or not, nationalism and longing for a nation-state are facts of modern life that many people are quite happy with. The nation is a pretty reasonable way to organize people.

The fault of nationalists—among them linguistic nationalists—is in thinking of the nation to the exclusion of all other identities, both bigger and smaller. For nationalists today, there are two enemies. The first is the domestic separatist, who claims his "Basque Country" or "Kurdistan" is a real nation worthy of a separate existence, just as real as the obviously important "Spain" or "Turkey." The second is the muddle-headed idealist who believes in bigger identities: Europe, the Islamic world community or, God forbid, the United Nations or the community of humankind.

In 2009, Newt Gingrich, the Republican former Speaker of the House of Representatives, attacked the latter view in a speech aimed at Barack Obama. Obama had addressed the Islamic world from Berlin in 2008, saying he was "a proud citizen of the United States and a fellow citizen of the world." Gingrich said a year later, "I am not a citizen of the world. I think the entire concept is intellectual nonsense and stunningly dangerous."

Never mind that every Republican's favorite modern president, Ronald Reagan, had pronounced himself a "citizen of the world" in 1982. What was Gingrich thinking? That citizenship had an upper boundary in the levels of hierarchy? Or that citizenship had only one level to begin with? Would he have denied, while in Congress, that he was a citizen of the state of Georgia? Of the city of Marietta, where I also hail from? And if he is a citizen of Marietta, of Georgia, and of the United States, how is he not also a citizen of the world?

There is nothing obvious about limiting loyalty to the nation alone. The quotation by Hobsbawm that begins this chapter sums up the problem eloquently. "We are all multidimensional beings." Another point made by Hobsbawm's Mr. Patel is that nationalism limits people to not only one vertical level of loyalty (the nation, as opposed to the region or the world) but to one horizontal sphere (nation versus religion, caste, or other group).

The problem is exclusivity; the solution is flexibility. I am a rabid Georgia Bulldogs football fan, and I pull for my team to beat anybody they play. But when Georgia isn't playing Georgia Tech, I pull for Tech, since they're from Atlanta. And if Florida, the hated regional rival, is playing in the national championship, I grit my teeth and pull for them: better a southeastern team than, say, Ohio State. As Hobsbawm saw, it's all about context.

Language works the same way. The traditional, prescriptive, nationalist view holds that there is only one correct variety of the language you speak, and you should speak it virtually all the time. But I speak a southern-accented English with a certain grammar and diction—plenty of "ain't"—with my family in the South. I speak a neutral American semiformal English at my office in New York. I find myself replacing "elevator" with "lift" and "line" with "queue" when I go to England. And I speak French in France and German in Germany, and whatever I can get by with when I don't know the native language of the country I'm in. None of them is the "real" or "right" me; different varieties are situationally appropriate, or they're not. Breaking the law doesn't come into it. It's a matter of feel and taste. (Sometimes, like most people, I get it wrong.)

My father used to tell this old joke:

A Georgia student visiting Harvard asks a passing student, "Excuse me, can you tell me where the library's at?" The Harvard man says, "Here at Harvard, we do not end a sentence with a preposition." The Georgia boy thinks for a second and tries again: "Sorry, can you tell me where the library's at, *asshole*?"

I love this joke for two reasons. First, though I'm among the few nerds who would care, it exposes the Harvard man's pedantry for what it is: a memorized superstition ("Don't end a sentence with a preposition") masquerading for a real, if unfounded, rule that he doesn't really know or understand ("Prepositions should come before the words they relate to and not at the end of clauses"). The Georgia boy wins by being just as superficial: if I can't end a sentence in a preposition, why not just add another word?

But the real joke is this: the Harvard show-off really is being an asshole. To reply to an honest question that is perfectly understood with grammatical outrage is a sin against decency. It shows that the stuck-up Ivy League man is really grasping, insisting on the letter of the law rather than taking the casual syntax of the Georgia student as a gesture of friendliness and solidarity. The joke isn't that Georgia boys are dumb but that Harvard assholes don't know when to insist on the rules. (The linguist's bonus joke is that the rule is stupid anyway.)

Before we leave nationalism and the modern nation-state, we have to think about one more painful question. The world has about six thousand languages in it. In a century, according to many projections, about half of those will be extinct. According to more pessimistic forecasts, just six hundred of the six thousand will survive.

We have seen a few threatened languages in this book. Tuyuca, the language we met that has "evidentiality," for example, is spoken by a tiny number of Indians in the Amazon.

As such regions develop, more and more languages will go. Linguists point to fascinating features such as evidentiality to argue that losing languages means losing a precious resource: a valuable insight into how human language can work and, with it, insights into our brains themselves.

Some linguists even compare the importance of linguistic diversity with the importance of biodiversity. And some take the comparison quite literally: natural habitats are destroyed when native cultures are destroyed, and vice versa. Daniel Nettle and Suzanne Romaine argue that these "primitive" cultures include invaluable knowledge about the plants and animals in the ecosystem surrounding them. Destroying those cultures and their languages could mean missing out on a host of scientific knowledge, including potential treatments for human ailments.

For the linguist, the need to preserve nearly all the world's languages is virtually an article of faith. But it is often forgotten that linguistic diversity, unlike biodiversity, comes with a cost. Most obviously, people who speak differently are more likely to distrust one another. And when they speak totally different languages, they tend to try to become exclusive nation-

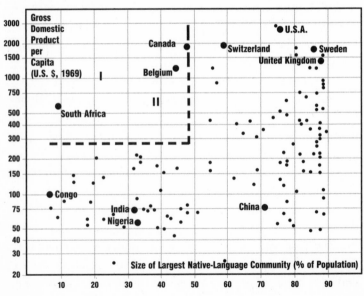

states, often getting into zero-sum competitions for land, resources, and population and even going to war.

But another cost is more literal. Countries where many languages are spoken widely tend to be poorer than countries where one or a few languages dominate. One of the first studies to find this (from 1969) simply plotted GDP per capita against the size of the largest single language group.

Countries dominated by a single language can be poor (Bhutan, Yemen) or rich (Norway, Sweden). And poor countries range from highly monolingual (Haiti) to highly plurilingual (Congo). But one finding was striking: no highly multilingual country was rich. The closest examples were Belgium and South Africa, and both were oddities. Belgium, a semiartificial creation of the European great powers in 1830, is roughly half French-speaking and half Dutch-speaking. The two halves are so independent and so mutually antagonistic that in 2008 a lengthy political crisis had commentators wondering whether the country would survive or split into two. And South Africa in 1969, of course, was dominated by two imported languages, while most blacks spoke an African language at home. South Africa's 1969 wealth per capita figure concealed the fact that nearly all the wealth belonged to the members of the white minority who spoke English or Afrikaans as their mother tongue.

A follow-up study in 2000 found much the same: the greater the percentage of people who spoke the country's biggest language, the richer, on average, a country was. Few linguistically fragmented countries make it to the richest tier. Moreover, linguistic fragmentation was even more strongly correlated with shorter human life spans than with poverty.

This finding has to be interpreted carefully. It may mean two very different things, or it may mean nothing at all. One possibility is that multilingualism hampers development. But this does not seem obviously to be the case. Belgium here is instructive. Novel political engineering—in Belgium's case, devolving a lot of power to local regions rather than concentrating it all in the national capital, can mean that a linguistically divided country can prosper. Switzerland—where the biggest language (German) is spoken by only about two-thirds of the people and four languages are official—is even richer. It too prospers without language conflict. A big reason is probably its Belgian-like devolution of power to its twenty-odd cantons (the units of local government), with few powers restricted to the national government in Bern.

The causation may in fact run the other way: economic development may decrease language diversity. We have seen France, over its past few hundred years, developing into a powerful, prosperous, centralized modern state, and we have also seen the squeezing out of non-French languages. Do we see this elsewhere? Do states get more monolingual as a natural part of modernization?

One 1974 study looked at countries over time and claims to find no evidence of this. But we really don't have enough data over the time frames we would need. There are few premodern linguistic censuses out there—who really has good data on who spoke what language in Zambia in 1500?—providing the information we would need to test this hypothesis. Such data would be limited geographically to the developed and Western world, not to mention the fact that some states— like most in Africa—came into being as a result of imperialist boundary drawing, while others—like those in Europe—came into existence as products of homegrown nationalism. It's hardly any surprise that African countries are both poor and multilingual, but this doesn't mean that their linguistic diversity caused their poverty or vice versa.

So the short version is that we may never know if economic development pushes countries to become linguistically more homogenized. At the very least, we won't know for some time. However, those who study dying languages work as if they knew this to be true: development kills languages. As countries get richer, people move to the cities, put their kids in school, and adopt habits such as newspaper reading and so forth that all put the squeeze on tiny languages: those least likely to be supported by urban concentration, education, or media.

The dilemma is that these habits (education, reading newspapers, etc.) are also usually considered to be good things. Those linguists racing to save dying languages—urging villagers to raise their children in the small and threatened language rather than the bigger national language—face criticism that they are unintentionally helping keep people impoverished by encouraging them to stay in a small-language ghetto.

Can there be any compromise between the imperatives of development and the desire to save beautiful and fascinating small languages? Only partially. Not all languages can be saved; not even the most hopeful linguist thinks so. Those that can indeed be saved are those whose speakers have the wealth, numbers, and geographic concentration to be viable as semi-self-contained communities.

There are a few modern examples. Wales is part of a political unit, the United Kingdom, where the dominant language is also the most important language on Earth. Yet improbably enough, the number of speakers of Welsh, once thought moribund, has not only stabilized but grown. Welsh cultural nationalism benefits from the fact that Welsh-speakers are concentrated geographically, belong to a modern polity that politely blesses Welsh revival, and are rich enough to afford bilingualism: the teaching of Welsh in school, where children might be spending those class hours on another subject.

Ireland has made the same decisions, with roughly the same success. Irish is co-official with English in the republic, and students are required to study it for years in school. Though few people speak Irish fluently, fewer speak it natively, and no one is monolingual in Irish, the language is no longer on life support. And remember that the Irish even successfully insisted on making Irish an official language of the European Union. When it did, many non-Irish Europeans may have balked at the new cost of €3.5 million (about $4.5 million), needed to translate all new EU documents into Irish. But the European Union sucked it up, all in the name of diversity.

Wales, Ireland, and the European Union pull this off because they are already rich democracies. They can afford to. The same applies to many other tiny languages in Europe, whether Letzeburgesch, Frisian, or Sami. But what of a small tribal language in a poor country that is threatened by the new factory, mine, or oil rig that has recently come to the region, which might bring, along with jobs, the need to learn a bigger regional or national language? Only communities with the size, concentration, and wealth to be economically secure can also guarantee the future of their language. Saving every language is not possible.

So how do we save as many as we can, while not sacrificing poor peoples' right and need to grow richer? The challenge, essentially, is to jump on the right side of the line in the graph on page 270, to flatten it out a bit—to lessen the trade-off between language diversity and economic prosperity. The examples of our rich democracies—and a few developing ones—show how that might happen.

The short answer is multilingualism. Again, the few rich and middle-income countries where no language dominates are instructive. Why are they outliers? Partly because they are chockablock with polyglots. Most people in Belgium learn both French and Dutch, not to mention a third language (usually English). The same goes for Switzerland, where whatever the first language, students learn another national language (French, German, or Italian) plus English. Multilingualism removes the trade-off between diversity and economic efficiency. If people can't talk to one another, larger and more efficient economic networks can't grow. If they learn multiple languages, they can develop economically without crushing cultural homogenization as a side effect.

If we want to preserve both diversity and development, there is no way around the need for more people to learn more languages. India is one poor but growing country that has shown a way. It educates small children in one of dozens of local languages, teaches bigger regional languages as the children advance, and teaches Hindi to as many students as can learn it (with the goal that Hindi be the national language) and English to all those who need it for advanced study. This is the ideal and certainly doesn't pertain everywhere—many local languages are not in fact preserved by teaching in school, and many regions have resisted Hindi. But the model, at least, is one to admire. It combines the virtues of diversity (protecting the little languages), nationalism (promoting Hindi), and economic internationalism (English).

In the course of writing this book, I asked dozens of people in casual encounters which languages they spoke and how they felt about them. One was Miguel, whom I chatted up while on a train into Paris. Miguel, who works for a wind-power company, is from Barcelona, and his first language is Catalan. But he also speaks Spanish, German, and English, as well as decent French. I tried to draw out any Catalan nationalism in him— many Catalans are famously insistent on using their language, and some are known to say they come not from Spain but from Catalonia. But Miguel wouldn't bite. Pragmatically, he knew all the languages that he needed to, and was happy with the room each one took up in his life. When I brought up Franco's repression of Catalan, he shrugged and said, "That was a long time ago." (He looked as if he had been born about the time Franco died.) More revealing was his attitude toward the European Union, of which he was a big fan. Europe has given minority nations such as Catalonia the multitiered identity that is the best hope for solving language conflict: Miguel was Catalan, Spanish, European, and internationalist, all at the same time, and so calmly so that he hadn't even really thought about it. He seemed to find my eager questions kind of odd. Europe has made such diversity and flexibility banal. It may be expensive, but it works.

- - - - - - - - - - - -

Accepting diversity isn't just a matter of accepting minority languages. Remembering how much "correctness" was invented recently, recalling the debates of sticklers versus scholars, and keeping in mind the controversies of Ebonics and "diglossia" in other parts of the world, it is clear that diversity means far more than multiple languages in passports or on street signs. It means acceptance that language is not a single law code but a human behavior that varies from place to place and situation to situation.

Cases of "diglossia," the situation where two varieties of a language coexist, typically one with "high" and one with "low" functions, include standard versus dialectal Arabic, standard versus Swiss German, and *katharévousa* versus *dhimotiki* Greek. In the Greek case, the diglossia is disappearing over time with the triumph of *dhimotiki*. In the Arabic case, many Arabs remain unhappy that the language they speak every day isn't a "real" language like the standard Arabic of books and newspapers. Many endure a feeling of distance from written culture and nagging linguistic insecurity. This is an ironic result of extremely successful prescriptivism: the standard language was frozen by prestigious grammar codifiers, but the spoken language moved so far along that a thousand years later, writing and speaking require two different languages. (English and French prescriptivists, take note: this is what "success" looks like in the long run. You can freeze writing, but you will never be able to freeze speech.)

But the Swiss case is far happier. The German-speaking Swiss vary effortlessly from the Swiss German of their town or region—used to talk with friends at the beer garden or family at the dinner table—and High German, used to deal with international colleagues, give a lecture, or debate in parliament. Again, variety and adaptability are so commonly accepted that most people don't even think about it most of the time. Nobody is told to stop speaking that gutter German and start speaking "real" German. The Swiss like their local Germans, and they find High German useful too.

This is how we should think about correctness in every language. Black English isn't a broken, rule-free mess. It's a rule-bound dialect of English, with intermediate steps between a relatively pure form of Black English and standard written English. Why don't we just call it diglossia? Accept that there is one language for the barbershop or the hip-hop record and another for high-school economics class and job applications? That one is mainly spoken, for solidarity and joking with friends and family, and the other is more formal, for wider communication and the business meeting? Why can't what works for Bern and Basel work in Brooklyn and the Bronx? The excuse that "we can't afford so many languages" is belied by Switzerland, one of the most prosperous countries on Earth.

The only thing between us in the United States and that happy future is a difficult-to-make change in attitude. Even many black leaders, including many who proudly support the idea of a unique black identity, frown on "Ebonics." Bill Cosby has said:

> I can't even talk the way these people talk—"why you ain't," "where you is"? I don't even know who these people are. And I blamed the kid until I heard the mother talk, and then I heard the father talk. . . . Everybody knows it's important to speak English except for these knuckleheads.

In a similar vein, Malcolm X described his early self-education in prison, copying words out of a dictionary to improve his handwriting and vocabulary. He said that when learning to read and write standard English, alongside coming to Islam, he felt that "I had never been so truly free in my life," even behind bars. No more of what he called "slang"—we would now call it Black English—for the burgeoning black separatist.

Fortunately, modern linguistics has taught us better. Different dialects and registers can and should happily coexist. That goes for southern American English, Glaswegian, Valley Girl, Surfer Dude, and any other variety you can think of. It's a staple of comedy that language-deprived kids can barely communicate because they don't use the grammar and larger vocabulary of standard English. In the movie *Baseketball,* Trey Parker and Matt Stone (the creators of the *South Park* TV series), two friends undergoing the movie's goofy third-act crisis, carry on the following conversation:

COOP: I'm not gonna do it, dude, end of story!

REEMER: Dude!

COOP: Dude!

REEMER: Dude!

COOP: Dude!

REEMER: Dude!

REEMER: Dude.

COOP: I guess you have a point.

Language is a lot more robust and flexible than people think. Making an argument with different intonations of the word *dude* wouldn't be right for the House of Lords. But it has its time and place.

Most people learn from the schoolteacher and seek to teach their children some version of "These are the *rules,* and rules are made to be observed without exception." What we really should think, and teach our children, is "There is a set of standard conventions everyone needs for formal writing and speaking. Except under unusual circumstances, you should use the grammar and vocabulary of standard written English for those purposes."

But the corollary of that must be "I don't care how you talk on the playground: in broad Scots or Black English—or even Spanish, Vietnamese, or Cajun." Do we truly want to lose these languages and dialects? To have everyone in the English-speaking world speak exactly the same way? Think of America's literary heritage without Mark Twain or Uncle Remus. Mentally replace the Glaswegian of the junkies in the movie *Trainspotting* with the English of Connecticut. Think of Louis Armstrong singing Duke Ellington's "It doesn't mean a thing / if you don't have that swing." In this world of homogenization—everyone speaking one standard language the same way, all the time—are we richer or better off? Not at all.

A truly enlightened attitude to language should simply be to let six thousand or more flowers bloom. Subcultures should be allowed to thrive, not just because it is wrong to squash them, because they enrich the wider culture. Just as Black English has left its mark on standard English culture, South Africans take pride in the marks of Afrikaans and African languages on their vocabulary and syntax. New Zealand's rugby team chants in Maori, dancing a traditional dance, before matches. French kids flirt with rebellion by using *verlan,* a slang that reverses words' sounds or syllables (so *femme* becomes *meuf*). Argentines glory in *lunfardo,* an argot developed from the underworld a century ago that makes Argentine Spanish unique still today. The nonstandard greeting "Where y'at?" for "How are you?" is so common among certain whites in New Orleans that they bear their difference with pride, calling themselves Yats. And that's how it should be.

Of course we could do without these, but do we want to? Even McDonald's tailors its menus around the world. You can buy a McLobster in Maine, a Maharaja Mac in Mumbai. Coca-Cola makes drinks from guaraná in Brazil and lychee in China. Do the defenders of "pure" language want even more dull homogeneity than that provided by those supposedly culture-destroying forces, McDonald's and Coke? No one who claims to love language should spend too much time trying to rid it of its endless, fascinating diversity. Doing so is not right and not needed. Worse, it's not a lot of fun.

ACKNOWLEDGMENTS

This book was a mess in my head until I sat down to write a proposal; Tanner Colby, with a better eye than mine for what people might find interesting, made it a sharper one and then introduced me to Peter McGuigan, the best agent possible to represent it. Peter got it from day one, and did a brilliant job finding Danielle Perez at Bantam, who got it too. The two of them and the talented and tireless Kerri Buckley made this a much better book than it otherwise would have been. Hannah Brown Gordon and Stéphanie Abou of Foundry also provided invaluable support. And I am grateful to my boss, John Micklethwait, for the time off from *The Economist* during which I wrote this. Some of the material appeared in different form in the pages of that publication.

Numerous friends and experts read chapters, catching errors and infelicities: İlker Aytürk, Robert Greenberg, Prashant Keshavmurthy, Parag Khanna, Victor Mair, Prune Perromat, Don Ringe, and Ann Senghas. Stewart James-Lejárcegui gave a particularly sharp and helpful read of the whole thing. Bill Poser answered questions about China and Japan, as did Mohamed Maamouri about Arabic, and Geoff Pullum has been a lively correspondent over the years. Cameron Sinclair kindly helped organize the notes. The usual disclaimers—that any remaining mistakes are mine, not theirs—apply.

Jean-Mathieu Pasqualini and Joan Martí i Castell let me interview them at length about their beloved languages, French and Catalan, and too many others to mention let me quiz them about how they feel about the languages they speak. Beyond them, I have had more language teachers over many years than I could possibly thank, but I hope the modest efforts in this book might find their way into the hands of a few of my favorites: Thomas Starnes, George Cummins, Almir Bruneti, Ahmed Eissawi, and Karam Tannous.

Three people stand out as having taught me so much about language that when they see their influence on this, I hope they will take it as homage and not larceny. Steven Pinker's writings were responsible for the original "aha" moment when I stopped thinking about languages and started thinking about *language* and wondering if I had anything interesting to say about it. He kindly provided edits and research help. Mark Liberman answered endless questions and provides a free public good in his tireless nonsense-detecting writing at Language Log. Few people keep a cooler head when writing about hot topics. And John McWhorter has helped me more than he signed up for when I shamelessly befriended him. His thinking about language change, languages in contact with one another, and the anguished politics of both has been an obvious influence on mine.

In my own little world, Daniel Arizona made me laugh as we wrote together and kept everything in perspective when I couldn't. The lovely Eva Høier Greene not only was my favorite language teacher, but was also my wife and an outstanding pair of eyes on this work. Her English would be the envy of many natives, and I'm grateful for our late-night editing sessions; her subtle suggestions and pointed questions made this book tighter and smarter than it would have been. I spent less time with my family, including my mother, Sherry, and my son, Jack, than I would like to have while I was getting this done. Jack, Mom, Eva, and you too, Hank: each of you deserves a book, but I know you'll understand why this one's for Dad.

NOTES

CHAPTER 1: BABEL AND THE DAMAGE DONE

8 **"*X* people have no word for":** From Language Log, www.languagelog.com.

9 **"muscatel" and "musk":** *Merriam-Webster's Dictionary,* accessible at www.merriam-webster.com. The *Oxford Concise Dictionary of English Etymology* (Oxford, England: Oxford University Press, 1986) gives a somewhat different explanation for "musk," saying that the Sanskrit *muská,* "scrotum," may have come to cover for "musk" because of the similarity to a deer's musk bag.

12 **"*X* cannot be translated":** Ibid.

13 **"I'm no linguist":** BBC interview of Ronald Reagan by Brian Widlake, October 29, 1985. Full text at the website of the Reagan Library, at www.reagan.utexas.edu/archives/speeches/1985/102985d.htm.

13 **tongues of preliterate or indigenous societies:** In fact, small languages seem to be systematically more complicated than ones spoken by large numbers; see the author's article "Babelicious," *The Economist* online, January 25, 2010, www.economist.com/sciencetechnology/displayStory.cfm?story_id=15384310&source=hptextfeature

14 **Tuyuca encodes this information:** Daniel Nettle and Suzanne Romaine, *Vanishing Voices: The Extinction of the World's Languages* (Oxford, England: Oxford University Press, 2000), pp. 60–61.

Notes

6

CHAPTER 2: A BRIEF HISTORY OF STICKLERS

22 **Thomas Jefferson's apostrophes:** Mark Liberman at Language Log, June 9, 2004, http://itre.cis.upenn.edu/~myl/languagelog/archives/001034.html.

23 **"For we English men":** David Crystal, *The Cambridge Encyclopedia of the English Language* (Cambridge, England: Cambridge University Press, 1995), p. 57. I have put the text into modern English. Note that "mete" in Caxton's text, though it is the source of the modern English "meat," meant simply "food" in his time.

24 **Dryden said he liked to compose:** *Merriam-Webster's Dictionary of English Usage* (Springfield, Mass.: Merriam-Webster, 1994), p. 764.

32 **twenty-one editions in Britain:** Rollo Laverne Lyman, quoted in Charlotte Downey's introduction to *English Grammar* (Ann Arbor, Mich.: Scholars' Facsimiles and Reprints, 1981).

33 **first prohibition against the split infinitive:** Jack Lynch, *The Lexicographer's Dilemma: The Evolution of "Proper" English, from Shakespeare to South Park* (New York: Walker, 2009), p. 97.

34 **one 1931 study:** George Curme, *A Grammar of the English Language,* vol. 2, "Syntax," cited in *Merriam-Webster's Dictionary of English Usage,* p. 867.

35 **"If you do not immediately":** Crystal, *Cambridge Encyclopedia,* p. 195.

36 **Henry Watson Fowler:** Biographical information from Jenny McMorris, *The Warden of English: The Life of H. W. Fowler* (Oxford, England: Oxford University Press, 2001).

39 **10 million copies:** *The Letters of E. B. White,* ed. Dorothy Lobrano Guth (New York: HarperCollins, 2006), p. 368.

42 **"Life as a textbook editor":** Ibid., p. 423.

48 **"At some point":** Cicero, *Orator* 48 [160], available at www.thelatinlibrary.com/cicero/orator.shtml and translated by the blog Sauvage Noble at http://sauvagenoble.blogspot.com/2004/10/scientiam-mihi-reservavi.html.

49 **"In reading carefully":** Quoted in Otto Jespersen, *Language: Its Nature, Development and Origin* (New York: Macmillan, 1922), p. 42. I have rendered Grimm's *altdeutschen* as "Teutonic" rather than Jespersen's "Old Gothonic."

50 **E. B. White was a fine writer:** Geoff Pullum was the original source of this point: that White's excellent writing belies his misguided usage advice.

CHAPTER 3: ANOTHER WAY TO LOVE LANGUAGE

56 **Men talk (on average) slightly more:** Liberman's findings are at http://itre.cis.upenn.edu/~myl/languagelog/archives/003607 .html.

56 **A study published in** *Science:* Matthias Mehl et al., "Are Women Really More Talkative Than Men?," *Science,* July 6, 2007.

56 **Liberman was at it again:** Language Log, http://languagelog.ldc .upenn.edu/nll/?p=1495#more-1495

64 **"this book is too interesting":** Noam Chomsky, *Some Concepts and Consequences of the Theory of Government and Binding* (Cambridge, Mass.: MIT Press, 1982), p. 45.

66 **"The Sanskrit language":** Quoted in Pieter A. M. Seuren, *Western Linguistics: An Historical Introduction* (Oxford, England: Blackwell, 1988), p. 80.

71 **"Behavior alters the environment":** B. F. Skinner, *Verbal Behavior* (Acton, Mass.: Copley, 1957), pp. 1–2.

72 **"A typical example":** Noam Chomsky, "A Review of B. F. Skinner's Verbal Behavior," *Language* 35 (1959): pp. 26–58.

74 **"The very language":** David Foster Wallace, "Tense Present: Democracy, English and the Wars over Usage," *Harper's*, April 2001, pp. 39–58.

74 **"The things mentioned above":** Language Log, http://itre.cis .upenn.edu/~myl/languagelog/archives/000918.html.

80 **Geoffrey Sampson:** "Grammar Without Grammaticality," *Corpus Linguistics and Linguistic Theory* 3 (2007): pp. 1–32.

83 **"They set forward, every one":** This example and others from the King James Bible were assembled by Wayne Lehman at http://englishbibles.blogspot.com/2006/09/singular-they-in-english-bibles.html.

85 **William Labov:** The discussion of New York English that follows is taken from William Labov, *The Social Stratification of English in New York City* (Washington, D.C.: Center for Applied Linguistics, 1966).

87 **"a decade of work":** John Joseph et al., *Landmarks in Linguistic Thought,* vol. 2 (New York: Routledge, 2001), p. 144.

88 **"Por eso cada, you know":** William Labov, " 'System' in Creole Languages," in *Pidginization and Creolization of Languages,* ed. Dell Hymes (Cambridge, England: Cambridge University Press, 1971).

88 **Studies of code switching:** The classic article on this is Shana Poplack, "Sometimes I'll Start a Sentence in Spanish y Termino en Español: Towards a Typology of Code Switching," *Linguistics* 18 (1980): pp. 581–618.

90 **Diglossic pairs include:** Ronald Wardaugh, *Sociolinguistics,* 3rd ed. (Oxford, England: Blackwell, 1998), pp. 87–93, which draws heavily on Charles Ferguson, "Diglossia," the foundational treatment in *Word,* 1959, pp. 325–40.

92 **Words and phrases from *katharévousa:*** Wardaugh, ibid., and Anna Frangoudaki, "Diglossia and the Present Language Situation in Greece: A Sociological Approach to the Interpretation of Diglossia and Some Hypotheses on Today's Linguistic Reality," *Language in Society* 21 (1992): pp. 365–81.

95 **Illiteracy is 40 percent:** Mohamed Maamouri, "Literacy," in *Encyclopedia of Arabic Language and Linguistics* (Leiden: Brill, 2005–2009).

95 **Maamouri relates:** Mohamed Maamouri, "Language Education and Human Development: Arabic Diglossia and Its Impact on the Quality of Education in the Arab Region," paper presented to the World Bank's Mediterranean Development Forum, 1998.

CHAPTER 4: MORE EQUAL THAN OTHERS

101 **"do" has an idiosyncratic function:** John McWhorter explains why this might have arisen in *Our Magnificent Bastard Tongue* (New York: Gotham, 2008).

103 *The New York Times* . . . **rejected several op-eds:** John Rickford, "The Ebonics Controversy in My Backyard: A Sociolinguist's Experiences and Reflections" www.stanford.edu/~rickford/papers/ EbonicsInMyBackyard.html. The linguists included Rickford himself, Geoff Pullum, Salikoko Mufwene, and Gene Searchinger.

103 **bold headlines reading:** Geoffrey Nunberg, "Double Standards," *Natural Language and Linguistic Theory* 14 (1997), pp. 667–75.

104 **it produces apathetic readers:** Maamouri, "Language Education and Human Development."

105 **A child cannot be taught:** "If Black English Isn't a Language, Then Tell Me, What Is?," *The New York Times,* July 29, 1979.

108 **One recent study showed:** Ann Senghas and Marie Coppola, "Children Creating Language: How Nicaraguan Sign Language Acquired a Spatial Grammar," *Psychological Science* 12 (2001), pp. 323–28

109 **"When I shout 'Fire!' ":** Mark Halpern, *Language and Human Nature* (Piscataway, N.J.: Transaction Publishers, 2008), pp. 20–22.

110 **Kwaio:** Roger Keesing, *Kwaio Grammar* (Canberra: Pacific Linguistics, 1985), quoted in John McWhorter, *Language Interrupted* (Cambridge, England: Cambridge University Press, 2007), p. 23.

111 **Russia must envy:** McWhorter, *Language Interrupted,* p. 36.

111 **English has both:** Ibid., p. 23.

113 **"Human beings do not live":** Edward Sapir, "The Status of Linguistics as a Science," *Language* 5 (1929): pp. 207–14.

116 **Russian painters make death female:** Lera Boroditsky, "How Does Our Language Shape the Way We Think?," *Edge,* June 12, 2009, accessed online. Boroditsky cites her papers "Do English and Mandarin Speakers Think Differently About Time?," *Proceedings of the 48th Annual Meeting of the Psychonomic Society* (2007); and "Sex, Syntax and Semantics" in D. Gentner and S. Goldin-Meadow, *Language in Mind: Advances in the Study of Language and Cognition* (Cambridge, Mass.: MIT Press, 2003).

117 **The academic debate over Whorfianism:** Nicholas Evans and Stephen Levinson, "The Myth of Language Universals," was published in *Behavioral and Brain Sciences* (October 2009), reformulating the neo-Whorfian challenge to "universal grammar." Stephen Pinker and Geoff Pullum were among the writers of twenty-five response articles printed along with it.

123 **"becoming sensitive to mere solecisms":** Halpern, *Language and Human Nature,* p. xxvi.

125 **"Not all languages have":** *Le Devoir,* July 2, 2008.

130 **Languages shake off bits and pieces:** Gary Lupyan and Rick Dale, "Language Structure Is Partly Determined by Social Structure," *PLoS ONE* 5 (2010): e8559. doi:10.1371/journal.pone.0008559.

CHAPTER 5: WELCOME TO *X*. NOW SPEAK XISH

131 **You could continue:** This discussion of dialect continua in pre-modern Europe is based on Sue Wright, *Language Policy and Language Planning* (New York: Palgrave, 2004), p. 21.

136 **the 1841 census:** John O'Beirne Ranelagh, *A Short History of Ireland* (Cambridge, England: Cambridge University Press, 1994), p. 118.

138 **Even tyrannies educate their people:** Ernest Gellner, *Nations and Nationalism* (Ithaca, N.Y.: Cornell University Press, 1983); "coal face of nature," p. 33.

139 **"even tailors and shoe-makers":** John Lewis Nuelsen, *Luther: The Leader* (New York: Eaton and Mains, 1906), accessed online at www.archive.org/stream/lutherleader00nuel/lutherleader00nuel_djvu.txt.

140 **German's center of gravity:** *dtv-Atlas zur deutschen Sprache* (Munich: Deutscher Taschenbuch Verlag, 1978), pp. 93–101.

141 **2 or 3 percent of newly minted "Italians":** Eric Hobsbawm, "Language, Culture and National Identity," *Social Research* 63 (1996), p. 1068.

142 **These efforts were sometimes farcical:** Jonathan Fishman, *Do Not Leave Your Language Alone* (Mahwah, N.J.: Lawrence Erlbaum Associates, 2006), pp. 48–49.

142 **Another purist, an overzealous Czech:** George Thomas, *Linguistic Purism* (London: Longmans, 1995), p. 87.

147 **"Then late one night":** From Ben Yehuda's autobiography *A Dream Come True,* quoted in George Mandel, "Resistance to the Study of Hebrew," in *Hebrew Study from Ezra to Ben-Yehuda* (Edinburgh: Horbury, 1999), p. 296.

148 **singing a Russian lullaby:** Mark Abley, *Spoken Here* (Boston: Houghton Mifflin, 2003), p. 231.

149 **the party's sole language:** Bernard Spolsky and Robert Cooper, *The Languages of Jerusalem* (Oxford, England: Clarendon, 1991), p. 59.

150 **it now has a distinctive accent:** Edward Ullendorff, "Hebrew in Mandatary Palestine," in Mandel, *Hebrew Study from Ezra to Ben-Yehuda*, pp. 300–06.

150 **The European backgrounds:** Ibid., p. 303.

150 **Israelis coin mongrel words:** Joel M. Hoffman, *In The Beginning: A Short History of the Hebrew Language* (New York: NYU Press, 2004), p. 201.

150 **"Ben Yehuda would be dismayed":** Ilan Stavans, *Resurrecting Hebrew* (New York: Nextbooks, 2009), p. 96.

150 **"Modern oddities":** Ullendorff, "Hebrew in Mandatary Palestine."

152 **demoting Arabic:** *Forward,* June 12, 2008.

153 **Franco was a centralizer:** Vincent de Melchor Muñoz, *El catalán: una lengua de Europa para compartir* (Barcelona: Universitat Autònoma de Barcelona, 2002), pp. 157–69.

165 **"Hind[ustani] is that language":** Robert D. King, "The Potency of Script: Hindi and Urdu," *International Journal of the Sociology of Language* 150 (2001): pp. 54–56.

166 **"I have no doubt whatsoever":** Robert D. King, *Nehru and the Language Politics of India* (Oxford, England: Oxford University Press, 1997), p. 86.

167 **Many more Pakistanis speak Punjabi:** Hamza Alavi, "Pakistan and Islam: Ethnicity and Ideology," *State and Ideology in the Middle East and Pakistan,* eds. Fred Halliday and Hamza Alavi (New York: Monthly Review Press, 1998), pp. 64–69.

172 **"I was back in Zagreb":** Ibid., Robert Greenberg, *Language and Identity in the Balkans: Serbo-Croatian and Its Disintegration* (Oxford, England: Oxford University Press, 2004), pp. 2–3.

172 **"Having landed at Sarajevo":** Ibid.

174 **"Among us young people"** Keith Langston and Anita Peti-Stantic, "Attitudes Towards Linguistic Purism in Croatia: Evaluating Efforts at Language Reform," in *At War with Words,* eds. Mirjana N. Dedaiç and Daniel Nelson (New York: Mouton de Gruyter, 2003), pp. 247–82.

CHAPTER 6: INSUBORDINATE CLAUSES

183 **An alphabet was now a crime:** "Language Reform: From Ottoman to Turkish," in Helen Metz, *Turkey: A Country Study* (Washington, D.C.: GPO for the Library of Congress), available at http://countrystudies.us/turkey/25.htm.

183 **one of the most concerted assaults:** This section draws on Geof-

frey Lewis, The Gunnar Jarring Lecture; Istanbul, February 1, 2002, available at www.srii.org/admin/filer/lecture2002.pdf.

186 **It remains a crime:** www.antenna-tr.org/mevzuat_devam.asp?feox =21&lgg=en

187 **Man or woman:** "Vive la Révolution," BBC News, January 9, 1998, available at http://news.bbc.co.uk/2/hi/in_depth/46227.stm.

188 **One scholar has counted:** Henriette Walter, "French: An Accommodating Language?," in *French: An Accommodating Language?*, ed. Sue Wright (Tonawanda, N.Y.: Multilingual Matters, 2000), pp. 31–36.

189 **The Academy is thus sometimes:** Tyrtée Tastet, *Histoire des quarante fauteuils de l'Académie Française depuis la fondation jusqu'à nos jours, 1635–1855,* vol. 1, pp. 11–12 (1844), cited in fr.wikipedia.org, "Académie française," accessed July 11, 2007.

189 **the average age of Academy members:** "L'Académie Française and Its Cultural Cul-de-Sac," *The Globe and Mail,* April 16, 2008, available at www.theglobeandmail.com/news/world/article680397.ece.

189 **"Well-taught French":** *Le Figaro,* March 18, 1996, quoted in Dennis Ager, *Identity, Insecurity and Image* (Philadelphia: Multilingual Matters, 1999), p. 235.

190 **In 1794 theater directors:** Ferdinand Brunot, *Histoire de la langue Française des origines à nos jours* (Paris: Colin, 1966), vol. 9, p. 685.

190 **"The Citizens of Paris":** Ager, *Identity, Insecurity and Image,* p. 110.

192 **"scandalously poor piece of work":** Robert Hall, *External History of the Romance Languages* (New York: American Elsevier Publishing, 1974) quoted in Sue Wright, *Language Policy and Language Planning* (New York: Palgrave, 2004), p. 55.

192 **the phrase *madame la ministre:*** This method of research is more serious, and more effective, than it might seem. Professional linguists are using Google to mine the tremendous "corpus" of perhaps 10 trillion words that exists on the Internet. Research has shown that search engines such as Google return results comparable to traditional corpora such as, for example, newspaper databases. See "Corpus Colossal," *The Economist,* January 25, 2005, and Frank Keller and Mirella Lapata, "Using the Web to Obtain Frequencies for Unseen Bigrams," *Computational Linguistics* 29 (2003), pp. 459–84.

193 **another borrowing is far more prominent:** Searches performed though Google, using Advanced Search and selecting only pages in French, in October 2009.

194 **The Ministry of Culture commissioned:** Ager, *Identity, Insecurity and Image*, p. 154.

195 **which is the "real" Norwegian:** Kristin Grøntoft, "Brenner nynorsk-bok i tønne," *Dagbladet*, available at www.dagbladet.no/nyheter/2005/08/17/440490.html.

197 **When not inventing words:** George Thomas, *Linguistic Purism* (London: Longmans, 1995), p. 78.

197 **"I cannot help it":** Quoted by E. M. Forster in the introduction to *William Barnes: One Hundred Poems* (Blandford Forum, England: Dorset Bookshop, 1971), p. xv.

198 **He was a Little Englander:** Fr. Andrew Phillips, *The Rebirth of England and English: The Vision of William Barnes* (Swaffham, England: Anglo-Saxon Books, 1996). Phillips is the source of the claim that Barnes knew fourteen languages fluently, was familiar with seventy, and could learn the grammar of a language in two weeks. The latter claims are plausible, but most definitions of "fluent" would require the ability to comfortably have a conversation with a native speaker. Barnes would almost certainly not have had the kind of exposure to native speakers of most of those languages to learn them fluently.

198 **differences between American and British English:** David Crystal, *The Cambridge Encyclopedia of the English Language* (Cambridge, England: Cambridge University Press, 1995), pp. 80–81.

202 **Germany, Austria, Switzerland:** "Geschlichter Abriß der Reichtschreibung," available at www.schriftdeutsch.de/orth-his.htm.

205 **One experiment asked:** Asher Koriat and Ilia Levy, "Figural Symbolism in Chinese Ideographs," *Journal of Psycholinguistic Research* 8 (1979): 353–365. Interestingly, the related phenomenon of "phonetic symbolism" also operates; asked which of *zhong* and *qing* means "heavy" and which means "light," more than half of the test subjects correctly guessed that *zhong* is "heavy." The low vowel of *zhong* "feels" heavier. Steven Pinker, *The Language Instinct* (New York: HarperPerennial, 1995).

206 **the Chinese for "crisis":** Citations from Kennedy, Gore, and Rice

come from Benjamin Zimmer and Mark Liberman of the Language Log blog.

206 **But Victor Mair:** www.pinyin.info/chinese/crisis.html. Fortunately, this needed debunking is now the top Google result for "danger crisis opportunity."

208 **Estimates of the number in use:** This and the following draw on William Hannas, *Asia's Orthographic Dilemma* (Honolulu: University of Hawaii Press, 1997), especially pp. 125–152.

210 **Some Western linguists:** William Hannas, *The Writing on the Wall* (Philadelphia: University of Pennsylvania Press, 2003).

211 **Hannas, a former academic:** Hannas, *Asia's Orthographic Dilemma,* pp. 144–147.

212 **Modern computers are clever enough:** "Writing Chinese on the Windows Platform," http://newton.uor.edu/Departments& Programs/AsianStudiesDept/Language/chinese_write.htm.

212 **Japan's first notable advocate:** Japanese and Chinese names are routinely family name first, personal name second, and this will be followed here.

213 **Japan even stopped teaching English:** Tessa Carroll, *Language Planning and Language Change in Japan* (Richmond, England: Curzon Press, 2001), pp. 51–75.

213 **Some supported a switch to *kana:*** J. Marshall Unger, *Literacy and Script Reform in Occupation Japan* (Oxford, England: Oxford University Press, 1996), p. 60.

213 **Japanese proponents fell out:** Ibid.

216 **Mandarin speakers have a rhyming saying:** "Mandarin vs. Cantonese," www.chinese-lessons.com/cantonese/difficulty.htm cites this saying. This page also discusses the differences between Cantonese and Mandarin in more detail.

217 **Romanization nearly succeeded in China:** John DeFrancis: *Nationalism and Language Reform in China* (Princeton, N.J.: Princeton University Press, 1950).

218 **Chen Mengjia:** A fascinating account of this is Peter Hessler's "Oracle Bones," *The New Yorker,* February 14, 2004. An architect of the *pinyin* reforms told him that it was Stalin who told Mao not to use the Roman alphabet but to develop "national" forms instead. As this is one reporter's one-source citation for a

conversation the source was not present for, remembered fifty years later, Stalin's role should be considered possible but not definitive.

218 **"Your excellent mandarin":** http://itre.cis.upenn.edu/~myl/languagelog/archives/004898.html.

218 **the government has even objected:** Associated Press, December 4, 2004.

219 **George Thomas has collected:** Thomas, *Linguistic Purism,* pp. 19–23.

CHAPTER 7: THE MICROSOFT AND APPLE OF LANGUAGES

226 **"The role of English":** Samuel Huntington, *Who Are We?* (London: Simon & Schuster, 2005), p. 160.

228 **The royal language academies:** Shirley Brice Heath, "Why No Official Tongue?" *Language Loyalties,* ed. James Crawford (Chicago: University of Chicago Press, 1992), pp. 21–22.

228 **Benjamin Rush:** Ibid., p. 24. Italics in the original.

229 **large German-speaking communities:** Carol Schmid, "Historical Introduction," *The Politics of Language* (Oxford, England: Oxford University Press, 2001).

230 **It was the biggest period:** Raymond Tatalovich, *Nativism Reborn?* (Lexington: University Press of Kentucky, 1995), p. 72.

230 **11.7 percent in 2003:** Luke Larsen, "The Foreign-Born Population in the United States: 2003," U.S. Census Bureau, August 2004, available at www.census.gov/prod/2004pubs/p20-551.pdf.

230 **Some states and towns forbade German:** Schmid, "Historical introduction," p. 38.

230 **Washington McCormick, a congressman:** Dennis Baron, "Federal English," in Crawford, ed., *Language Loyalties,* p. 39.

231 **Exceptions were made for religious teaching:** Tatalovich, *Nativism Reborn?,* p. 52.

231 **The arguments were often:** Ibid., p. 4.

231 **"was to rear them":** Ibid., p. 58.

232 **"a desirable end":** Ibid., p. 61.

238 **The behavior of the bridge generation:** Rubén Rumbaut, Douglas Massey, and Frank Bean, "Linguistic Life Expectancies: Immi-

grant Language Retention in Southern California," *Population and Development Review* 32 (2006): pp. 447–460.

240 **Bilinguals show not just:** Alejandro Portes and Lingxin Hao, "E Pluribus Unum: Bilingualism and Loss of Language in the Second Generation," *Sociology of Education* 71 (1998) reviews the literature on cognitive abilities and bilingualism.

240 **warding off old-age dementia:** "Bilingualism Has Protective Effect in Delaying Onset of Dementia by Four Years, Canadian Study Shows," *Medical News Today,* January 12, 2007, available at www.medicalnewstoday.com/articles/60646.php.

243 **Shortly after the French Revolution:** Sue Wright, *Language Planning and Language Policy* (New York: Palgrave, 2004).

248 **"Provençal" and "Occitan":** Dennis Ager, *Identity, Insecurity and Image* (Philadelphia: Multilingual Matters, 1999), pp. 55–56.

249 **"France cannot retain its rank":** Ibid., p. 109.

251 **France Télécom was taken to task:** Ibid., p. 133.

251 **French law did take a big bite:** Philippe Desprès, "Foreign Firms' In-House and Technical Documents Must Be in French," *International Committee Newsletter,* American Bar Association, April 2006, available at www.abanet.org/labor/newsletter/intl/2006/Apr/france3.html.

252 **My magazine, *The Economist*** "What's the French for Cock-up?," *The Economist,* August 12, 1995.

252 **Some opponents of the Toubon Law:** Elizabeth Manera Edelstein, "The Loi Toubon: Liberté, Egalité, Fraternité, but Only on France's Terms," *Emory International Law Review* 17 (2003), pp. 1127–1201.

CHAPTER 8: CLOUDS, NOT BOXES

259 **"Human mental identities":** Eric Hobsbawm, "Language, Culture and National Identity," *Social Research* 63 (1996): p. 1068.

270 **Some linguists even compare:** David Nettle and Suzanne Romaine, *Vanishing Voices: The Extinction of the World's Languages* (Oxford, England: Oxford University Press, 2000), pp. 60–61.

271 **Countries where many languages are spoken:** J. Pool, "National Development and Language Diversity," in *Advances in the Sociol-*

ogy of Language, vol. 2, ed. Jonathan Fishman (The Hague: Mouton, 1972), pp. 213–30.

271 **A follow-up study in 2000:** Daniel Nettle, "Linguistic Fragmentation and the Wealth of Nations: The Fishman-Pool Hypothesis Reexamined," *Economic Development and Cultural Change* 48 (2000): pp. 335–48.

272 **One 1974 study:** Stanley Lieberson and Lynn Hansen, "National Development, Mother Tongue Diversity, and the Comparative Study of Nations," *American Sociological Review* 39 (1974): pp. 523–41.

277 **"I can't even talk":** Quoted in the *Oakland Tribune,* August 8, 2004, available at http://www.snopes.com/politics/soapbox/cosby.asp with a somewhat modified transcription.

277 **"I had never been":** Malcolm X, "Coming to an Awareness of Language," in *Language Awareness,* 6th ed., eds. Paul Escholz, Alfred Rosa, and Virginia Clark (New York: St. Martin's Press, 1994), pp. 9–11.

INDEX

Index

About the Author

ROBERT LANE GREENE is an international correspondent for *The Economist,* and his writing has appeared in *The New York Times,* on Slate, and in other publications. He also wrote a biweekly column for *The New Republic* from 2002 to 2004. Greene is a frequent television and radio commentator on international affairs, an adjunct assistant professor in the Center for Global Affairs at New York University, and a term member of the Council on Foreign Relations. He speaks nine languages and was a Marshall Scholar at Oxford University, where he earned a M.Phil. in European politics and society. Greene lives in Brooklyn with his wife, Eva, and his son, Jack.